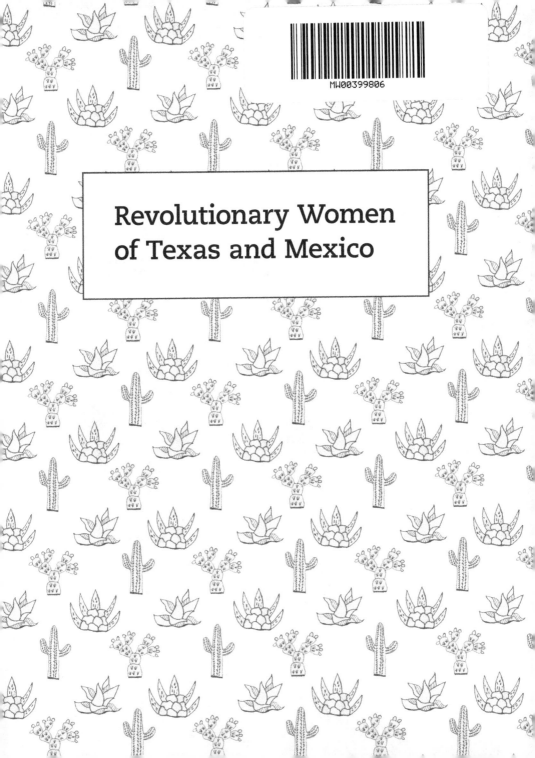

Revolutionary Women
of Texas and Mexico

Revolutionary Women of Texas and Mexico

Portraits of Soldaderas, Saints, and Subversives

Edited by
KATHY SOSA,
ELLEN RIOJAS CLARK,
and JENNIFER SPEED

Foreword by
DOLORES HUERTA

Afterword by
NORMA ELIA CANTÚ

Illustrations by
KATHY SOSA
and LIONEL SOSA

MAVERICK BOOKS
TRINITY UNIVERSITY PRESS
San Antonio, Texas

Published by Maverick Books, an imprint of
Trinity University Press
San Antonio, Texas 78212

Book design by BookMatters, Berkeley
Cover design by Erin Mayes
Cover illustration by Kathy Sosa

ISBN 978-1-59534-925-5 paperback
ISBN 978-1-59534-940-8 hardcover
ISBN 978-1-59534-926-2 ebook

Trinity University Press strives to produce its books using methods and
materials in an environmentally sensitive manner. We favor working
with manufacturers that practice sustainable management of all natural
resources, produce paper using recycled stock, and manage forests with
the best possible practices for people, biodiversity, and sustainability.
The press is a member of the Green Press Initiative, a nonprofit
program dedicated to supporting publishers in their efforts to reduce
their impacts on endangered forests, climate change, and forest-
dependent communities.

CIP data on file at the Library of Congress

24 23 22 21 | 5 4 3

For all of the revolutionary women in our lives

CONTENTS

FOREWORD

Reflections on Revolutionary Women

DOLORES HUERTA

WHO IS A REVOLUTIONARY WOMAN? A REVOLUTIONARY WOMAN WANTS change, not mere cosmetic change but change to the status quo, and she is willing to sacrifice to make this happen. We have some extraordinary examples: Sojourner Truth, Las Adelitas, Frida Kahlo, Sor Juana Inés de la Cruz, Dorothy Day, Malala Yousafzai, Coretta Scott King, and others. The stories of revolutionary women need to be heard because they are inspiring and because they are courageous. By telling these stories, we encourage women not to be held back by their own inhibition, their own self-doubt, their own belief that they lack the capacity to be revolutionary women. We need to offer these examples of women who made huge sacrifices so that others can say, "I can do something, too."

Historically, stories of revolutionary women have been minimized or even left untold. Women's accomplishments have often been diminished, or men have usurped their accomplishments and claimed them as their own. If we don't highlight these stories, we all lose. These women will be lost to history, and their good works will go unknown. Everyone, but especially women, needs to have knowledge of these stories.

I was fortunate to have women in my life who were revolutionary and put a light in front of my path. My mother had the courage to divorce her husband during the Great Depression and bring us to California from New Mexico. She worked two jobs and saved enough money to start her own business. She was ahead of her time, and she was always pushing me out of my comfort zone. My Girl Scout leader, Katherine Kemp, made it a point to recruit young women of color. Both Eleanor Smeal, who is head of the Feminist Majority, and Gloria Steinem inspired me. I drew strength from Rebecca Flores, who led farmworkers in organizing for better pay and working conditions in Texas in the 1960s. Women like Rebecca are rocks. She and others were so strong, and willing to go to jail, and take their children with them to the picket line—and still do everything that was expected of them at home. They are all remarkable women.

I firmly believe that young women today can be revolutionary women. They are brave, and they are marching, and they know about women's rights and reproductive rights. In many communities, and in colleges and high schools, Latina women are really at the front line— and they are on fire. They get angry about situations that exist, and they become activists. We get frustrated because we do not always know how to change things, but then we find there is a way, and we can learn how to organize. When we use the tools we've learned, we can make a difference.

There are many tools at our disposal. We can bring about change through labor unions, even if they are under attack these days and women have a hard time even getting to the stage. We have devices and platforms for grassroots organizing that we didn't have in the past, like social media. We can educate and mobilize people quickly with our computers and cell phones. Sometimes women think that they do not have the capacity to do something, and they understandably do not want to be criticized or threatened. Organizing is about trying to get people to lose their fear so they know that they have power, and letting them know they don't have to go it alone—they can form a group and then a movement. And then they can bring about change.

When I speak to young women I try to remind them that we will never have peace in the world until women take power. But it is going to take all of us working together, standing up together. Women have been taught to be dependent on men, to wait for Prince Charming to save them. They are told not to get their dresses dirty or to wrestle with their siblings because it isn't ladylike. I want to remind women that the lioness is more ferocious than the lion. The only reason we are not as ferocious as we can be is that we've been stifled to think that we shouldn't be ferocious.

We need to protect ourselves and support ourselves. Once women realize that they have independent power, they don't let anyone subjugate or dominate them. Everyone on this earth came from the body of a woman. By owning their strength and power, women learn to fight for their dreams and overcome the obstacles others put in their way. Part of developing that power, and becoming revolutionary, means learning to accept advice that can make us stronger, even if we can't act on that advice in the moment. And women have to develop emotional fortitude. They have to become strong internally and psychologically; learning how to organize is like exercising. If your muscles get sore, you are exercising and getting stronger. If you feel butterflies in your stomach, those feelings shouldn't tell you to stop, because it's okay to be nervous. You keep on going, because the more we engage, the more we can offer and the stronger we become.

Once you get involved with helping others, you start to work on issues that are larger than you are. All of your personal issues diminish because you don't have the time or energy to focus on them, and many of those personal problems will solve themselves. When you are working with others on conflicts that are bigger than you, you can see that you, along with other people, do have the power to make changes. When you are part of the change, you open yourself to a whole different world. Women don't always want to take credit for the work they do because they don't want to seem conceited. I tell young women, "Channel your inner Oprah Winfrey." I tell them to stand up and say, "This was my idea, my project, my creation." And be proud of it. Women often say that they are not trying to make history, they are just trying to make a change. But that's how you make history.

Women have it in us to be revolutionary, even today. My dad's parents are from Mexico, and I was born not long after the Mexican Revolution ended. When I was a child in New Mexico, people were still talking about the revolution. And it had an influence on me because I learned that poor people could change the government. Coretta Scott King said that women have to get involved, take power, and create peace in the world. But it may not happen all at once. Remember the song lyrics, *"No hay que llegar primero, pero hay que saber llegar."* Be a revolutionary woman—you don't have to get there first, just get there.

PREFACE

KATHY SOSA

SOMETIME IN 2009, I WAS GIVEN AN ESSAY WRITTEN BY MY FRIEND LANCE Aaron, pointing to the then-imminent hundredth anniversary of the Mexican Revolution (1910–27) and the Cristero War that extended conflicts through 1929, both of which threw Mexico into violence and chaos and turned the Mexican political and social orders inside out. There were many significant outcomes of the revolution in Mexico, and these have been well documented. But what wasn't well known, he said, was the huge impact of Mexico's revolution on the United States, on our home state of Texas, and on our multicultural yet very Mexican hometown of San Antonio. This cataclysmic event drove an entire population—hundreds of thousands, perhaps even a million people—north to the United States. The vast majority never returned. In the process, our borderland home became irrevocably transformed, became more densely and fundamentally Mexican, and the Latinization of the United States began in earnest.

Not only did this essay open my eyes, but it also stirred memories of my husband's stories of his grandmothers, both of whom had come to San Antonio to escape the revolution, both alone with several small children. I was already somewhat familiar with the *soldaderas*, the Mexican women who underwrote the revolutionary armies' success by providing their supply lines and food, taking up arms when necessary, but it occurred to me that the story of the revolution, and its impact on both Mexico and Texas, was to a great extent the story of "revolutionary women": those who left Mexico and those who stayed, their courage amid brutality and disorder, their willingness to assume roles and take actions previously reserved for men, and their ability, through those actions, to change the course of history. Yet so little was written or known about them, unfortunately.

Jennifer Speed, my historian friend and future collaborator, explained the project's importance to me this way: back when biography was in favor as a means of recounting history, it was overwhelmingly the biographies of "great men" that were written (by male historians, no doubt). Women were overlooked, taken for granted. As the traditional biography format falls out of favor, we must address the silence around these subjects and begin to fill this void, so that women's stories will not go untold.

Thus an obsession with telling the stories of the women of the Mexican Revolution was born, along with a broader concept for a project that would tell the stories of other formidable women in the history of Texas and Mexico. Mis grandes amigas, Sandra Cisneros and Ellen Riojas Clark, who have been trusted advisers and guides on previous creative journeys, gathered with me to discuss the merits of the project, brainstorm it, and bring form to the idea. This book is the result of my collaboration with Sandra, Ellen, Jennifer, and a group of talented and accomplished authors. It tells the stories of remarkable women who lived in different times and were revolutionary in different ways, but all lived in the Texas–Mexico region, a community with shared geography, history, culture, and DNA.

In what context are we to consider the subjects of this book revolutionary? Granted, the most common use of "revolutionary" may be in the context of war and politics, an area where women have historically gone unacknowledged. For this book, we adopted a broader definition of "actions threatening to the established order." Herein we consider revolution, in Jennifer's words, as "a transformative process that makes the society new." This more expansive concept of revolution gives clarity to just how revolutionary women are and always have been.

At the heart of this project is women and their stories from the Mexican Revolutionary period, 1910 to 1927. This led us naturally to ask the question: Who are the spiritual godmothers of these women? *Quiénes son las antepasadas*, the earlier female figures from this region whose example or inspiration put wind beneath the wings of our early twentieth-century subjects? This question led to others: What is their legacy? Who are the spiritual daughters of revolutionary-era pioneers and heroines in more contemporary times? These questions were the rough structure for the book, and we began to refine the list of subjects and to find authors to write about each one.

Our contributors range from scholars to literary figures and journalists. We sought authors who are passionate about or have a keen insight into their subject, believing that these qualities were more important than consistency of style. And the style of the essays, or "portraits," varies widely. Each one stands on its own, like sisters—all in the same family but each with her own point of view and personality. The collection, of course, does not represent a definitive compilation. Our intention, instead, is to offer a sampling of compelling exemplars, thereby spurring interest and further examination of the topic.

INTRODUCTION

Setting the Scene of Revolutionary Women in Texas and Mexico

JENNIFER SPEED

THE HISTORICAL CENTER FOR THIS COLLECTION IS THE ERA OF THE MEXICAN Revolution, from 1910 to 1927, and the Cristero War (La Cristiada) that followed, from 1926 to 1929. The geographical center is Texas and Mexico, given their shared history and culture. The revolution shaped the lives of women from nearly every profession and background. These essays are reflections not only on how the revolution affected women but also on how women shaped the revolution. Women actively participated in the revolution under many different guises as soldiers, journalists, nurses, scouts, political activists, and telegraph operators, to name only a few roles. In other ways, they embraced the revolution's promises for liberty and sought to extend those promises to marginalized persons who had the most to gain from a political revolution. In that spirit, women revolutionaries fought for fair labor practices and better access to education in the same way that they fought for political access.[1] Here we make women's connection to the revolution explicit and seek to understand their efforts in context.[2] From the era of the Mexican Revolution we look backward and forward along the historical continuum that extends from the Texas–Mexico colonial era until today. Without a doubt the revolution's origins are to be found deep in its colonial history, and much of that history is well known. In bringing revolutionary women from Mexico's premodern past into the foreground, we seek to broaden the conversation about women and revolutionary change.

Our use of the terms "revolution" and "revolutionary" is necessarily expansive. Revolution is generally understood to be a violent struggle that leads to regime change. The focus on governmental, or constitutional, change is an ancient one, for that is how Aristotle first defined it more than two millennia ago. The outcome of this regime change is freedom from oppression, to use Hannah Arendt's language, with stress on participation in the public sphere.[3] For most of the twentieth century, studies on revolution were largely directed toward either exploring the violence of revolution or the actual overthrow of the state. There has been little room for women in this schema until more recently.[4] Even though women have often been involved in armed struggles throughout history, they have typically been in the minority—making it easy to discount their contributions.[5] By the nature of the upheaval that revolutions cause in society, women are often drawn into nontraditional and more public roles, but these largely fall outside of the domain of military conflict.[6] Additionally, women historically have had a small share in the leadership and elected roles at the level of the nation-state relative to their numbers in the population, whether their nation has seen a revolution or not. They are party neither to the regimes that are overthrown nor the regimes that immediately follow.[7] As a result, women's activities in the midst of revolution are easy to overlook, especially since their wartime freedoms are often undone by new, more oppressive regimes.[8] A case in point, women were first popularly elected to office in Mexico during the 1920s in the Yucatán, but political upheaval and regime changes prevented them from either taking office or exercising their elected duties.[9]

Women's absence from formal warfare and politics, however, does not mean that they haven't shaped the cultures and communities in which revolutions have unfolded, often in extraordinary ways. In framing the idea of revolution as a transformative process that makes a culture anew, we are affording an opening for women in revolutions and as revolutionaries. In these essays, we understand revolution to be a political turnaround as well as a social and cultural transformation that may extend over a long historical period. The era of the Mexican Revolution and Cristero War marks a considerable transformation in Mexican society, but those events are also historical markers along Mexico's long journey from Spanish territorial conquest to a liberal-democratic nation-state.

COLONIAL-ERA MEXICO AND TEXAS

The Spanish conquest of what is now Mexico and Texas began in earnest in the early sixteenth century. In ventures formally authorized by Queen Isabella of Castile and her successors, private expeditions first seized islands in the Caribbean and then began their westward expansion. One of the most influential expeditions was led by Hernán Cortés, who set out from the island of Hispaniola in 1519. Lured by tales of wealth and accompanied by a contingent of soldier-adventurers, he and his companions attacked, and then toppled, the Aztec Empire and its capital at Tenochtitlán, now Mexico City. Although the speed with which Cortés carried out the conquest is startling, it is in many ways not surprising. Cortés benefited greatly from European weapons and horses. He also held two other sources of significant advantage: translators and local peoples who loathed their Aztec overlords. As to the former, Cortés depended heavily on the political negotiations made possible by a pair of translators, a shipwrecked Spaniard who learned a native language and a Tlaxcala woman, Malintzín (or La Malinche), who had learned a number of indigenous languages in the course of being traded from one tribe to another as a slave. Cortés also found willing allies among the Aztec's subject peoples. They aided him, of course, without being fully cognizant of the consequences for their own survival. Fewer than three decades after Christopher Columbus had first set foot in the New World, the first Mesoamerican empire fell victim to Spanish dreams of expansion. Following Cortés's hasty conquest, the Spanish crown took over from soldiers and adventure-seekers and assumed the more difficult work of colonization and settlement. Over the next two centuries, Spain set about establishing and controlling a vast overseas empire known as New Spain.

Brought to New Spain were cadres of royal officials whose primary work was directed toward matters of justice and taxation. In the company of royal officials, but obliged to pay their own passage, came the artisans and laborers who established Spanish settlements. The shipping manifests of this era tell an important story about who did not come on those voyages: women. Overwhelmingly, single working-class men who came to the New World and stayed would partner and create families with indigenous women. The children of these unions, mestizos with mixed European and indigenous heritage, would gradually become the predominant ethnic group in Texas and Mexico.

Together, Spanish settlers and officials laid out orderly towns with churches at their centers and built modest homes, bakeries, and workshops. To supply the food needs of their communities, they established farms and gardens outside the walls of the towns, echoing the pattern of European communities. Where the Spanish crown granted large estates known as *encomiendas,* their *encomanderos* set up farming operations for cash crops. Supplying the labor were indigenous persons—women, men, and sometimes children—now bound to the land and obligated to work. Mostly male slaves bought and shipped from Africa would expand the ranks of the laboring classes. As both the papacy and the Spanish crown came to forbid the enslavement and exploitation of indigenous peoples, they permitted even worse exploitation of African slaves. Those who survived and eventually gained freedom often intermarried with indigenous women.

It is hard to overstate the cultural importance of religion for both the indigenous people of Mexico and the Spanish who brought their Catholic traditions and beliefs with them. In many areas, native religious practices were almost entirely stamped out; in others, some syncretic practices developed, to include traditions from Africa. Devotion to Our Lady of Guadalupe emerged from this tension between native and Catholic beliefs. She was said to have appeared at Tepeyac in 1531, a site where the goddess Tonantzin has been worshipped and which

Spanish conquerors had destroyed shortly after their arrival in central Mexico. Many clerics, especially Franciscan friars, initially resisted devotion to the Marian apparition at Tepeyac because they feared it was neither orthodox nor authentic. Their objections hardly mattered, or perhaps their objections actually fueled the flames.

Devotion to the Marian apparition of Guadalupe surged among people who saw in her an image that spoke to their own needs—in their faith lives, in their suffering, in their resistance to oppression of all kinds, and in their identification with indigenous culture. When Spanish settlers and clerics pushed northward, they brought their devotion to Guadalupe when they founded the first parish church in San Antonio in 1738.[10] Eventually, the protection of the Virgin would be invoked by parties involved in the Mexican War of Independence, the Mexican Revolution, the Cristero War, and the Zapatista uprising of the late twentieth century. Her popularity, her malleability, and the ways in which her image has been invoked in revolutions of all kinds make the Virgin of Guadalupe an ideal subject for our collection of essays.

In the rigid religious and cultural environment of colonial Mexico, the activities of persons of every class and profession were severely circumscribed by law as much as by custom. Mexican society was rigidly patriarchal and hierarchical; women were thereby doubly limited. Mexico's rigid caste system, based on race, further delineated women's roles. In this volume, we recognize some of the challenges that they faced in a race-based culture by calling attention to the ways in which women broke racial barriers and expectations. Regardless of ethnicity or class, though, women had the onerous burden of household responsibilities and childbearing and were explicitly excluded from the political and ecclesiastical decision-making of any kind. Upper-class urban women could consider convent life instead of marriage, but even in a community entirely of women, nuns were under the authority of local bishops and the Holy Office of the Inquisition. Sor Juana Inés de la Cruz, for example, is one woman who used the feminine space of the convent to carve out a distinctive identity for herself. She used the safety of that space, and her friendship with the viceroy of New Spain, to advocate for women's education. Women who followed the typical path of married life moved from the guardianship of their fathers to that of their husbands or even their sons or brothers; in only the rarest of instances do we find women who were completely independent of male authority. When the war for independence began in 1810, women who rebelled against the status quo in colonial Mexico did so under extraordinarily oppressive conditions.

NINETEENTH-CENTURY MEXICO AND TEXAS

Mexico's War of Independence from Spain raged from 1810 to 1821 and resulted in the declaration of Mexico as an empire, which lasted just over a year before giving way to Mexico's First Federal Republic. At the time of independence, Mexico's territory extended southward all the way through Central America and northward, comprising what is now most of the western United States as far as the modern-day border with Canada. As part of Mexico's earliest territorial and political reorganization in 1824, the government formed the State of Coahuila and Texas, which persisted as a territorial unit for just over a decade until Texas won its own independence from Mexico in 1836. In that war, too, women played an important part.

From the time of independence up through 1876, Mexicans suffered through sustained periods of armed conflict, including wars with France and the United States, along with five major governmental changes. These upheavals had important implications for women, including those who were directly involved in combat as spies, as fighters, or as political dissidents. During the period of the French Intervention, women in areas like Oaxaca acted as the only link between the Mexican government in hiding, and women who were caught were beaten or jailed for their dissidence.[11] Women such as Jane McManus Cazneau acted as correspondents and smugglers on both sides of the Rio Grande during the U.S.–Mexico War. Moreover, frequent warfare and the deaths of so many soldiers tipped the gender balance in some areas, such as Mexico City, in favor of women. Many young married women were widowed before they had the chance to bear children, and others became heads of households following the deaths of multiple male relatives.[12] Women were also part of the conflicts in large numbers as soldaderas who accompanied troops and filled vital support roles that were not staffed by the army proper. Many took part in active warfare. Their stories are featured in this collection. When the troops suffered, so did soldaderas. As many as 1,500 women and children accompanied General Antonio López de Santa Anna on his campaign to defend Texas, but only 300 returned home. The others died of starvation, thirst, or exposure.[13]

Liberal reforms of the nineteenth century, such as the secularization of education, offered more avenues for women to engage in the public sphere. Schools were established for training teachers, with women enrolling in significant numbers. In general, the newly circumscribed role of the Catholic Church and expanded roles for women in other labor sectors also allowed women greater room for self-determination during the nineteenth century.[14] These freedoms would once again be sharply curtailed under the long administration of Porfirio Díaz.

THE PORFIRIATO AND OUTBREAK OF THE REVOLUTION

The Mexican Revolution was the direct result of the social and political tensions that emerged from decades of rule by Porfirio Díaz, a period known as the Porfiriato. Díaz had risen to national prominence as a military leader who helped bring an end to French intervention in Mexico, which lasted from 1861 to 1867. However, he also initiated several rebellions against his own elected government. Díaz formally entered political life as a representative to Congress from Veracruz. He became president after leading an armed rebellion that toppled the government in 1876 and presented himself as a liberal reformer. After generations of warfare within Mexico and against foreign invaders, he paved the way for the so-called Pax Porfiriato, much needed by the entire nation. As has happened the world over, though, that kind of peace demanded the trading away of personal and civil liberties. Díaz curbed factionalism, which included making some groups enemies of the state, created a strong central regime with himself at the center, and built up a network of regional strongmen and appointees who owed their power and prestige to him alone.[15] He also realized that the restrictions placed on the Catholic Church were deeply resented by many Catholics. Díaz earned the favor of some Catholics by choosing not to enforce such restrictions rather than abolish them. Ironically, activism rooted in "social Catholicism" would come to play a significant role in challenging Díaz, especially in the northern state of Chihuahua.[16]

One of Díaz's signature achievements was the launch of large-scale industrial and economic development, but that development came at a high cost. Major investment in industry by foreign firms was accompanied by the massive displacement of indigenous communities in Mexico's north. Water was appropriated for industrial development, thereby affecting the livelihood of rural, indigenous people, and workers who labored on industrial or mining projects often suffered under dangerous, deplorable working conditions. U.S. companies played an important part in this displacement, and their continued activity in Mexico was directly supported by President Howard Taft's administration. As critics became more vocal, some of whom fled to the United States to escape Díaz, Taft's and Wilson's administrations increasingly supported Mexico's efforts to track down dissidents and either return them to Mexico or imprison them in the United States.

Some of the opposition to Díaz arose out of the rapidly changing labor environment within Mexico as the country became more industrialized. For example, mutual aid societies, or *mutualistas*, came to play a role in supporting workers and their families after confraternities and guilds had been abolished by the 1857 constitution.[17] Following the outbreak of the Mexican Revolution in 1910, many women-led mutualistas formed to provide social and financial support for revolutionaries and refugees who settled in Texas and elsewhere in the southwestern United States. Also, rising educational levels across

Mexico fueled demand for a lively press, some of which turned against Díaz. Newspapers and broadsheets made for an easy means of communicating discontent about working conditions and political developments. Juana Belén Gutiérrez de Mendoza, for example, founded a protest newspaper, *Vésper: Justicia y libertad*, as a means of challenging Díaz and was forced underground—with her printing press in tow—in order to carry forward her work. Teresa Urrea, too, challenged the Díaz government indirectly, making her a target of both the U.S. and Mexican governments.

The tide began to turn against Díaz around 1900 and worsened with a worldwide economic crisis in 1907. Alongside the steady opposition of presses from around the country and within Mexico City, and worker agitation coming from all directions, moderate liberals regrouped and attempted to challenge Díaz's hold on power through the creation of political clubs. The Flores Magón brothers, with their socialist and anarchist bent, found supporters in some sectors, while Francisco Madero, with his more moderate and measured brand of the liberal opposition, found backers in others. Ultimately, Madero's upper-class connections helped him gain a following among Mexico's landed establishment. Madero ran for office in 1910 against Díaz, but Díaz had Madero jailed to prevent his participation in the election. Madero escaped while he was under house arrest and fled across the border to Texas. From his base in San Antonio, Madero and his supporters hatched the Plan de San Luis Potosí in early October 1910 to overthrow Díaz. Armed rebellions subsequently broke out the following month, marking the start of the Mexican Revolution. Just as quickly as major rebel coalitions emerged, so too did women soldiers and leaders appear among their ranks. Less than a year into the revolution, a U.S. paper, the *Washington Herald*, featured a story with the headline: "Mexican Rebels Have Girl Leader." After noting that "the entire state of Morelos, except the city of Cuernavaca, rose up against the government," the article calls out Margarita Neri and Esperanza Echevarría for their command of more than a thousand indigenous troops.[18] Off the battlefield, women arranged for the smuggling of money and arms as well as communications across the U.S.–Mexico border.

As Mexicans rebelled against Díaz and his allies, they tried to overturn a deeply entrenched legacy of political and social injustices. A point worth underscoring is that while discontent with Díaz and his decades of rule was widespread, there was considerable disagreement among his opponents about which features of Mexican life and politics were most in need of fixing. Was it the influx of foreigners and foreign investment in infrastructure? Regional rule by *caudillos,* or strongmen? Mistreatment of indigenous people? The outsized influence of the Catholic Church? Legal, educational, and reproductive freedoms for women? The rejection of the liberal reforms in the post-independence decades? Unjust appropriation of land and natural resources? What had begun as a regime change with Francisco Madero's election and attempts to unseat Díaz devolved into civil and military chaos. Within less than a year of the outbreak of the revolution, Emiliano Zapata and his supporters issued their Plan de Ayala, challenging Madero's authority and commitment to genuine reform. Madero's forced resignation and assassination in 1913, followed by the dictatorship of Victoriano Huerta, marked the start of the civil war that plagued Mexico on and off for the next seven years. During the war, many women, like Cristina Jimenez Sosa and Leonila Barrios Ortiz, fled Mexico with their children and set up businesses in Texas and elsewhere.

The ascendancy of Venustiano Carranza to the presidency in 1915 and the remarkable fact that he remained alive and in office for five years given the short tenures of his predecessors brought a measure of political stability in the midst of chronic warfare. The promulgation of a new constitution in 1917 was a tentative sign of a return to political normalcy, but Mexico was still battered and broken—and would be for years to come. Although women made considerable strides in pressing for their rights at the national level, their demands were not reflected in the new constitution. Zapata was assassinated in 1919, thereby removing one rebel leader from the national scene. Carranza survived an assassination attempt but was either killed, or committed suicide, during an ambush in 1920. That same year, Pancho Villa agreed to cease his rebellion and largely retreated from public life, but he would be assassinated in 1923. Estimates of the revolution's toll vary, but it is likely that more than 1.5 million people died as a result of warfare.[19] To put this number in context, it is more than twice the total number of all casualties during the U.S. Civil War.[20]

THE CRISTERO WAR

The early 1920s saw only sporadic fighting, but the presidency of Plutarco Calles marked the return of open warfare.[21] One of Carranza's signal achievements was the Constitution of 1917, but it carried forward old resentments, especially with regard to the role of the Catholic Church in Mexican society. The liberal Constitution of 1857 had sharply limited Catholic influence, especially in the sphere of education. Díaz had largely chosen to ignore the constitution's restrictions on the church, leaving regional and local leaders to exercise discretion. The Constitution of 1917 reaffirmed the free exercise of religion, but article 3 declared that education should be compulsory at the elementary level, democratic, free, and entirely secular. Church and state were to be unequivocally separate, to include a prohibition on clerics or consecrated religious holding office of any kind or inheriting property, except close relatives. Women such as María Concepción Acevedo de la Llata were caught up in this battle and fought back. Also, the state reserved the right to appropriate church lands (article 24) or declare them part of the national heritage. A holdover from Mexico's colonial era, the church was the single-largest landholder in Mexico, which allowed prelates and congregations to treat residents of their lands as little more than serfs, and businesses and other enterprises therein as their personal property. That same article also limited worship services to taking place within religious buildings, thus preventing large-scale religious gatherings.

Carranza's successor, the revolutionary general-turned-politician Álvaro Obregón, followed Díaz's lead in ignoring the anticlerical provisions of the 1917 Constitution, but President Calles took a more aggressive stance. In office from 1924 to 1928, and ruling from behind the scenes from 1928 to 1936, Calles was a student of social democracy and international labor movements. He tried to implement some of the revolution's aims, including the redistribution of land and worker organization. He was also a staunch atheist and argued that the Catholic Church was standing in the way of social and political progress. Calles went beyond upholding the basic provisions of the 1917 Constitution and worked vigorously to expand them by depriving clerics of the right to jury trials and fining those who wore their clerical garb in public, among other restrictions. Once the employment of priests came under public control, regional leaders were able to sharply limit the number of active priests in areas under their control. Hostilities and resentments simmered as bishops and laypeople voiced their objection to government restrictions. In 1926 the umbrella group known as the National Defense League for Religious Liberty, or LNDLR (Liga Nacional Defensora de la Libertad Religiosa), formed to unite the efforts of more than thirty-five thousand people from religious clubs and groups across Mexico, including the Knights of Columbus, and groups representing women, youth, and workers. At first, the LNDLR promoted peaceful means of resistance to the government, to include a boycott of tax payments. The first armed conflict between the government and its opponents broke out on August 3, 1926, when a group of at least four hundred armed men and women holed up in a church in Guadalajara and tried to fight off government forces. Guerilla warfare broke out elsewhere, and government forces were ill-prepared to respond. The following year, the LNDLR launched its military opposition to the Calles government.

Once again, Mexican women distinguished themselves as revolutionaries who genuinely agitated for regime change. Some women continued the tax boycotts and others launched peaceful protests, while others directly carried out guerilla warfare or supported those who did. The Feminine Brigades of Saint Joan of Arc (Las Brigadas Femeninas de Santa Juana de Arco) grew from a group of fewer than two dozen young women in 1927 to thousands of women by 1929 who formed a network of fighters and smugglers whose activities extended throughout Mexico. The war came to an end in 1929, when the United States and foreign Catholic bishops helped broker a truce that the Cristeros largely honored; for its part, the Calles government had thousands of rebels executed after the war. María Concepción Acevedo de la Llata (Madre Conchita) is one woman who was drawn into the Cristero War, indirectly when she was forced out of her cloister and then more directly when the man who assassinated Álvaro Obregón named her as his co-conspirator. The death toll was staggering: upward of eighty thousand lives were lost, and perhaps three times as many fled Mexico and settled mostly in Texas and California. Once again, Mexico's history became U.S. history.

THE POSTREVOLUTIONARY ERA

The end of the Cristero War coincided with major social and cultural upheavals around the world. Women in Texas and Mexico had distinguished themselves during the long period of revolution and continued to do so outside the theater of war. Much as women had challenged conditions for workers in Mexico before the war, Emma Tenayuca led a strike of more than ten thousand Mexican American workers in San Antonio in the 1930s. In the interwar and postwar period, both Alice Dickerson Montemayor and Genoveva Morales attacked institutional racism and discrimination that deprived Mexican Americans of public services, including education. They fought against deeply entrenched hostility toward women and Latinos but eventually prevailed. Women in other arenas, such as Frida Kahlo and Nahui Olin, used art—written and visual—to challenge social conventions about both creative activity and sexuality. We understand their contributions to be revolutionary in every sense of the word.

Our collection concludes with the most revolutionary of women, namely, women who write and women who fight: Gloria Anzaldúa and the Zapatistas. Anzaldúa reimagined the meaning of the border, not as a place between "us" and "them," but as a space in which we all live and that lives in us. She grounded her identity in the indigenous women's act of rebellion and then theorized that identity-making for other women to explore.[22] The Zapatistas are carrying forward the promise of the revolution, but this time they are bringing to the fore the needs, strengths, and ambitions of the indigenous women who refuse to be left behind ever again.

THE COLLECTION

The essays here offer written portraits of extraordinary women in a broadly chronological fashion. The first part features women who lived prior to the era of the Mexican Revolution and the Cristero War. The second part brings to life women who lived or were active as revolutionaries during the era of the revolution. The final part offers portraits of women who lived after 1930. The book does not pretend to be definitive. Some of the women included are simply our favorites. Others we thought would either resonate with our audience or had a story that really needed to be brought to the foreground. We hope that this collection prompts you to reflect on a revolutionary woman in your own orbit and that you, too, find a way to tell her story.

ONE

Women Revolutionaries During the Era of the Mexican Revolution of 1910

Juana Belén Gutiérrez de Mendoza (b. San Juan del Río, Durango, Mexico, 1875; d. Michoacán/Mexico City, Mexico, 1942), a journalist and militant, began her government protests while a young miner's wife in Coahuila. She sent essays to opposition newspapers in protest of the horrible living and working conditions for miners, angering both Porfirio Díaz and the powerful mining company owners. Later she endured multiple arrests not only for her newspapers, like *Vésper: Justicia y libertad* (which she printed as well), but also for her role in a military insurgency that tried to bring Francisco Madero to power. After the war she fought to bring about a social and economic revolution for Mexico's poorest citizens.

Juana Belén Gutiérrez de Mendoza

CRISTINA DEVEREAUX RAMÍREZ

Through her newspaper *Vésper: Justicia y libertad*, she was the first woman to speak out against the poor treatment of miners, factory workers, and women.

A COLORFUL MURAL OF MEXICO'S HISTORY BEDECKS THE WALLS OF THE Palacio de Gobierno in the heart of downtown Durango, Mexico.[1] The mural recounts the history of Durango and Mexico with bold images of indigenous slaves, architects, Franciscan monks, intellectuals, and community leaders. On another wall, bloody scenes of the Mexican Revolution surround an image of Pancho Villa mounted high on his horse. A daughter of Durango is missing from these scenes of Mexico's history: Juana Belén Gutiérrez de Mendoza. Born in the same small pueblo as Pancho Villa, Juana was an activist, journalist, and revolutionary. She did not pick up a rifle to fight for the rights and land of Mexico's displaced people; she was not the traditional soldadera. Instead, Juana played the role of revolutionary through her rhetoric. Through her protest paper, *Vésper: Justicia y libertad*, she was the first woman to speak out against the poor treatment of miners, factory workers, and women. Juana maintained correspondence and political relations with some of the most influential revolutionaries and politicians of her time. She also wrote for many other newspapers, known as *papeles volantes* or "flying papers." The ideas she espoused earned her several jail sentences. Her writing carried a harsh, defiant, and rebellious tone, a verbal and rhetorical stance that was not acceptable for women at the time. This would become her discursive and revolutionary signature.

Juana's role as a writer of rhetoric in the Mexican Revolution was not acknowledged alongside such male contemporaries as Ricardo Flores Magón, Camilo Arriaga, Juan Sarabia, Antonio Díaz Soto y Gama, and Enrique Flores Magón, who have been touted as the intellectual instigators.[2] Their individual and collective writings in *Hijo del Ahuizote* and *Regeneración*, and their organization of the Partido Liberal Mexicano in 1905, earned them the titles of Mexican revolutionaries. In portrayals of the Mexican Revolution in mainstream writings, Juana and other women have only recently been included. This distortion of history is not surprising, according to historian Martha Eva Rocha: "The process of turning the revolution into a masculine, patriarchal event began as soon as the bullets stopped flying."[3] This essay aims to reinstate Juana to her rightful place in the intellectual history of the Mexican Revolution.

By the turn of the twentieth century, from 1876 to 1911, Mexico was in an era known as the Porfiriato, which referred to Porfirio Díaz's dictatorship. During this period few women were granted a credible space in the public arena of journalism, and none were granted one in the political realm. Women such as Laureana Wright de Kleinhans (1842–1896) and Laura Méndez de Cuenca (1853–1928) gained some literary and journalistic clout through their writing in and leadership of women's magazines and their continued writing throughout their lives. But as historian Joel Bollinger Pouwels notes, they "were pioneers, but not revolutionaries. They favored gradual cultural reforms, and avoided writing about politics, still a wholly male domain."[4] In 1897, as a young writer and journalist, Juana became the first woman to formally take part in the social movement that led up to the Mexican Revolution. Her early writings signaled the beginning of a long career as an activist and revolutionary.

A REVOLUTIONARY IS BORN

María Juana Francisca Gutiérrez Chávez was born on January 27, 1875, in San Juan del Río, Durango, to parents of little means. Her father, Santiago Gutiérrez Lomelí, was a carpenter and blacksmith. Her mother, Porfiria Chávez, was devoted to her family and claimed a maternal lineage to the Caxcan Indians.[5] The family moved to San Pedro del Gallo, Durango, where Juana and her sister, affectionately known as Yova, attended school for several years.[6] Like most girls, Juana did not have the privilege of attending school for long, but this time in school provided her with a crucial introduction to literacy and its value.

Following the unexpected death of their father, the sisters found work as domestic servants in Durango. At the age of seventeen, Juana married Cirilo Mendoza and moved to Sierra Mojada, Coahuila, where he found a job as a miner in La Esmeralda mine.[7] During the years that she lived among the miners, Juana gave birth to three children: Santiago (1893–?), Laura (1895–1975), and Julia (1899–1933); she taught her husband how to read and write; she witnessed the miserable, degrading conditions the miners endured and the menial pay they received. Juana's husband died from complications related to the abuse of alcohol, leaving Juana alone to raise the children. Tragedy soon struck the young widow again when her infant son, Santiago Mendoza, died. Inspired by the harsh material realities she had faced at an early age, Juana started her life of political activism and writing.

Her first published articles denouncing the treatment of the miners appeared anonymously in early opposition newspapers, including *Diario del Hogar* and *Hijo de Ahuizote* in Mexico and *Chinaco* in Laredo, Texas.[8] In 1897 authorities from the mines discovered Juana's connection to the antigovernment publications, resulting in the first of several jail sentences she would endure throughout her life.[9] Instead

of deterring her activism, the time in prison only intensified her resolve to depose Porfirio Díaz and to live a life of activism. It may also
have increased her credibility and notoriety by showing that she was
speaking not from a place of privilege but from one of risk-taking and
a willingness to suffer the consequences of speaking to power. Spend-
ing time in jail also taught Juana that simply deposing Díaz would not
change the cruelty of Mexican life.

At the turn of the twentieth century, Mexico experienced a time
of rising political discourse, although there was no physical place to
gather and debate political issues. Instead, debates flared in the newspapers. There were 227 newspapers in Mexico by 1888, 385 in 1889,
and 531 in 1898.[10] Within this male-dominated scene, Juana openly
challenged the sociopolitical conditions and defied social norms and
patterns. She claimed her revolutionary voice and identity through the
social structure of the journalistic scene that was gaining strength at
the time. Through journalism, the influence of her discourse expanded, and she was able to intersect and disrupt the power structures of
patriarchy, government, and the Catholic Church. If her rhetoric was
powerful enough to draw attention to the authorities and land her in
jail, then it had the power, as government officials must have feared, to
change Mexico's political and social climate.

FORGING A REVOLUTIONARY VOICE

Throughout his dictatorship, Díaz had tried to silence all dissent
against the government. He did so most notably with an amendment
to the Constitution of 1857, which limited "absolute 'freedom of the
press, only to be limited by respect for private life, public morality,
and public order.'"[11] The original constitutional wording guaranteed
the public the right to free speech, but Díaz manipulated this right by
pressing for his own interpretation of "private life, public morality, and
public order" by shutting down presses, jailing journalists, and having
others killed. "As fast as old opposition newspapers were closed down,"
James Cockcroft writes, "new, more militant ones opened up." Yet the

journalists continued to write in the face of this opposition. The threat of being arrested or even killed did not deter Juana from writing and speaking out about the dictator, the government, or its flawed policies. In the late 1890s, she felt compelled to continue writing and speaking to and about the oppressive Mexican regime. Finally, in 1900, Juana moved with her two young daughters, Laura and Julia, to Guanajuato, where it occurred to her to start her own opposition newspaper, *Vésper: Justicia y libertad.* In 1901 she began selling issues, even parting with cherished belongings to fund the paper.[12]

The year *Vésper* launched, it was hailed as a serious contender amid the flurry of discussion and debate being voiced in the many publications. In May 1901 Ricardo Flores Magón, one of the main intellectuals challenging Díaz, published an article in *Regeneración* acknowledging Juana's early rhetorical efforts. He claimed that her confrontational voice put others to shame—namely, her fellow citizens who lacked the courage to challenge tyrants.

Her participation in this Mexican assembly of newspapers was an anomaly. Her rhetoric conformed to the deliberative and confrontational tone of other major revolutionary and intellectual writers such as Flores Magón, Camilo Arriaga, Juan Sarabia, Antonio Díaz Soto y Gama, and Filomeno Mata,[13] yet it presented its own feminist agenda within this genre of male-dominated writing. Juana's newspaper articles created a critical space for female political action and established a rare feminine voice in opposition to Díaz; her organic intellectualism remained tied to the poor and disenfranchised.

Juana shared the goal of her male intellectual counterparts in wanting to depose Díaz from office. As such, she felt her rhetoric had to produce a keen awareness of the *científicos*, "the tyrants" that Flores Magón referenced. Juana's distinctive use of opinion essays, a unique linguistic style, and a harsh and belligerent voice had a persuasive effect on her audience. For example, she directly addressed the dictator in her early 1903 *Vésper* writings, titled "Al General Díaz."[14] This approach of speaking directly to her audience came to be her revolutionary and discursive mark.

AN INTELLECTUAL REVOLUTIONARY

Juana's early writings struck a nerve with powerful officials of the Catholic Church. Due to growing disapproval from the archbishop of Guanajuato regarding her opposition to the church and its renewed connections with the government, Juana's stay in Guanajuato would only last a year. On November 9, 1901, her press was confiscated, but she later avoided arrest because a supporter and friend warned her of the police's ensuing action.[15] Within two months she was in Mexico City, where she would become deeply involved in the growing movement against the regime, including the liberal clubs that were becoming increasingly relevant in the movement. The liberals were highly political and striving to be perceived as a legitimate force in the ideological battle being waged against the Mexican regime. This led many of the clubs to give formal appointments to members. Accordingly, Juana became involved with the Club Liberal Ponciano Arriago as first or lead speaker at the forefront of nine men.[16] Her work in the club may have included the writing of public protests, manuscripts for the newspapers, and speaking openly at meetings. Such a speaking role was rare for a Mexican woman. Gaining the role as lead speaker revealed her tenacity and strength as an influential and public figure.

Juana also represented the Zaragoza Liberal Club of Cuncamé at the Liberal Congress in Zitácuaro, where in 1902 she was named honorary vice president and presented a rare public speech.[17] This political club served as a forum where members could exchange political ideas and engage in formal debates. As the movement escalated, clubs were forced to meet in secret locations due to the regime's increased control; however, debates continued to take place in the hundreds of newspapers that circulated throughout the country.

DISCURSIVE DEVIANT

In the years leading up to the revolution, Juana became more involved in journalistic, militant, and anti-Díaz activities. She continued to employ a radical voice, such as that of the May 1903 article "¡Ecce Homo!," in which she addressed the audience as if she were Pontius Pilate, sole judge and jury of the people.[18] She presented Díaz, the dictator, to the people of Mexico declaring, "Flatterers! Here is your man as he is." Her tone, though, is not one of praise but of scorn: "What Porfirio Díaz figures is that his most humble servant, Juana B. Gutiérrez de Mendoza, wants to snatch away his title of local thug."[19] To add insult to injury, she claimed that Díaz would be "the first man to be afraid of women."

In an article from July 1903, "Un discurso bulneriano," she employed a play on Bulnes's name. Bulnes was one of Díaz's supporters who gave a flattering speech in praise of the dictator, and she converted his name into an adjective, *bulneriano*, which made reference to the type of speeches that Bulnes delivered.[20] Juana pointed out that "the claims Mr. Bulnes makes toward Esquire Porfirio in praising him are the same we make in accusing him."[21] In 1903, after the publication of radical open letters to the public and lengthy high-rhetorical editorials, she was thrown in jail for the second time, along with her friend Elisa Acuña y Rosete.[22]

In Latin America, separation of men and women in prisons was a common practice.[23] Many of these female prisons were run by nuns and functioned as reform institutions meant to "enable them [the women] to support themselves without committing crimes."[24] In Mexico, many of the women were charged with crimes of sexual deviance and placed in hospitals that functioned essentially as prisons. Juana, however, was charged with discursive deviance, never with sexual deviance. The authorities considered her infraction of speaking out to be a male offense, not necessarily a feminized crime. Instead of being sent to a women's prison, she was assigned to the infamous Belén prison, which at the time housed male revolutionaries such as the Flores Magón brothers, Camilo Arriaga, and Santiago de la Hoz.[25]

NO REFUGE FOR THE RADICALS

After her 1903 incarceration, Juana sought freedom of speech in the United States and left Mexico for Laredo, Texas. There she would again convene with a group of revolutionary intellectuals that included Ricardo and Enrique Flores Magón, Camilo Arriaga, Juan Sarabia, Sara Estela Ramírez, and Elisa Acuña y Rosete. The group would gather at Ramírez's home, holding meetings around the kitchen table.[26] From these discussions, serious differences about the direction of Mexico's politics began to emerge.[27] Ricardo Flores Magón's solution to the problems of Mexico leaned toward a socialist and anarchist ideology, while Camilo Arriaga's ideas included the tenets of democracy and the principles of the Mexican Constitution of 1857. The ideological differences between the Flores Magón brothers and Arriaga eventually resulted in a parting of ways. Juana may have been a radical thinker and writer, but she did not espouse anarchy, and in this ideological battle she sided with Arriaga.[28]

In 1904 Juana and her friend Elisa followed Arriaga to San Antonio, Texas, where the two women continued to circulate *Vésper* in Mexico and the United States. They also published a phantom newspaper, *La Protesta Nacional*, which indicated on the broadsheet that it was being published in Saltillo, Mexico, so as to confuse the Mexican authorities. Although able to write freely, Juana never felt comfortable with people in the United States; thus she continued to address her people in Mexico. Juana and Elisa remained only two years in the United States because they felt that their physical exile was not conducive to their social struggle in Mexico. Time spent in San Antonio solidified Juana's negative views of the United States, which served to further separate her from mainstream liberals. Shortly before returning to Mexico, Juana and Elisa stayed with Sara Ramírez in Laredo, where they continued to write and publish their articles.

Upon Juana's return to Mexico in 1905, her once staunch supporter, Ricardo Flores Magón, began to speak out against her. Though he would remain in exile in the United States for the rest of his life, Flores Magón tried to discredit her revolutionary efforts. Possibly as a backlash against disagreeing with his politics, he accused her of being unpatriotic and, worse yet for that time, a lesbian, two claims that she fervently resisted in various articles. She responded to the accusations with bold counterallegations of her own. On July 1, 1906, in an article titled "Redentores de la peseta," she discounted the claims against her and accused Flores Magón of not living up to the movement's ideals.

She rejected his personal "slander and attacks" against her and argued that the Flores Magón brothers "are the insulters of women who bellow with rage and bitterness because we have been very worthy and we love our homeland dearly so as not to take its misfortunes to the marketplace, and sell its adversity for a peseta."[29]

Juana must have known that this exchange would likely damage her image in the public's eye, but she showed a spirit of relentless courage. With her rhetorical knowledge, she turned the tables on the situation and used it as an opportunity to solidify her beliefs and her love of country. Other liberals called for reconciliation between the two, but the divide ran too deep, and they were never reconciled.[30] Juana then allied herself with others with whom she more closely identified.

The years 1907 to 1911 were filled with a flurry of activism and collaboration with many revolutionaries and politicians. In 1907 Juana collaborated again with Sara Estela Ramírez in the reorganization of Ramírez's newspaper, *La Corregidora*, and helped establish another newspaper, *El Partido Socialista*, which had ties to a group of industrial workers.[31] She also worked with Dolores Jiménez y Muro, José Edilberto Pinelo, Elisa Acuña y Rosete, and other liberals to organize the workers union Socialismo Mexicano. In keeping with Juana's character, she utilized the power of discourse to circulate the union's ideas and cofounded and edited its weekly paper, *Anáhuac*.[32]

Another emerging periodical, *El Partido Socialista*, commissioned Juana to interview the main leader of the movement against Díaz's reelection, Francisco I. Madero.[33] Madero believed in true democracy for Mexico, which made him attractive to other socialists and activists, including Juana and her collaborators.[34] Because of a growing realization that the efforts of so many activists had failed to make political headway, Juana may have shifted her thinking from action and change through discourse to transformation by means of armed revolt. Through personal interaction with Madero, she was convinced that he was the most qualified leader to replace Díaz. If he agreed to lead the revolt against Díaz, she would place her full support behind him, with the clear understanding that her support and articles could once again land her in jail and potentially lead to personal injury. After her interview was released in 1907, she continued with Maderista activities and was again jailed in 1909 in the Belén prison.[35] After her release, she encouraged other women to become politically active in Mexico City, and she was instrumental in the organization of a feminist Maderista political club, Club Político Feminil Amigas de Pueblo. She was also part of another political feminist club, Hijas de Cuauhtémoc, led by well-known activist Dolores Jiménez y Muro.[36]

In 1910 the political frustration increased exponentially, which motivated Juana to revive her protest newspaper *Vésper*. Even as the government sought to arrest or harass Maderistas, in the May 8, 1910, issue, Juana continued to fully support Madero. In an editorial, "Don Francisco I. Madero: Candidato a la presidencia de la República," she praised Madero, not for standing up to Díaz, but for standing "up in front of these people like a citizen with rights and duties to carry out."[37]

Some newspapers caved under the pressure of censorship. On May 1, 1910, for example, *Evolución*, a newspaper published by workers in Mexico City, fully supported Madero's candidacy in the Anti-Reelectionist Party.[38] The printer, Rafael Quintero, who later became the leader of Casa del Obrero Mundial, a major workers union, urged workers to "reclaim their rights and fulfill their duties as worthy citizens of a country that…celebrates the triumph of democratic institutions."[39] But within the first month of the publication, Quintero and the newspaper minimized their strong discourse and "instead proposed a protagonism among workers in the defense of citizenship rights. The very real possibility of repression forced critics of the government to use rhetorical, elliptical, and abstract arguments and above all to avoid direct attacks on President Díaz."[40] As others acquiesced, Juana embraced a more politically dangerous approach, intensifying her attacks on activists such as Quintero for his cowardice and chastising Díaz for being politically obstinate.

REVOLUTION BEGINS

On November 20, 1910, at the urging of Madero in the Plan de San Luis Potosí (which read, "Fellow citizens, do not hesitate, even for a moment!

Take up arms, throw the usurpers out of power, recover your rights as free men"), the Mexican Revolution began.[41] The uprising was the beginning of the long and bloody conflict that would evolve into an extremely complex and overwhelming war.[42]

Few men in Mexico and even fewer women were as brazen about their political ideas as Juana, and her participation in the revolution would prove to be the true embodiment of her rhetoric. In March 1911, toward the beginning of the revolution, she took part in the Complot de Tacubaya, a conspiracy to overthrow the Díaz regime. The plot was betrayed, and Juana was again jailed and later released after Madero had become president.[43] With Madero in power (1911–13), she received compensation for the printing press, which Díaz had confiscated. Amid this revolutionary environment, she left Mexico City in 1912 for Morelos, where Zapata was engaged in fighting.[44] Juana remained active there in the latest revolutionary politics. Along with the group she had organized in 1909, Amigas del Pueblo, she wrote a manifesto protesting Madero's assassination by Victoriano Huerta's men and featured it in *El Voto* and *Vésper*.[45] In the manifesto, she issued a call for women's involvement in the revolution, not as helpmates to men but as independent women.

In doing so, Juana again rejected the traditional perceptions of women. Her rhetorical defiance, at times, seems to have been actualized and carried out in isolation from other women; however, many women did come together in support of Madero and the revolution that was the genesis for a feminist movement, which was not well known.[46] With Huerta now in power, a lack of sympathy prevailed for Zapatistas and their supporters. In 1914 Juana was again imprisoned, this time for ten months, after she was captured while carrying out a mission commissioned by General Zapata.[47] Upon her release, she returned to the rank and file of Zapata's followers, where the general honored her, named her a colonel, and made her the leader of the Regimiento Victoria.[48] This title was of little comfort to Juana, who saw her desire for justice crumble as she witnessed the disintegration of a movement she once believed would lead to practical solutions.

The assassination of Zapata in April 1919 dismantled the efforts of the agrarian movement. Two months after Zapata's betrayal and assassination, Juana readdressed the direction of her mission, which conflicted with the sentiments of President Carranza, who remained in power. Through the publication of her new paper, *El Desmonte*, Juana endeavored to clear out the chaos of the present and to foster a new direction. In the article "¡Por la tierra y por la raza!" Juana promised to keep Zapata's movement alive.[49] She wrote that "*Desmonte* will know how to keep the flag aloft that was taken up from the field of battle; *Desmonte* will know how to carry on with dignity the motto of a dreamer of his people."[50]

For Juana, the revolution, with its myriad shifts in power, killings, and battles, did not bring about solutions to societal problems. In particular, she felt that a politician's words did not accomplish anything for the people. In another *Desmonte* article, "Hechos, no palabras," she defined revolutionary rhetoric as empty talk; only when it was infused with action and change would the words become meaningful. "Revolutions are not made with desires, neither with speeches nor with printed paper," she wrote. Further, they are "absolutely ineffectual when everything is reduced to that."[51] On more than one occasion in the new newspaper, Juana offered a critique of the men in power and verbalized her philosophy about the power of discourse. She stated that social change, such as that induced by the revolution, could not be created solely through orations nor the printed word. Her understanding of the nature of rhetoric assumed that one's discourse should bring about some social action. For the next twenty-two years of struggle, she would live by her philosophy.

Seeking approval was not her style, and Juana never extended an apology for her definitive rhetorical stances. Witnessing and sharing in the struggles of indigenous people amid a violent revolution, and enduring countless broken promises extended to her people, served as her reasons to write unapologetically. Her frank rhetoric may have contributed to the reasons she has been overlooked in Mexican history. In much the same way, the Mexican government refused to validate the works and efforts of *las soldaderas*. Juana's inclusion in Mexican and American rhetorical history, and in this collection of other extraordinary women, serves as an acknowledgment of the importance of women's roles in the discursive and intellectual realm of revolutionary movements.

Although this essay centers on Mexican historical events, the rising numbers of Mexican Americans living in the United States blurs the line of what is considered "our" American history. Investigating our sisters to the south makes U.S. history more democratically inclusive and respectful of other cultures. Few mainstream Mexican histories acknowledge Mexican women's discursive participation, mostly because the public domain offered limited possibilities for them. Although several histories counter the stereotyping of Mexican women at the turn of the century and in contemporary times, the collective conscience of society today does not carry these narratives. Juana's writings add to previous scholars' evidence that women in Mexico in the early twentieth century did take an active role in launching and participating in the Mexican Revolution.

Juana had fulfilled the promise she made early in *Vésper* when she announced, "*Vésper* siempre ocupará su puesto."[52] The newspaper, synonymous with its founder's identity, stormed onto the male-dominated political-journalistic scene and occupied a distinctive discursive space. With so much rhetorical activism, Juana was eventually recognized as an influence in the formation of Mexican political journalism, but she seems to have for the most part been forgotten.[53] She was active for over forty years in the struggle to give workers, the poor, the marginalized, and women a public voice. "I will never be silenced!" she proclaimed in 1935, seven years before her death. In one of her last publications, *Alma Mexicana*, she claimed that "thirty-five years of incessant fighting and sixty years of living can put anyone out of combat, or at least serve to justify indifference or to disguise cowardice."[54] For her, the intimate awareness of so many poor and disenfranchised people in Mexico "only had one solution: to continue [her] work, although bearing the sad conviction that it is all in vain."[55] In analyzing Juana's scholarly, activist, and revolutionary writings, it is clear that none of her discourse or activism was spoken or written in vain.

Soldaderas The *adelita* (activist) or *soldadera* (soldier) of the Mexican Revolution is in some ways hard to characterize, for her image in life and in art is often hard to separate. Usually lacking supply and medical units, Mexican armies were utterly dependent upon soldaderas—women hired by or related to soldiers—as their quartermasters in the army. Soldaderas, sometimes with children in tow, followed the troops on foot, set up camp, foraged for food and firewood, washed and mended the soldiers' clothing, tended the wounded, and even buried the dead. In life and in song, soldaderas became the romanticized sweethearts of and helpmates to their soldiers as *valentinas* (brave ones) and adelitas.

Las Soldaderas

**They use their *rebozo* (shawl) to carry babies or
ammunition. Whether standing or sitting, they are
the image of resistance.**

"I'll bring you water."
"I'll carry pots and pans to make your food."
"I'll delouse you."
"I'll pack up your things."
"I'll wash your clothes."
"I'll get wood to make a fire."
"I'll oil your rifle."
"I'll light your smokes, and if there's no regular tobacco I'll roll up
some of the wild stuff in these corn husks."
"I'll carry your Mauser and your cartridges."
"I'll keep your powder dry."
"I'll make a home for you on the battlefield."
"I'll be your mattress, you can lie on my guts."
"I'll have your baby in the trenches."

The soldaderas followed the troops and rode on the roof of the rail-cars because the horses had to be protected. "The horses travel inside the wagons," as ordered by Pancho Villa. The loss of a mare was an irreparable setback, but the loss of a woman, well, who knows. At their man's side, the soldaderas endured the northern snow, the frost, and the early morning dew until the wind and the first rays of sunshine dried their clothes. The sun, as everyone knows, is a blanket for the poor; it shines on everyone no matter how late it rises. The soldaderas were both sunshine and blanket, covering legs and arms, heads and eyes, baskets and rifles; they were a huge rebozo spread over the shaggy troops that marched without knowing how, nor where to, nor what for.

The soldaderas clambered on board the train of life, the train of combat, the train of destiny. They didn't let the train leave them behind, unlike the respectable women who took shelter from harsh conditions, sitting at the window with a cup of tea in their hands and a handkerchief to dab their eyes. Soldaderas were equipped with the most important attribute in this life: two legs that are willing to walk. When they heard the cry, "The detachment is moving out!" they came to the station with their cooking pots, their bowls, and their child who would soon curl up against a basket and fall asleep. They also brought their fierce dog, or the pig they were fattening up, three chickens, or a lark in a cage, or a mockingbird to keep covered at night and listen to during the day.

Most of the soldiers were teenagers, barely fourteen or fifteen years old. The soldaderas were also quite young, although historians and novelists have depicted them in the same disparaging terms they used to describe the writer Nellie Campobello (1900–1986). Very few were like La Pintada, Juana Gallo, María Pistolas, La Adelita, La Valentina, or La Cucaracha. In the movie *La Generala*, the actress María Félix plays a rough-and-tumble tomboy who, with an arched eyebrow and a cigar between her teeth, calls the shots for herself and for everyone else as well. Was there ever such a soldadera? There is no record of one.

On the other hand, photographer Agustín Casasola (1874–1928) shows women who toil as patiently as ants, carrying water and patting tortillas, keeping the fire going, lugging the portable cooking stove and the *metate*—the flat stone used to grind corn (who knows what it's like to carry a metate for miles across the open country?)—and the bowl for the *atole*, which is a hot maize drink, or coffee they take to their man, saying, "Don't worry, I'll do it." And who, at sundown, cross themselves, their fingers like insects briefly perching on forehead, mouth, and chest, good-luck charms to ward off misfortune and death.

The filmmaker Salvador Toscano (1872–1947) shot thousands of meters of film showing scenes of women, their brown hands holding a grocery bag or giving their man his Mauser and cartridge belt. With their percale skirts and straw hats, their rebozos, and a quizzical look in their dark eyes, they look nothing like the brazen, vulgar, foulmouthed women portrayed by some of the authors who have written about the Mexican Revolution. On the contrary, these soldaderas remain discreetly in the background; when they are at the forefront it is because they have chosen to impersonate a man. They use their rebozo to carry babies or ammunition. Whether standing or sitting, they are the image of resistance. Their diminutive size helps them survive, and their determination shows as they look straight into the camera. When they travel on the roof of a railcar, they talk to the clouds sweeping past them overhead, and at night, when the fighting stops, the soldiers come looking for them and call them *mamá*. Those who do not have a woman are only half a soldier, half an orange, half a horse.

When a soldadera's man dies, she will bury him and make a cross out of stones or with maguey thorns. When night falls she will use her dog-eared cards with pictures of saints to make an altar on the nearest wall or on the ground and light a candle for him. Ernest P. Bicknell, an official with the Red Cross, was at the Presidio, Texas, campground one night and was deeply moved to see the countless candle flames flickering in the darkness and hear the sweet murmur of human voices rising up from the fields. They were praying to Jesus Christ or to the Virgin, beseeching their guardian angel not to forsake them, not to take his eyes off them, not to abandon them because without him they would be lost.

The soldaderas walked all day because, as I said, the horses were for the men. The women were sent on ahead to collect wood, make a fire, and cook the food. They went to the villages to beg for chickens, corn masa to make tortillas, and beans for the stewpot. When people refused to give them these things, the women stole them. It's not that they were brawny and aggressive; on the whole, they were slightly built. But theirs was a hunger that could not be satisfied; they were hungry for change. General Álvaro Obregón (1880–1928), who later became president of Mexico (1920–24), used to send the women and their children ahead of the soldiers, and they often acted as a shield for his troops. They called them "the impediment," but rather than create an impediment they provided protection for the artillery.

Without the soldaderas, the men who were pressed into service would have deserted. During the Spanish Civil War in 1936, militiamen on both sides saw no reason to remain in the barracks or the trenches and just walked off to sleep in their own beds at night. The same thing would have happened in Mexico in 1910 if the women had not been there. Without them, the soldiers would not have eaten, bedded down at night, or stayed to fight. When Mexican troops were deployed they took their soldaderas, who were their little stoves that provided food and warmth. If those soldiers had been unable to carry their homes with them into battle, there would have been no armies.

Nellie Campobello, a great writer, published *Cartucho* (*Cartridge*) in 1931. Her explosive book was more like a grenade that laid bare the tragedy of the Mexican Revolution. In a succession of brief chapters, Nellie sketches a cruel, stark picture of the uprising as seen through the eyes of a little girl who was born before original sin. There are dead men—killed in battle or executed by firing squad—on every page. The girl eagerly watches from her window as men are shot down, and their corpses become her toys. When her favorite one is finally taken away, she misses it because it has entertained her for five days.

Many years later, in 1967, Jesusa Palancares concludes that waging war to make peace is a colossal lie. She counts the bodies left lying on the battlefield with their eyes open and their guts spilling out, and writes that armies were made up of "people who were rounded up at random." According to Jesusa, "The generals grabbed whomever they could find and sent them into battle as cannon fodder because while they were still learning how to carry a rifle, they'd be shot and killed. The young ones, who didn't understand, went straight to the front where they were cut down, their bodies left strewn on the field. They were like little pigs being led to slaughter. One day we shot some reinforcements who'd been sent to join us. I think the war has been misunderstood because what people say about different groups killing each other—saying that there were fathers against their children, brothers against brothers, Carranza's troops, Villa's troops, and Zapata's troops—that was just nonsense because they were all the same wretched kids."[1]

If Nellie Campobello had not recorded her experiences, we would have been deprived of the most creative view of the Mexican Revolution ever written. Yes, I know, we have the writers Mariano Azuela, Martín Luis Guzmán, Rafael F. Muñoz, and the boring Francisco L. Urquizo, but there is no one as authentic as Nellie, no one who could say, as she did: "Such a terrible thing! My eyes had become accustomed to seeing people killed by hot lead that exploded in their bodies. A woman wearing a skirt was left lying on the ground, trussed up like a bundle of clothes. A young boy was placed carefully beside the railway track, without a mark on him; he was pale, his eyes open. I wondered why he was staring like that, he looked as though he was still alive. They threw a handful of dirt on his face and covered his staring eyes." / "Cartridge found what he was looking for." / "Hit the target, hungry for death." / "Chagua dressed in mourning for a while and then became a woman of the streets." / "Mama's eyes, aged by the revolution, shed no tears." / "The sentry in her eyes held the threads of her life." / "A woman came to the door and shouted at one of the officers: 'Hey, you bastard, bring me a bone from Villa's injured knee to make a relic.'" / "Men coming and going, a milling crowd of people. It's amazing, so many men, there are so many people in the world! said my childish mind." / "They killed him quickly, that's how it is with horrible things we don't want to talk about." / "They took the Portillo boys to the Luis Herrera cemetery one quiet afternoon that has been erased from the history of the revolution; it was five o'clock." / "He became my friend because one day we smiled at each other. I showed him my dolls, he smiled, there was hunger in his laughter, and I thought that if I gave him some flour *gorditas* (small, fat tortillas), I would please him." And this surprising portrait of Pancho Villa: "He had tight little curls all over his head; he looked up at Mama with his huge yellowish, almost chestnut-colored eyes that changed color according to the time of day." These excerpts and her other descriptions are as simple as they are accurate, as when she says that there is now an anthill where they buried the revolutionary fighter Nacha Ceniceros.

Why were Nellie Campobello's contemporaries so dismissive of her, when she had seen the revolution with her own eyes? Why were the soldaderas so obviously ignored? The writer Friedrich Katz described Pancho Villa's army as "a folk migration," and the anthropologist Eric Wolf said that "there were women and men, *coronelas* and colonels in Emiliano Zapata's army." Rosa E. King, who lived in Morelos during the revolution, wrote *Tempest over Mexico: A Personal Chronicle*, in which she said that "the Zapatistas were not an army, they were a people who had risen up in arms."

The journalist John Reed asked a soldadera why she was fighting with Pancho Villa's army. The rail-riding woman pointed at her man and replied, "Because he is." Another was more explicit: "I can clearly remember when Filadelfo called me one morning, saying, 'Come on, we're going to fight because our good man Pancho Madero was assassinated today!' We had only been lovers for eight months, our first child wasn't born yet, and I said: 'Why should I go too?' He replied, 'Am I to starve to death? Who will make my tortillas, if not my woman?' It took us three months to travel up north, and I got sick and the baby was born in the desert and it died because we had no water."

"Have you found yourself a woman yet? Who will look after you?" (In the 1980s, the poet Renato Leduc still introduced his wife as "the woman who takes care of me.") They were often abducted, which is why village women were locked up like chickens so that they wouldn't be taken to satisfy the soldiers' most urgent needs.

Women who were taken or raped had no alternative but to become soldaderas. They were tied up and strapped onto the men's horses, and their screams could be heard as their captors galloped away from the village. Spiteful gossips said that sometimes they were screams of pleasure. According to Mariano Azuela, when revolutionaries came to a village the first things they wanted were women and money. It was only later that they demanded horses, food, and weapons.

When rebels attacked landowners and their families and held them prisoner, they threatened to take the women if they were not paid a ransom. They would then take them anyway, with or without a ransom. "The men had their way with all of them, regardless of age, color, religion, or social position." Soldiers serving under General Venustiano Carranza (1859–1920) once abducted fifty nuns and, in due course, dropped them off at a hospital "so that they might have their babies."

People set up guard boxes on the roads leading into their village: "Here come Carranza's soldiers!" "Here come Villa's horsemen!" "Here come the Reds!" "The bad guys are here!" No matter who they were, they all helped themselves to the pretty girls, and the ugly ones too. And older women. Village women who didn't want to be raped or abducted had three options: they could pretend to be men, they could barricade themselves in a stone building, or they could head for the hills. Some of them chose not to wait for rebel troops to arrive but went looking for them. "Before I became a soldadera, I lived an ordinary life," says Jesusa Palancares. "But life is great now and so am I, thanks to the blessed revolution."

Pancho Villa treated women very badly and, according to Jesusa, was a heartless man. This opinion is confirmed by Colonel José María Jaurrieta and the writer Rafael F. Muñoz, the author of the novel *Se llevaron el cañón para Bachimba* (*They Took the Cannon to Bachimba*). The book provides a vivid portrait of Villa, with its memorable description of his steely, wide-set eyes, his full mustache, his teeth "like a mastiff's, crammed into his broad jaw," his skin burned by the northern winter winds, and his innate cruelty.

On December 12, 1916, according to the novelist, Villa's cavalry—Los Dorados—captured the Santa Rosalía railway station in Camargo, Chihuahua, from Carranza's troops, and sixty soldaderas and their children were rounded up and taken prisoner. One of the women in the group fired a shot that struck the Centauro del Norte's sombrero. (Villa was known as the Centaur of the North.) As Muñoz tells it, Villa let out a roar, his eyes aflame.

"You women, who fired that shot?"

No one replied. Then he gave the order.

"Shoot them one by one until they tell us who it was."

None of them moved. They preferred to die than to betray one of their own.

Rafael F. Muñoz then describes how the women clustered even closer together. Villa drew his gun and held it up over his head.

"Women, who fired that shot?"

An old, pockmarked woman raised her arm and shouted: "We all did. We all want to kill you!"

The rebel leader drew back. "All of you? Well, you'll all die before I do."

The soldiers tied the women together, four, five, or six to a bunch. They tied the ropes tight, cutting into their bodies. Soon all sixty women were bound up in ten or twelve bundles of human flesh, some standing upright, others lying on the ground like cords of wood, like barrels.

The wood was dry and the wind was blowing, so the human pyre burned quickly. The women's skirts caught fire first, then their hair, and soon the air was filled with the smell of burning flesh. But the soldaderas never stopped cursing Villa. And as they were engulfed in flames, he heard a hoarse voice screaming from the pyre: "You dog, you son of a bitch, you'll die like a dog!"

One of Villa's Dorados shot the woman, and she fell back onto the bonfire. The Dorados rode back to the village in silence until their leader spoke up, saying, "Damn, those lying women would not shut up! They sure insulted me! They were really starting to piss me off!"

Colonel José María Jaurrieta, the Centauro del Norte's faithful secretary, wrote that this massacre reminded him of Dante's inferno and that the horror of seeing those women slaughtered by Villa's men left him permanently scarred.

Friedrich Katz quotes Jaurrieta, who suggests that Villa acted in self-defense. Or almost. One of the soldaderas tried to kill him, so Villa had them all killed. In *The Life and Times of Pancho Villa*, Katz says: "The massacre of those soldaderas and the rape of the women at Namiquipa were the greatest atrocities Villa committed against civilians during his years as a revolutionary. They marked a fundamental change compared to his behavior prior to his defeat in 1915. Until then, almost every observer had been impressed by Villa's discipline and by his efforts to protect civilians, especially the lower classes."

In 1914 some federal troops ran away from Paredón, Coahuila, abandoning more than three hundred soldaderas. Within twenty-four hours the women had taken up with the single men in Villa's ranks. And with those who were not single, too.

According to the *El Paso Morning Times*, in 1914 there were seventeen thousand men and four thousand women in Pancho Villa's army, but there are many other statistics that show that, without the soldaderas, there would have been no Mexican Revolution.

Petra Herrera went to war ahead of everyone
Bravest girl you ever saw and deadly with a gun.

Petra rose to the rank of *generala* because she was able to convince everyone that she was a man. She rode her horse at a gallop on the front lines, and the soldiers shouted "Come on! We're with Pedro Herrera." She was an excellent shot, which earned her the admiration of Carranza's troops. She passed herself off as a man "in order to remain in active service and rise up in the ranks." In the morning she pretended to shave. "My beard is just starting to grow," she explained. She suffered from goiter, and her eyebrows almost met, like Frida Kahlo's.

As "Pedro Herrera," she blew up bridges and showed great leadership skills as a member of Pancho Villa's army. Alongside four hundred other women, she fought in the second Battle of Torreón on May 30, 1914. Cosme Mendoza Chavira, who was in Villa's ranks, claims that "she took Torreón and turned out the lights when they entered the city." History does not acknowledge her because Villa never gave any woman any credit, and covered up the role she played in the capture of Torreón.

Recognized as an "excellent soldier," she finally came out as a woman, standing in front of the troops to shout: "I am a woman, and I am going to continue to serve as a soldier under my real name: Petra Herrera."

The lack of recognition prompted Petra Herrera to form her own brigade that grew from twenty-five to a thousand women. Male soldiers were forbidden to enter the brigade's campground. Petra would take guard duty at night and shot anyone who tried to approach her women's army. If she came across any man on her rounds, she'd shoot him without so much as a "Who goes there?"

Petra ended up as a waitress in a cantina in Ciudad Juárez, where she worked as a spy for Carranza's people in Chihuahua. One night, a group of drunks harassed her and shot her three times. She survived the attack but died "because the wounds got infected."

There was another Petra—Petra Ruiz—who was nicknamed *el echa balas* (spitting bullets) because of her surly nature and because she fired her carbine from behind adobe walls and was more accurate than a torpedo. She had a violent temper. One day three soldiers were arguing about who would be first to rape a girl they had kidnapped, when "Pedro Ruiz" rode up, firing her gun and shouting, "Let her go, this one is mine." Afraid of her skill with a gun and a knife, the soldiers backed off and let her take their prize. Petra then swung the girl onto her horse and galloped off to take her back to her village. The girl was terrified and would not stop trembling, so Petra stopped in a secluded place along the way. "Stop crying," she said, "we're going to dismount here." Hiding behind some bushes, she took off her hat and, to the girl's astonishment, opened her shirt and exposed her breasts. "Don't be scared, nobody is going to hurt you. I'm a woman, just like you."

Petra Ruiz led one of the battalions that defeated the federal army in Mexico City, and she was promoted to the rank of lieutenant. Later, when Carranza was reviewing his troops, she confronted him and said: "I want you to know that a woman has served you as a soldier."

There was a rumor that women would be expelled from the army, but before that could happen, Petra Ruiz resigned her commission and quit the service.

There were many soldaderas, many Chabelas, Chelas, Chepas, Choles, Chonitas, Chuchas, Conchas, Dionisias, Eufrosinas, Eustaquias, Felizas, Isidras, Joaquinas, Juanas, Lupitas, Modestas, Nachitas, Otilias, Panchas, Pelanchas, Petras, Tomasas, but history mainly remembers those who attained some measure of celebrity. Most of them came from the north because Villa's victories over the federal army in Chihuahua swayed public opinion and convinced whole families that social change was possible, so why not join the scramble to make it happen? Long live Mexico!

Manuela Oaxaca fell in love with Francisco Quinn and followed him as his soldadera because she thought love and war were romantic adventures, but when she realized that her husband was neither romantic nor particularly considerate, she was sorely disappointed.

Francisco Quinn thought the revolution would lead to heaven on earth; for Manuela, it was all about the screams of the wounded and the smell of gunpowder. She saw no idealism in all those people fighting just to fill their bellies. And she never imagined that the son she gave birth to in 1915 in Chihuahua—Antonio Rodolfo Quinn Oaxaca—would become Anthony Quinn, the actor. One night, one of the many she had spent waiting for her husband, Manuela Oaxaca Quinn decided to leave him and get a job so that she could support her newborn baby, though the couple eventually reconciled. When Elizabeth Salas interviewed Manuela for her magnificent book *Soldaderas in the Mexican Military*, Manuela explained that being a soldadera had stripped her of all her illusions about romance and adventure: "The very first battles changed her view of love. Being a soldadera was a nightmare. Her husband was not a fairy tale knight in shining armor who would come riding to her rescue. On the contrary, Manuela lived in constant fear that at any minute the black horseman of death would appear. Love turned out to be nothing like what she had expected it to be; instead, it meant being suspicious of everything and waiting endlessly for things to happen. Love meant cooking food and mending clothes for a soldier who had to report for duty on the front line. Love meant thanking God that he was still alive."

Manuela Quinn also never imagined that, many years later, her son Anthony would be cast as Jesús Sánchez, the patriarch of *The Children of Sánchez*, in the movie version of the book by Oscar Lewis. This role was a perfect fit for the actor who, as a child, had suffered the same hardships that Sánchez and his children were still suffering fifty years after the revolution that only brought justice for those who betrayed it.

The locomotive was the main protagonist of the Mexican Revolution, but the Adelitas and Valentinas came a close second. They could be cut down by a bullet at any moment, of course, but they did have one advantage: they could always find another man and make a new life for themselves when the battle was over. Maybe that is why the song begs "Adelita" not to go off with someone else.

Popular ballads, or *corridos*, made up for the way history ignored the soldaderas, and "La Adelita" is still popular to this day. The writer Baltasar Dromundo collected one version of the song, but there are several others. They all mention buying Adelita a silk dress or a rebozo and taking her to the dance at army headquarters. And they all include the memorable verse that advises "following her on land or sea; if by sea in a warship, if by land in a military railway train."

Nellie Campobello—who wrote two novels, *Cartucho* and *Las manos de mamá* (*A Mother's Hands*)—was never granted the legendary status she deserves despite the fact that she is the only woman to have authored works about the Mexican Revolution. Her colleagues never acknowledged her nor paid her tribute of any kind, so much so that we are unsure exactly when and how she died. I would anoint her as a priestess, make a cross with her rifle and cartridge belt, and appoint Juan Rulfo and Elena Garro as her acolytes. Martín Luis Guzmán and Mariano Azuela would be altar boys to hold the censer.

The soldaderas may have been ignored by history, but that has in no way diminished their role. To this day, on Mexican national holidays, girls in government elementary schools still sing:

I ride the rails and Juan is my man
he is my darling and I am his love.

When the train is leaving, he will say:
"Goodbye my rail-rider, your Juan's going away." (...)

My ivory-handled pistols are ready to attack
whenever there is shooting / along the railway track. (...)

Courage like mine is seldom seen
in the heat of battle I'm still the queen.

I am a soldadera with Juan at my side.
He's one of a kind, he's my joy and my pride.

Valientas The Mexican Revolution wreaked havoc on families throughout the country. Husbands and fathers disappeared, victims of conscription, casualties of battle, or consumed by a desire for adventure. The women who accompanied their men to war gained notoriety as *soldaderas*, actively functioning as supply lines and joining the fight. But waves of their sisters chose another path: to escape war-ravaged Mexico for los Estados Unidos. Many had small children in tow. Many settled in Texas, starting new lives from nothing. Their descendants became leaders in cities like San Antonio, transforming communities into hubs of Latino culture. Unlike the soldaderas, this group's role in history has gone virtually unnoticed. We will christen this group with the name they deserve: *las valientas* (the brave ones). Leonila Barrios Ortiz and Cristina Jiminez Sosa, *las dos abuelas* of Lionel Sosa, were two such valientas. This is their story as he reimagines it.

Two Women, One Story

LIONEL SOSA

**These brave women, who have always been
overlooked by history, now have a name—**
las valientas.

I HAD TWO GRANDMOTHERS. THEY NEVER SPOKE, THEY NEVER MET. YET BE-
cause they were similar in so many ways, they could have been mistaken for the same woman. Cristina Jimenez Sosa was born in Puebla,
but the family soon moved to Mexico City, the place she called home.
My maternal grandmother, Leonila Barrios Ortiz, was a proud *norteña*,
from Monterrey, Nuevo León. Neither planned to leave Mexico, yet
both did. Neither planned to become single mothers. Both managed the
transition. Neither had the intention of becoming hyphenated Americans, yet there they were—*San Antonianas* in a strange country, with
kids to raise, no job, no home, and no idea what the future might bring.

Although I had always known, by family lore, how they each came
to Texas, it never occurred to me that their similar circumstances were
more than random coincidence. Until the centennial of the Mexican
Revolution of 1910, I was ignorant of their history, the forces that
drove their decisions, and the impact they and others made. Over

the past decade, I've encountered some readings about the topic, and I have come to realize that my two grandmothers were just two of hundreds of thousands, part of a large wave of emigrants, *refugiadas de la revolución*, who fled Mexico and made the United States their new home. Some came with husbands; some joined husbands who had come to the United States ahead of them. But many came *solitas*, on their own—or like my *abuelas*, on their own with little ones.

The fact that I didn't imagine until recently that my grandmothers were part of *una gran migración de las valientas* is not as odd as it seems, because they were virtually invisible. No references were made to them in the Texas history we read. No celebrations were held in their honor. No romantic, iconic photographs were recorded by Casasola. There were only the stories, passed down across dining tables or on back porches. The proof, the ephemera, of their journeys existed only in scrapbooks or cardboard boxes tucked away in the closet or stashed under the bed.

So here we are, putting a name to a large group of women who did nothing less than change the course of history in not one, but two, countries. These women were brave enough to leave Mexico with all the odds stacked against them and make it in a new country. Sick of the war at their doorstep, and of the destruction and devastation all around them, they finally lost (or found) hope and came north to Texas, many vowing never to return. These brave women, who have always been overlooked by history, now have a name—*las valientas*—courtesy of this book devoted to telling their stories.

Cristina and Leonila were part of a demographic tsunami that changed the face of Texas between 1910 and 1927, the years of the Mexican Revolution. Here in San Antonio, most of our friends of Mexican descent—fellow artists and civic and community leaders from many fields—had a mother or grandmother who arrived during the *revolución*. My wife, Kathy, and I set up camp at a Mexican restaurant popular with our friends to ask them. The answer, unfailingly, was yes. Cristina and Leonila were not alone. They were members of a vast and secret society, a great unheralded history that deserved the light of day.

Las valientas, some like Carolina Munguía, were high-profile leaders and activists in their time. Henry Cisneros's grandmother formed the first recognized association for Latina mothers devoted to child welfare and education reform. Other women were leaders in their churches, among their neighbors, and certainly in their homes, raising a generation of entrepreneurs, civic leaders, and elected officials who would become professors, university presidents, activists and organizers, city councilmembers, members of the state legislature, and members of the U.S. Congress (like Joaquin Castro), and mayors (like Henry Cisneros and Julián Castro, who were both later named cabinet secretaries).

As for Cristina and Leonila, both of their husbands had disappeared near the end of 1910. Men who left their family weren't unusual in those days. They were routinely drafted to fight in the army. Others were conscripted into renegade fighting units led by revolutionaries like Pancho Villa and Emiliano Zapata. Some came back. My grandfathers did not. One left to become a bandleader in the U.S. army, and the other fled to escape the responsibilities of raising a family with no job.

What I know of my grandmothers' journeys is what I was told by my mom and my dad—and in the end, it isn't nearly enough. I never met Leonila, who died when my mother was sixteen. I did know my father's mother, Cristina, whom I was afraid of as a little boy. Not knowing her as a young woman, I can't say if she was grumpy by nature or if her long, hard journey made her so. I will tell their stories as I remember them.

CRISTINA JIMENEZ SOSA, THE CHAMELEON

Cristina was a brave and independent woman who could do it all. She started out as a mother and wife. Over the course of her life, she worked as a laundress, entrepreneur, midwife, nurse, and, finally, just a grandma.

When my grandfather disappeared, she was left with no means of support and four children all under the age of fourteen. She had no place to go and no way to earn a living. Growing desperate, she remarried quickly in an effort to find security for herself and her children, Fernandito, Alicia, Herlinda, and Roberto, my father. The marriage didn't work out, and Cristina divorced Señor Nuche. She made her way north with her brood to Monclova for a year, where she took in laundry to make ends meet. When the battles of the revolution reached their doorstep for a second time, the family would be forced to move again.

They traveled north, reaching the next town, Piedras Negras, which is on the Texas border. Cristina and her children waited several months in hopes that the war would end so they could return home, but waiting was an exercise in futility. The bombs were still exploding nearby, the bullets still flying, the soldiers still falling, the innocent still dying. Fearing for their lives again, the family finally crossed to Eagle Pass, on the U.S. side of the border.

No más. No more. Cristina gave up on Mexico. Although the main battles of the revolution had subsided, things were still unsafe. At last she could say it out loud: "To hell with you, Mexico, and all the pain you've caused us." As a teenager, I heard her curse Mexico more than once.

Like so many Mexicans, Cristina settled in San Antonio, a welcoming and prosperous city where many spoke her language. She started a home laundry in a black and Mexican neighborhood near downtown. She and her four children washed and ironed clothes for the neighbors and, after a few years, scraped enough pennies together to move to the all-Mexican side of town.

Now committed to the United States, Cristina worked even harder, studied, became a midwife, and then a nurse. She was a devoted churchgoing Protestant (unusual in the days when most Mexicans were Catholic) who expected her children to be good, honest U.S. citizens. She taught them personal responsibility and family values and encouraged them to become self-sufficient, productive adults. She never married again, devoting the rest of her days to the family.

The year was 1935. My mom and dad were in their teens. They met in a night school class and fell in love. I still have some of their love letters. My favorite is a Valentine card from my dad expressing his love for his beloved Anita. The card is full of pictures of flowers, and his handwriting is perfect, as if a calligrapher had penned it. The two married on May 15, 1938, at the Iglesia Cristiana on El Paso Street. Cristina paid for the wedding and insisted they marry at her church, even though she knew my mom would have preferred a Catholic wedding. The two were always at odds about one thing or another.

That same year, my dad, at the young age of twenty-one, opened his first and only business, the Prospect Hill Cleaners, on the city's west side. He didn't see the move as a big risk. After all, he'd had years of experience doing laundry. Cristina's entrepreneurial spirit had rubbed off. In the very back of the cleaners was a single large room where we lived. My brother Robert and I were born there and delivered by our grandmother, Cristina, who was now a respected midwife.

The Prospect Hill Cleaners was good to the Sosa family. After three years of living in the back of the shop, Dad bought us a three-room house at 245 Pendleton Street, located by the railroad tracks near a giant meatpacking house that stunk twenty-four hours a day. My youngest brother, Dan, was born there. Now the family consisted of Mom, Dad, and us three boys.

The truth about what happened to Cristina's husband, Fernando—my grandfather—remains a mystery. Some claimed he died young, a victim of the flu epidemic of 1918, and is buried in the Basilica de Nuestra Señora de Guadalupe in Mexico City. Others say he found a new love and went on to become a successful businessman. Regardless, after he disappeared, Fernando ceased being real and became this huge romantic legend in our family lore.

My dad's brother, who was also named Fernando, chose a different path. He wanted to do something besides laundry. He went back and forth across the border for years until age twenty-five. That's when his wife in San Antonio found out he already had a wife in Mexico. She turned him in and had him deported. "Tío Fernando" made the most of it in Mexico. He literally willed himself to become a sophisticated intellectual—a lover of art, architecture, fine food, literature, and everything deemed cultured and stylish. To make a living, he put his artistic talents to work designing and manufacturing expensive dolls for the wealthy.

Once every three or four years he would drive to San Antonio. His arrival was always a big deal. He'd pull up in a beautiful antique Mercedes-Benz he called Meche (short for Mercedes), wearing a fine suit and huge scarf. To us, it seemed like a Picasso or a Dalí had just arrived at our doorstep. I wanted to be just like him.

Looking back, I realize how unfair it is that these men, with their unquestionably exciting and colorful lives, are the stars of the family history. Cristina, who quietly accomplished whatever she set her mind to, changing from laundress to midwife to nurse, and who assumed the work of the men by paying for my parents' wedding, was background. But she was the infrastructure of the family, something no one ever appreciates or even notices, until it breaks or disappears.

LEONILA BARRIOS ORTIZ, THE TOUGH-LOVE WOMAN

Leonila, her younger sister, Mariquita, and an older brother, Raul, took a train to San Antonio when they could no longer stay in Mexico. Leonila's husband, Eduardo, had deserted the family to join the U.S. army, not the Mexican army, to fight in the First World War. He never made it to the front lines. When a high-ranking officer heard him playing the clarinet one evening, he reassigned him to play in the U.S. Fourth Army band. Once there, he wrote letters to the family on occasion. Then one day the letters stopped.

Leonila and her siblings arrived in San Antonio in 1926. Leonila's brood included two grown boys, Goyo and Beto, and my mother, Anita, who was twelve. The extended family moved into a *vecindad*, a shantytown compound close to downtown. The family raised cash for the day-to-day expenses by doing small construction jobs and handiwork. Their tiny, two-room apartment had no electricity or running water. An old water pump and small, dilapidated outhouse could be found in the backyard for the families to share.

Leonila was the woman in charge, keeping the family focused on achieving the American Dream. She assumed the alpha role in the family, and she was good at planning and steering the family in the right direction. My uncles, Goyo and Beto, both became successful carpenters and contractors who helped build some of San Antonio's historic buildings, including the Texas Theatre.

A third brother, Raul *chiquito*, was born in San Antonio from an affair between Leonila and her mysterious lover, El Señor Caballero. It was taboo in those days to acknowledge having children outside of marriage, so Raul was always considered a full brother and not a half-brother.

Both Goyo and Beto lived to be more than one hundred. They were alert and healthy to the very end. Leonila died much younger, at age forty-six, from complications of a gallbladder operation. Anita, my mom, was sixteen at the time and took her death very hard. She felt lost and alone, as if she'd lost her best friend.

Perhaps my mother channeled her grief by carrying Leonila's influence forward. As it turned out, Mother had a knack for real estate. Every few years she would sell our home at a nice profit and buy another. We moved from Pendleton to Salinas Street, where my sister, Mary Christine, was born in 1946, on a night when it hailed golf balls. After another move, we settled down at 2506 Buena Vista. This is the place my siblings and I look back on as the house where we grew up.

LOOKING BACK

Now, as I look back on my two wonderful grandmothers who braved the ravages of war, the uncertainty of a life in a foreign country, the persecution of women before suffrage, and the discrimination against Latinos in a time long past, I am thankful. They taught us all valuable lessons, including the importance of family and of helping one another. But they also taught us to be independent and self-sufficient, to have the strength to overcome any obstacle, and to have the confidence to understand and seize the opportunities before us. Today we are secure in knowing that honesty, love of good, hard work, and dedication to the task at hand can make anything possible.

My grandmothers were only two of the many thousands of women who made a difficult journey in a dangerous time. In the process, not only did these *valientas* revolutionize their families' histories, but in time their progeny revolutionized the American Southwest and the United States itself. I wish my *abuelitas revolucionarias*, my revolutionary grandmothers, could come to life again, if only for one day, so I could ask them the questions I never asked and hear the stories I never knew.

Preservationists The preservation movement west of the Mississippi was born in San Antonio, Texas, in the early decades of the twentieth century, gaining momentum when a group of courageous women turned their wills to conserving historic sites, cultural landmarks, and natural habitats. Their influence would lead to the 1924 establishment of the San Antonio Conservation Society, and in the decades since, many preservationists, mostly women, have continued the cause. Today the missions they fought to save have earned UNESCO World Heritage Site designations, and the city is renowned for protecting its historic assets. Adina De Zavala, teacher and granddaughter of Lorenzo de Zavala; Emily Edwards, artist, author, and friend of Diego Rivera; and Rena Maverick Green were three of the movement's earliest leaders.

Adina De Zavala, Rena Maverick Green, and Emily Edwards

LEWIS F. FISHER

Adina De Zavala overcame great odds to expand the footprint of the hallowed Alamo, pioneered preservation of San Antonio's outlying Spanish missions, identified historic structures, and turned up another rare Spanish landmark in serious danger.

SAN ANTONIO'S DISTINCTIVE AMBIENCE OWES MUCH TO THE EFFORTS OF three pioneering preservationists in the early twentieth century. Adina De Zavala, Rena Maverick Green, and Emily Edwards were activists who found their single marital status an asset in a time when married women were legally subjugated to their husbands. Wives were referred to not by their given names but by their husbands' names, preceded by "Mrs." They could not sign legal documents unless their husbands co-signed, limiting their ability to transact business and handle finances. Although their right to vote was emerging, many had to enjoy independent life outside the home as members of proper women's social clubs, though federations of these clubs could muster enough clout to allow some opportunity for real civic contributions.

Adina De Zavala never married, thus always used her maiden name. She could sign checks and legal papers on her own, as could women who no longer had husbands, though there were certain other distinctions. Rena Maverick Green, widowed at thirty-three, kept her late husband's surname, preceded both by her maiden name and by "Mrs." She was no longer Mrs. Robert B. Green but Mrs. Rena Maverick Green. Emily Edwards divorced in midlife. She could drop her ex-husband's name altogether and revert to her maiden name, always preceded, unlike a widow's, not by "Mrs." but by "Miss." With the fine points of their marital identities thus sorted out, these three women were freer than their married counterparts to forge ahead on their own, fortified as they were against some obstacles of living in what was still a man's world.

First of the three to make her mark was the stern schoolteacher Adina De Zavala. Her effectiveness was often dulled by "her forthrightness, her tendency toward stubbornness, which bordered upon intractableness if she thought she was right," and by, added her biographer, L. Robert Ables, "a quick tongue." Her one non-Anglo-American grandparent was Lorenzo de Zavala, first vice president of the Republic of Texas. Miss De Zavala often spoke with pride of this Hispanic heritage. Despite latter-day suggestions that she suffered ethnic discrimination, no contemporary evidence can be found that she did, nor that the subject even occurred to her. Noted her biographer: "It is an anomaly in the history of the State of Texas that a woman of Spanish-Mexican ancestry should have such an intense desire to preserve and illuminate Texas history while many of her Anglo contemporaries did little or nothing."[1]

Adina De Zavala's public role in preserving Texas history began in 1887, when, at the age of twenty-five, she gathered a group of "patriotic women" to stir up interest in the state's past. Six years later these women helped form the San Antonio chapter of the recently organized Daughters of the Republic of Texas. It was named the De Zavala Chapter, and Miss De Zavala was elected president.

The Alamo by this time had become a cause célèbre. The Alamo church was uncompleted at the time the Spanish mission San Antonio de Valero closed in 1793. It was known as the Alamo by the time its Texian defenders lost the Battle of the Alamo in 1836. After six years of a community-wide preservation effort—led by Mary Adams Maverick, widow of Texas Declaration of Independence signer Samuel A. Maverick—the old church was bought by the State of Texas in 1883. It was the first landmark west of the Mississippi purchased by a public body simply to save it. The City of San Antonio was handed custody, hired a caretaker, and opened it to the public. The former mission's adjacent two-story *convento* remained in private hands.

While the city dealt with maintaining the Alamo church, Adina De Zavala, a devout Roman Catholic, led her Daughters of the Republic of Texas chapter in the first effort to preserve San Antonio's four other eighteenth-century Spanish missions nearby. The ruins of Mission San José's church were her first target. In spring 1902 Miss De Zavala commandeered a friend's horse-drawn buggy and made the rounds of merchants, collecting donations of bricks, lumber, cedar posts, and fence wire, then headed the five miles south to begin repairs. A wooden brace she had built behind the roofless church's entrance helped stabilize the front wall and its distinctive Spanish Baroque doorway. Six months later the bishop gave her DRT chapter a lease on the mission complex then in poorest repair, San Juan Capistrano. She reached out for mission restoration pointers from the successful work of the Landmarks Club of California.[2]

Preservation of San Antonio's missions, however, soon took a back seat after one of the public affrays that have punctuated the modern history of the Alamo. Remains of the Alamo's two-story stone convento projected past the Alamo church into Alamo Plaza and were for sale. The structure was considered unsightly by progressive businessmen who wanted it cleared away for a park that would enhance both the plaza and the view from a large hotel planned to the rear of the convento. Adina De Zavala, in her characteristic style that bordered on the grandiose, had her DRT chapter call for a Congress of Patriotism to turn the convento into a "Texas Hall of Fame—a Museum of History,

Art, Literature and Relics." Membership was open to "anyone of good moral standing interested in the objects of this organization."[3]

But the price of the convento was today's equivalent of $1.8 million. A flurry of fundraising by Adina De Zavala could raise barely 10 percent of that amount. She had, however, been introduced to an attractive young, high-spirited ranching heiress from Corpus Christi named Clara Driscoll. Together they cooked up the notion that, since more fighting in the Battle of the Alamo had taken place in the convento than in the church, what should be called the Alamo was not the church but the convento. Therefore, when Clara Driscoll loaned the balance to purchase the convento, she became known as the Savior of the Alamo. Miss Driscoll was reimbursed a year later by the State of Texas, which added the title of the convento to its ownership of the adjoining church and conveyed custody of both to the DRT's De Zavala Chapter.

The partnership of dour, stubborn schoolteacher and attractive, vivacious heiress soon broke up. Clara Driscoll decided that the original convento actually "fell to pieces long ago," and that the current structure needed to be cleared away. As De Zavalans and Driscollites went at it, Adina De Zavala once barricaded herself inside the convento for three days in an attempt to protect the building. Driscollite Daughters of the Republic seceded from the De Zavala Chapter and gained custody of the Alamo for their new chapter, the Alamo Chapter, and Adina De Zavala was expelled from the state organization. In 1913 Driscollites got all but the lower shell of the convento razed, though it turned out, in fact, to have been an original mission structure.

Adina De Zavala and her allies regrouped as the Daughters and Sons of the Heroes of Texas and also organized the Texas Historical and Landmarks Association, its "Founder's Chapter No. 1 of San Antonio" known, unsurprisingly, as the De Zavala Chapter. Building a statewide organization was not easy. "We have not an organized chapter in Austin," she wrote a preservationist who had returned to Houston. "While our members there are patriotic they have been ill a great part of the time and are very timid, so have not always made themselves known to you on your visits."[4]

The Texas Historical and Landmarks Association placed plaques on numerous landmarks, marking most for the first time. A network of various chapters and auxiliaries appeared. Then in 1915, a major endangered landmark was identified, on the western edge of San Antonio's Military Plaza: the moldering home of the captain of the Spanish presidio that had somehow survived since 1749. This Adina De Zavala romanticized as having been the Spanish Governor's Palace, an "old relic of imperial Spain." She vowed that the "old walls of the palace will ring again with laughter as in the old days when the representatives of the Court of Spain held their entertainments." Such would be accomplished when a second story was added and the "palace" could substitute for her failed Alamo convento proposal and become a Texas Hall of Fame. But fundraising barely sputtered along. No Clara Driscoll could be found to pick up the slack.[5]

While Adina De Zavala was being sustained by force of will, the historic preservation movement was maturing throughout the nation and in San Antonio as well. Miss De Zavala had overcome great odds to expand the footprint of the hallowed Alamo, pioneered preservation of San Antonio's outlying Spanish missions, identified historic structures, and turned up another rare Spanish landmark in serious danger. But women more accustomed to the effectiveness of working in concert with others were now appearing. They were well equipped to take up the cause.

One of those emerging was Rena Maverick Green, fifty, a granddaughter of Samuel and Mary Maverick. She was one of the first women elected to the San Antonio Board of Education and a suffragette whose husband, once a judge, was serving in the state senate at the time of his death. On a San Antonio street corner in 1924 she chanced to meet schoolteacher Emily Edwards, thirty-five, a onetime social worker at Chicago's Hull House and an artist who would study art with Diego Rivera in Mexico. The two lamented the news that one of the city's distinctive landmarks, a Greek Revival market house built in 1859, was to be torn down for the widening of Market Street. They decided to organize. On March 22 they gathered eleven other women to form the San Antonio Conservation Society. Unlike the usual run of preservation groups elsewhere in the country at the time, the Conservation Society was bent on saving not just individual landmarks but the general cultural heritage of the city as well.

The transition from Adina De Zavala's pioneering if uneven preservation leadership did not go smoothly. "She was furious," Emily Edwards remembered. "That was her field, there was just room for nobody else." After a meeting between Miss De Zavala and another Conservation Society member came the report to the new society that "there were many tears, but we will be permitted to exist."[6]

Adina De Zavala kept scolding city hall for inaction on the "Governor's Palace" but soon found herself marginalized. The city passed a bond issue providing funds to purchase and successfully restore the landmark—with no new second story—but oversight of the effort went to a board representing six local historical organizations, only two of them controlled by Adina De Zavala. Several representatives also happened to belong to the Conservation Society. Rena Green, whose late husband had served in the state senate with the mayor, was named chair of the board, though the chore was so fraught with frustrations and interpersonal conflicts that she had to keep a "Diary of Insults" to read and laugh at to maintain her equanimity. The women of the San Antonio Conservation Society would dominate preservation issues in San Antonio for the remainder of the century, while the Texas Historical and Landmarks Association continued on with a lower profile until after the death of Adina De Zavala in 1955, age ninety-three, its president for life.[7]

The Conservation Society's efforts to save the Greek Revival market house failed, but a growing range of effective women, undaunted, branched into broader areas affecting the city's character. Rampant growth was successfully addressed in an effort, led in part by Rena Green, to get the city to commission its first master plan in 1929. Nor did Mrs. Green hesitate to take things into her own hands when necessary. She was walking down Villita Street when she saw workers from the city water board knocking down the Spanish-era Cós House, notwithstanding the marker placed on the building by the Texas Historical and Landmarks Association. Santa Anna's brother-in-law had surrendered in the house months before the Battle of the Alamo. She made the workers stop and called the head of the water board, who hurried over and ended the destruction.

But among the group's most significant preservation efforts was rescuing San José Mission. It was mainly a women's effort. Men were slow coming to the preservation table, though they would eventually recognize the importance of the movement in building San Antonio's tourism industry, critical to the city's economy. San José would become a key component of San Antonio Missions National Historical Park and, in 2015, of the San Antonio Missions UNESCO World Heritage Site, the first World Heritage Site named in Texas.

The Catholic Church had kept ownership of all San Antonio mission churches but the Alamo's. In 1924 Concepción's church was in good repair, San Juan's and Espada's less so. But the finest of all, San José's, had lost its dome when the roof collapsed, taking most of the north wall with it. Half of the landmark tower soon split and fell to the ground. Across the way, the mission's vault-ceilinged granary was in poor condition. Remains of the compound's walls had disappeared as roads crisscrossed the old mission plaza and small houses sprung up within. Worse, the entire site was threatened by creeping development from the city.

Four months after the Conservation Society was organized, Rena Maverick Green was named head of its effort to preserve not just the decaying mission churches but the property around the churches, recognizing that "one of their chief attractions is the open natural country surrounding them." Preserving more than just a historic building was a radical idea in the United States at that time, although in Great Britain, where Mrs. Green frequently visited, founders of the National Trust had long recognized the importance of preserving historic landscapes.[8]

Several years of trying to cajole Catholic bishop Arthur J. Drossaerts into giving the Conservation Society leases to restore the mission churches, like the ones the church in California had provided preservation groups and those Adina De Zavala had obtained more than twenty years earlier, proved fruitless. "The church has no funds for preservation or restoration, but only for saving souls," the bishop said. So Rena Green's committee focused on the surroundings. "Our first step was to buy pieces of land—a few feet at a time—surrounding the mission and granary and save the buildings from threatened encroachments of little homes, stores, filling stations," recalled one member, Amanda Cartwright Taylor. She added that their lawyer "thought we were just a little crazy to buy the land without being able to get a clear title, but we said, 'If we couldn't get title nobody else could,' and went right ahead." What the society couldn't buy "we just fenced, since nobody seemed to own it."[9]

The society purchased ruins of the large stone granary from two of the three families who lived in it, but the resident of the third, Ignacio Salcedo, whom Adina De Zavala had hired nearly three decades earlier to guard what was left of the church, refused. Suddenly, he was arrested for bootlegging and gambling and needed today's equivalent of $35,000 to stay out of jail. If the ladies of the society could come up with that amount, they could have the rest of the granary.

Rena Green and two Conservation Society members went to the National Bank of Commerce for a loan. The other two were married women, known legally as Mrs. Perry Lewis and Mrs. Lane Taylor. They were told "very gently and politely that husbands had to sign a note with wives. We were terribly crestfallen," they continued, "as we had to confess to our husbands and beg them to sign. They did, under duress, calling us the most impractical women of their acquaintance." By the time the persuasive ladies were done, both the president of the bank and its chairman had joined the husbands in "signing a note whose collateral was a pile of rocks."[10]

The granary was rebuilt with the help of federal Depression-era funds, which were also used to begin restoration of the church. By the time restoration funding for the church was canceled due to concerns over separation of church and state, the preservationists had won over Bishop Drossaerts, who finished the job in the belief that "every soul with a living faith" would "be glad to see this monument to religion restored to some at least of its past glory and dedicated anew to its original sacred purpose, the praise of God and the salvation of souls."[11]

Rena Green's daughters remembered their mother's frustrations in dealing with the inadequacies of the time. As improvements spread to other missions, "nobody could control the work or watch it," nor could archaeologists be found to help. A seven-foot skeleton found within the foundations of San Juan's octagonal sacristy was in a bushel basket by the time Mrs. Green arrived, with no specific records made. Nor could provision be found to care for "shards of china, coins, and even Spanish bridle bits," and "many of the artifacts were picked up by tourists. That just drove Mama crazy."[12]

Rena Maverick Green's highest preservation profile may have come through her work with the Spanish missions, though her civic credentials also included a role in keeping a parking garage from being built beneath Travis Park, a victory won five years before her death in 1962 at the age of eighty-eight.

A different legacy was left by Emily Edwards, her cohort in organizing the San Antonio Conservation Society.

Emily Edwards was elected the society's first president in 1924. Her creativity as an art and drama teacher at Brackenridge High School led her to draw some of the first illustrated historical maps of San Antonio and to promote the heritage of the city through a celebrated puppet show aimed at those in a position to make a difference, the city commissioners. At a commissioners' meeting, she sketched each member, then made puppets personifying each one. She wrote a script in loosely written verse in which the commissioners formed a jury hearing a case between Mr. San Antonio, who wanted to kill a goose sitting on five golden eggs, and Mrs. San Antonio, who wanted to save the eggs. Each egg represented an element of San Antonio's charm: Heart of Texas, Missions, History, Tourists, and Beauty.

The puppet show was presented to bemused city commissioners following the close of a regular meeting in September 1924. "Civic pride" won the day and the goose was spared. The performance boosted preservationists' morale but had little practical effect, as landmarks kept falling. Thirty years later, during the controversy over a bridge planned across the San Antonio River Walk to a parking garage, Emily Edwards rewrote the script to emphasize the need for saving the River Walk. The bridge was built anyway, though the commotion launched a groundswell that eventually revived the River Walk, now one of the world's most noted linear parks.

Although Emily Edwards lived away from San Antonio for thirty-three years, returning in 1959, she remained, like her fellow preservationists, an egalitarian activist to the end. From her window in a retirement home northwest of downtown San Antonio, she looked out over Woodlawn Lake, then choked with weeds. "Why is Woodlawn Lake being abandoned to the water lilies?" she asked in a letter to a local newspaper. When nothing was done, six months before her death in 1980 at the age of ninety-one she wrote the Conservation Society, pointing out that the lake needed to be skimmed and "returned to its usefulness. This is a workers neighborhood, and the lake has a special value for fishing, rowing, sailing, swimming."[13]

María Concepción Acevedo de la Llata (b. Santiago de Querétaro, Mexico, 1891; d. Mexico City, Mexico, 1978), a Capuchin nun, was caught up in the violence connected with the Cristero War. Acevedo de la Llata, also known as Madre Conchita, was convicted as the intellectual author of and accomplice to the assassination of President Álvaro Obregón in 1928, but the trial was later judged to be a sham. Following her release from the Mexican penal colony of Islas Marías, Madre Conchita spent the rest of her life advocating for religious liberty and the rights of indigenous Mexicans, especially the Otomi people.

María Concepción Acevedo de la Llata

JENNIFER SPEED

The police arrested her for violating federal law on public worship, the famous *Ley de cultos*, and made a spectacle of carting an abbess and more than a dozen nuns to prison.

REVOLUTIONS ALWAYS HAVE AT LEAST AS MANY UNINTENDED CONSE-quences as they do unanticipated heroes and villains who emerge in the chaos. María Concepción Acevedo de la Llata, known as Madre Conchita, embodies both. She never intended to be in the public sphere at all, and probably never sought to engage in political opposition.[1] Nevertheless, the Mexican Revolution and the Cristero War (Cristiada, Guerra Cristera) came to her. Revolution forced her out of her cloistered religious convent, prompted her to engage in nonviolent political resistance as a consequence of pursuing religious life, and eventually drew her into the orbit of a political assassin. As a result of a sensational trial, Conchita's life was scrutinized in the Mexican and international press, as far, figuratively, from her intended life as she ever could have imagined.

The context for this interpretation of Conchita's life and her autobiographical life-writing lies at the intersection of major political upheaval and social transitions triggered by the Mexican Revolution, changing ideas about law and justice, deeply entrenched religious cultural and institutional norms, conflicts about the proper role of women in society, and the meaning of personal narrative writing. In order to challenge public portrayals of her life and character that were not of her own making, Conchita used the interpretive power of autobiography, in multiple iterations and versions and composed over decades, to praise God and reclaim the truth of her own life. This essay is not concerned with Conchita's guilt or innocence. I might even argue that it is not really concerned with the truth. Instead, it focuses on the ways in which Conchita reclaimed for herself the thread of meaning that ran through her own life story, especially her faith and her desire for martyrdom.

Conchita began interpreting her own life in writing no later than 1928, with her earliest texts focusing on the two-year period from the time of her trial as the co-conspirator in the assassination of Álvaro Obregón through her journey to Mexico's offshore penal colony, Islas Marías. She is the author of four books covering different stages of her life (published in 1957, 1962, 1965, and 1974), each with a different emphasis.[2] Her personal writings would eventually appear in print over a period of more than fifty years as new, revised, or reprinted editions. Conchita was also paid to publish portions of her life story in the Mexican periodical *Hoy* in serial format in 1944.[3]

Whereas many authors who choose the autobiographical form leave no explanation as to their literary impulse, Conchita self-consciously chose to write as a way of telling her truth. From her own vantage point, Mexico's apostolic delegate "provoked" her to write by acting against her. The same man who twice went into exile to protect himself from violent anticlericalism saw no moral conflict in excommunicating a nun whose only crime was persisting in her faith. In writing, she sought "to do nothing more than to defend the truth, with the few facts that are known and can be verified, because to defend myself would be a useless undertaking." She concluded by claiming that "lies should not live among us, and false deeds should not be written into history."[4] On another occasion, she says that she had begun to write "something like an autobiography" to her attorney, but was not able to finish it. She self-consciously claimed the right to tell her story, even an obligation to do so ("I believe that I must write"), because it was the truth.[5] Conchita's efforts to reclaim the public narrative about her faith and her life are the focus of this essay.

RELIGIOUS LIFE AS A RADICAL ACT

Conchita was drawn to religious life in her late teens. She overcame the objections of her parents and became a postulant of the newly established convent of the Discalced Sacramentary Capuchins in 1911 in her hometown of Querétaro. A year later, in December 1912, she made her final vows and embraced a life of silent contemplation and prayer within her cloistered community, "having only God as witness and confidant."[6] She expected to remain there for the rest of her life. That dream came to an end less than two years later when the convent's chaplain feared that constitutionalist forces led by Venustiano Carranza (*carrancistas*) would enter the convent by force.

Conchita's decision to become a cloistered nun was itself an act of defiance, given how deeply entrenched was the conflict between church and state when she came of age. Long-standing resentments over the Catholic Church's interference in secular affairs in Mexico led to a number of anticlerical provisions in Mexico's 1857 Constitution. Many liberals and reformers determined that the constitution did not go far enough in limiting the church's reach, prompting politicians to issue a number of reform laws to reduce ecclesiastical influence in government and public life. The reformers tried to completely separate religious and secular life, but, in fact, the government came to exercise control over important aspects of Catholic practice.

Under a reform law promulgated by President Benito Juárez in 1863, the Mexican government ordered the closing of all monasteries and convents, with inhabitants ordered to leave within eight days of the law's promulgation. The text of the decree hints at Juárez's discomfort with the idea of congregations of women, essentially outside of the law and under the "hand of the priesthood."[7] Although it is true that women's congregations had male confessors and chaplains, their members usually enjoyed independence and agency within a completely feminine space that was otherwise unavailable to them outside the convent walls. With that single reform law, Mexico tried to end a practice that had been a feature of Christian devotion since its earliest centuries—and Conchita knew it. At some point during her trials, she looked back and recalled reading the Desert Fathers, who also had sought to live apart from the temptations and demands of the world.[8] It was that life of religious seclusion, banned by federal law, to which Conchita had dedicated herself.

From late July 1914, when the *carrancistas* had prompted Conchita's community to evacuate, through the following decade, she and her fellow nuns were forced to confront Mexico's political reality. They perpetually faced the possibility of having to relocate or disperse on a moment's notice, and for an extended period they took up residence with another women's community that took in daughters of revolutionaries. Conchita recalled that those girls had arrived starving and infested with parasites, full of stories of "hatred, bloodshed, and cruelty without limits."[9] Eventually, in 1922, Conchita was given orders from the archbishop of Mexico to assume the role of mother superior, or abbess, at a convent in Tlalpan, a town near Mexico City.[10]

As abbess, Conchita (now "Madre Conchita") was not only responsible for the spiritual care and practical needs of her nuns; she also became the convent's liaison with the outside world.[11] And that came to matter more and more as Catholic institutions suffered one convulsion after another and Catholic institutions became the target of a new generation of anticlerical reformers. Conchita's convent served as a way station for priests in an underground network. The existence of the convent in Tlalpan was an open secret protected by family members and friends, the ecclesiastical hierarchy, and even local officials who ensured that the convent was left unmolested. Nevertheless, its safety depended on the vagaries of officials who chose whether, when, and how they wanted to enforce federal laws pertaining to religious practice.

CONFRONTING AND EMBRACING MARTYRDOM

In 1926 the tide turned against the convent. That spring marked the changing of the guard in Tlalpan, when a new slate of local officials assumed office and eventually ordered a raid on a house of women "suspected of piety." Forced out into the street in the middle of the night, the shoeless and penniless nuns were rescued by an influential family who fed them, laid out sleeping mats in their home, and set aside space for a makeshift chapel.[12] If officials had hoped to frighten these Capuchin nuns, their efforts only had the opposite effect. Conchita's resolve was simply strengthened: "We had no fear of going to prison on account of our faith."[13] Adding to tensions across Mexico, the infamous Calles Law (*la ley Calles*) was set to go into effect on midnight of July 31 of that year, with its radical interpretation of religious restrictions made possible by the Constitution of 1917. The Calles Law was named after President Plutarco Elías Calles, who was determined to enforce the spirit of the constitution, and even his understanding of the revolution itself, through a major revision of Mexico's penal code.[14] With uniform enforcement of the constitution would come harsh penalties for violations. The groundwork for restrictions on Catholics had been laid by Álvaro Obregón, who helped shape the new constitution and had served as president of Mexico from 1920 to 1924. During the Calles administration, Obregón was working behind the scenes and already planning his political comeback, thus he was a prominent target for those who opposed his anticlericalism.

By summer 1926, the Catholic hierarchy in Mexico had endured enough and, with the approval of the papacy, suspended all Catholic religious practices effective at midnight on July 31. On August 1, for the first time in more than four centuries, there was not a single public mass celebrated in all of Mexico.[15] Priests were withdrawn from service, bringing an end to all Catholic rites like baptisms, funerals, and celebrations of the Eucharist. Churches were shuttered across Mexico, and priests went underground or into exile. Tens of thousands of Catholics sought refuge in Texas alone.[16] In response, Catholics rose up in protest and built upon the work begun in earnest that year by the National League for the Defense of Religious Liberty (Liga Nacional Defensora de la Libertad Religiosa). The LNDLR organized a national boycott of nonessential goods and a refusal to pay taxes, hoping to deal an economic blow to the government. All the while, they continued to petition the government for political change. The movement drew in peasants, miners, student groups, workers, intellectuals, and even the Knights of Columbus.[17] Catholic women agitated for social and political change, putting thousands of them at the center of political protests.[18] Soon, ardent Catholics known as Cristeros, with their rallying cry of "Long Live Christ the King!" (¡Viva Cristo Rey!), took up active resistance against the government, either through armed warfare or through illegal Catholic observance. Conchita was accused of involvement in both.

Conchita's convent chapel once again became an important refuge for priests and devout Catholics in search of ordinary Catholic rites.[19] Some only needed a safe place to stay for the night, whereas others came to offer mass and confession. Still others found the convent chapel to be a safe place for exchanging messages and packages. Conchita always maintained that she did not ask, and did not know, what was exchanged. It was only her moral responsibility to offer a place for the mass: "My little chapel was always open to everyone."[20] What seems like a bustle of activity in Conchita's convent chapel may be hard to square with our idea of a cloistered convent, but it echoed the kind of hospitality Christian religious houses have offered for centuries. Even though most of the monks or nuns in a congregation did not interact with visitors, monasteries and convents had always accepted pilgrims, refugees, travelers, and people in need as short-term guests—especially those who had come to participate in daily mass on their travels. Conchita simply carried forward that tradition, albeit in the midst of heated church-state conflict, and she did so deliberately, calling to mind "the example of martyrs and anchorites of the first centuries of the Church."[21]

Conchita was adamant that male visitors only interacted with her in the presence of a priest or chaplain who had her trust, and no man was supposed to enter the convent without written permission from the bishop.[22] Two such men who received permission to enter the convent chapel were the Jesuit priest José Ramón Miguel Agustín Pro, who had been arrested for sedition for offering mass, and José de León Toral. Father Pro's first visit did not make much of an impression on Conchita, but she knew that he was a "priest who fought for the glory of God, for the salvation of souls, and he had a fear of neither death nor prison."[23] On a future visit to yet another temporary convent in September 1927, Father Pro heard Conchita's confession and personally encouraged her to make herself a personal sacrifice to "divine justice." She protested, saying she could only make such a commitment with the express permission of her spiritual adviser. After she approached her adviser, he counseled her that even though she and her community had suffered endless trials, she should "ask God to accept her sacrifice." Although a knot formed in her throat at the thought of what was to come, she wrote: "Within my soul I heard the singing of a thousand Alleluias."[24] When Father Pro returned a week later, he celebrated the mass and then summoned Conchita and another nun, reminding them that at the moment of consuming the consecrated host, he heard called out: "The sacrifice is accepted."[25] In interpreting the events of her life, she singled out this interaction with Father Pro as a turning point in her faith life and her martyrdom, namely, the moment when she was willing to make herself a sacrifice.

Two months later, in what Conchita called "one of the greatest injustices mourned by the Catholic world," Father Pro and three other men suspected of an assassination attempt on Obregón were put to death by firing squad—without a trial and even in defiance of a judicial order to halt the execution.[26] Upon learning of the news, Conchita and another nun insisted on seeing Father Pro's body. Seeing his naked body, still warm and with dried blood on his face in the shape of a cross, Conchita and her companions touched their scarves in his blood. "I also wished to be a martyr," she observed to herself, and she recalled "Father Miguel had offered his life, not once, but countless times...

and he had assured me that the offering of our lives, made to God in that memorable sacrifice of the mass on September 23, had been accepted [by God]."[27] She even acknowledged her own jealousy, because she "desired to be a martyr, giving up [her] own life as a consecrated religious woman, and had not died as Father Pro had."[28]

OBREGÓN'S ASSASSINATION

Conchita was written into public history owing to another visitor to her chapel convent, but her prior association with Father Pro would come to play a role in shaping opinions about her character and political motivations. Much like Father Pro, a man named José de León Toral did not make much of an impression on Conchita when he first came to the convent. He was not unlike "other young Catholics who came to hear mass and receive the sacraments." He returned multiple times with his family until Conchita's convent was forced to move once again—this time at the orders of the bishop.[29] Toral and his mother then sought out the new location. On the occasion of one visit, he was so insistent about serving alongside the priest at mass that Conchita came to see him as completely disagreeable—and could do little to hide it.[30] On yet another occasion, over two days in mid-July 1927, Toral insisted on serving with the priest again, and Conchita observed that he hovered around the altar, and then left without saying a word.

The following day, the nuns received word that a Catholic man had assassinated President-elect Obregón at a luncheon banquet in broad daylight, shooting him five times in the back, and made no effort to escape. They soon learned that the recent visitor to their convent had been accused of the crime. Toral declared to the police that he acted alone, but they were not persuaded. Only after extensive torture and threats against his wife and children did Toral give them the location where they could find his collaborator: rented space, inhabited entirely by women, in a Mexico City neighborhood. The police brought a bloodied and beaten Toral to Conchita's clandestine convent.[31] He later explained that the police were intent upon securing the name of a co-conspirator, and he was sure that if he gave them her name, they would meet her and realize how unlikely she was to be involved. Even the police were surprised when he led them to a woman.[32] As soon as he was brought before her, he declared that he had "worked alone, according to his own impulse, and without the counsel or involvement of anyone else."[33] The police arrested her instead for violating federal law on public worship, the famous *Ley de cultos*, and made a spectacle of carting an abbess and more than a dozen nuns to prison. As of that moment, Conchita would later realize that she had "completely lost [her] liberty…and set off down a path that not even Dante could have imagined. I don't understand, even now, how its course did not cause me to lose my mind."[34] Then began Conchita's martyrdom in earnest.

After enduring months of deplorable prison conditions, an attempt on her life by Obregón's nephew and other supporters, excruciating physical pain, and indignities inflicted on her by prison guards, Conchita was tried, alongside Toral, in November 1928 as the "intellectual author" of the plot to assassinate Obregón. She was accused not only of having plotted and planned the murder but also of having manipulated the gunman into doing her bidding. Moreover, she was accused of having weapons hidden in her chapel—including a gun and a syringe of poison.[35] Throughout the trial, her character and her faith were attacked by the state's prosecutors, by the crowds that filled the courtroom, and by people who witnessed her comings and goings from the prison and courtroom. People threw lit cigars at her, and "the police did nothing."[36] Her three lawyers received letters asking them to abandon her defense.[37] Even the jurors feared for their lives if they were to fail to convict Conchita.

Conchita never had a chance at a fair trial. The jury trial of the assassin and the nun, as many papers dubbed the pair, was a spectacle from the time of Toral's arrest. President Calles, who himself took a turn at interrogating Toral, could have demanded Toral's execution much as he had done for Father Miguel Pro, but he and his political allies used a full-blown trial to try and separate, in the public's mind, Toral's zealous Catholicism from the Cristero-state conflict that he was trying to bring under control. Calles had to make the crime seem like an ordinary homicide and not a political crime—which would have prevented Toral from receiving the death penalty. Toral, for his part, was happy to be part of the spectacle. He was unwavering: he had killed Obregón "so that Christ would reign over Mexico," and he seized the occasion of the jury trial, both as a platform for his antigovernment position and to publicize his own martyrdom.[38]

The trial spiraled out of control on November 5, the fourth day of the trial, when federal deputies feared that Toral and Conchita might be acquitted. They stormed the courtroom with plans to lynch Toral, and Conchita's leg was fractured in the melee.[39] In chaos, the defense concluded the trial in fear of their lives. It is easy to see why Conchita was never preoccupied with either defending herself or ever receiving justice after the trial and appeal concluded. Namely, state actors had made clear that neither justice nor truth were the goal of the trial. Toral was executed by firing squad, and Conchita was sentenced to twenty years in federal prison.

Even the church hierarchy had abandoned her. In their efforts to broker peace between the Cristeros and the government, Mexico's prelates tried to shape public opinion by arguing that Toral's and Conchita's crime was not religious in nature. Instead, it was a base crime committed by people who were of unsound mind. Leading up to the trial, Conchita was told that she had been excommunicated and denied association with her Capuchin community.[40] Her fellow nuns were strictly forbidden from having any contact with her.[41] Before the trial had even begun, she was ready to die. Quoted in the *New York Times* in August 1928, Conchita accepted punishment if she had done wrong in the eyes of God because "she could find happiness in God's will."[42] Within a few months, toward the end of the trial in early November, Conchita's faith was still intact, but her desire to live was faltering. With the "cries of her soul," she "asked for death in the Lord Our God; I wished to die at any cost." "My desire was not perfect," she acknowledged, because it was her own desire and not that of the will of God. This was not the sweet martyrdom of the saints that she wanted after Father Miguel Pro's death. Instead, she wanted death to relieve a profound "anxiety" and misery that could not be calmed.[43] Later, when Conchita revisited the memory of Father Miguel Pro's death, likely prior to her trial in 1928, she recalled that during the months that Father Pro was under a false accusation of sedition (before he was implicated in the plot to assassinate Obregón), he "never tried to defend himself because he had a perpetual obsession with martyrdom; that is the secret of his silence and of his valor, not shunning suffering or death."[44] The nature of her martyrdom would not be the same as his, but she could nevertheless follow his lead and offer up her suffering. Following his lead, she "offered to God the sacrifice of my blood and my life, the immense sacrifice of innocent and unknown souls." She believed that God accepted that sacrifice when she wrote, "I believed today more than ever that God loves me and I love God. I am spectacular in the eyes of the angels."[45]

By Conchita's own telling, there was more than one impetus for her to write her various autobiographies, but none related to defending herself from anything, and none pertained to public justice. All of her reasons were personal and were rooted in her faith, stemming from either her need to put her religious convictions in her own words or her desire to praise God. She lamented her suffering but recognized that it came from God. Even the people who injured her she saw as "God's instruments. How can [she] not love them?"[46] The idea of martyrdom presented itself to her as she matured, not only in the abstract from the stories of the early Christian martyrs, but also in the present, given that choosing religious life in early twentieth-century Mexico meant practicing one's faith against a backdrop of armed rebellion and the very real threat of firing squads.

Exploring autobiographical writings such as Conchita's can be a treacherous undertaking. A reader must investigate two faces of the same coin—author and subject—at the same time. It poses a fundamental question about the nature of autobiographical writing: "Is autobiographic life writing a construction or an authentic self?"[47] For Conchita's writings, I would argue both. Self-consciously, Conchita, at various points in her life, reflected on the events and trials of her life and derived meaning from them. She never intended to provide a biography or history, but that "which was recounted is historical."[48] As much as she offered up her life and body to God, she offered up her deepest reflections to the rest of us. We honor her memory by taking her at her word.

TWO

Las Antepasadas:
Women Revolutionaries
Prior to 1910

Malinalli, or Malintzín (b. Yucatán, ca. 1500; d. ca. 1529), as a young girl was traded to be a slave to Hernán Cortés following his defeat of a Mayan tribe near Tabasco. She served as Cortés's translator and an emissary as he made his way toward Mexico City and later bore two children with him. More frequently known as La Malinche, she is a highly contested figure in Mexican history, sometimes faulted for facilitating the Mexican conquest at the side of Cortés and other times honored as a true soldier and mother of the Mexican people. In this excerpt from Laura Esquivel's novel *La Malinche*, Malinalli, who has just begun to find pride in her position as an interpreter, is sexually humiliated by Cortés.

La Malinche

LAURA ESQUIVEL

**Never before had she felt what it was like to be
in charge. She soon found that whoever controls
information, whoever controls meaning, acquires
power.**

MALINALLI WAS WASHING CLOTHES IN THE RIVER, ON THE OUTSKIRTS OF
the town of Cholula. She was upset. There was too much noise. Far too
much. Not just the noise made by her hands when she scrubbed and
rinsed the clothes in the water, but the noise inside her head.

Everything around her spoke of this agitation. The river where she
washed the clothes charged the place with music through the force of
the waters crashing on the stones. Added to this sound was that of the
birds, who were as agitated as ever, the frogs, the crickets, the dogs,
and the Spaniards themselves, the new inhabitants of this land, who
contributed with the clamorous sounds of their armor, their cannons,
and their harquebuses. Malinalli needed silence, calm. In the *Popol
Vuh*, the Sacred Book of their elders, it stated that when everything
was at silence—in complete calm, in the darkness of night, in the darkness of the light—then would creation arise.

Malinalli needed that silence to create new and resonant words.

The right words, the ones that were necessary. Recently she had stopped serving Portocarrero, her lord, because Cortés had named her "The Tongue," the one who translated what he said into the Náhuatl language, and what Montezuma's messengers said, from Náhuatl to Spanish. Although Malinalli had learned Spanish at an extraordinary speed, in no way could it be said that she was completely fluent. Often she had to turn to Aguilar to help her to translate it correctly so that what she said made sense in the minds of both the Spaniards and the Mexicas.

Being "The Tongue" was an enormous responsibility. She didn't want to make a mistake or misinterpret, and she couldn't see how to prevent it since it was so difficult translating complex ideas from one language to the other. She felt as if each time she uttered a word she journeyed back hundreds of generations. When she said the name of Ometéotl, the creator of the dualities Omecíhuatl and Ometecuhtli, the masculine and feminine principles, she put herself at the beginning of creation. That was the power of the spoken word. But then, how can you contain in a single word the god Ometéotl, he who is without shape, the lord who is not born and does not die; whom water cannot wet, fire cannot burn, wind cannot move, and earth cannot bury? Impossible. The same seemed to happen to Cortés, who couldn't make her understand certain concepts of his religion. Once she asked him what the name of God's wife was.

"God doesn't have a wife," Cortés answered.

"It cannot be."

"Why not?"

"Because without a womb, without darkness, light cannot emerge, life cannot emerge. It is from her greatest depths that Mother Earth creates precious stones, and in the darkness of the womb that gods and humans take their forms. Without a womb there is no god."

Cortés stared intently at Malinalli and saw the light in the abyss of her eyes. It was a moment of intense connection between them, but Cortés directed his eyes somewhere else, abruptly disconnected himself from her, because he was frightened by that sensation of complicity, of belonging, and he immediately tried to cut off the conversation between them, for, aside from everything else, it seemed too strange speaking about religious matters with her, a native in his service.

"What do you know about God! Your gods demand all the blood in the world in order to exist, while our God offers His own to us with each Communion. We drink His blood."

Malinalli did not understand all of the words that Cortés had just uttered. What she wanted to hear, what her brain wanted to interpret, was that the god of the Spaniards was a fluid god, for he was in the blood, in the secret of the flesh, the secret of love; that he was contained in the eternity of the Universe. And she wanted to believe in such a deity.

"So then your god is liquid?" Malinalli asked enthusiastically.

"Liquid?"

"Yes. Didn't you say that he was in the blood that he offered?"

"Yes, woman! But now answer me, do your gods offer you blood?"

"No."

"Aha! Then you shouldn't believe in them."

Malinalli's eyes filled with tears as she replied. "I don't believe that they have to offer blood. I believe in your liquid god, I like that he is a God who is constantly flowing and that he manifests himself even in my tears. I like that he is stern, strict, and just, that his anger could create or make the universe vanish in one day. But you can't have that without water or a womb. For there to be songs and flowers, there needs to be water; with it, words rise and matter takes on form. There is life that is born without a womb, but it does not remain long on the earth. What is engendered in darkness, however, in the profundity of caves, like precious gems and gold, lasts much longer. They say that there is a place beyond the sea, where there are higher mountains, and there, Mother Earth has plentiful water to fertilize the earth; and here, in my land, we have deep caves and within them, great treasures are produced."

"Really? What treasures? Where are these caves?"

Malinalli did not want to answer him and said that she did not know.

His interruption bothered her. It proved that Cortés was not interested in talking about his religion, or his gods, or his beliefs, or even about her. It was clear that he was only interested in material treasures. She excused herself and went to weep by the river.

This and many other things made it difficult for them to understand each other. Malinalli believed that words colored memory, planting images each time that a thing was named. And as flowers bloomed in the countryside after a rainfall, so that which was planted in the mind bore fruit each time that a word, moistened by saliva, named it. For example, the concept of a true and eternal God, which the Spaniards had proclaimed, in her mind had borne fruit because it had already been planted there by her ancestors. From them, she had also learned that things came to exist when you named them, when you moistened them, when you painted them. God breathed through his word, gave life through it, and because of this, because of the labor and grace of the God of All Things, it was possible to paint in the mind of the Spaniards and Mexicas new concepts, new ideas.

Being "The Tongue" was a great spiritual duty, for it meant putting all her being at the service of the gods so that her tongue was part of the resounding system of the divinity so that her voice would spread through the cosmos the very meaning of existence. But Malinalli did not feel up to the task. Very often, when translating, she let herself be guided by her feelings, and then the voice that came out of her mouth was no other than the voice of fear, fear of being unfaithful to the gods, of failure, fear of not being able to bear responsibility. And truthfully, also fear of power, of taking power.

Never before had she felt what it was like to be in charge. She soon found that whoever controls information, whoever controls meaning, acquires power. And she discovered that when she translated, she controlled the situation, and not only that but that words could be weapons. The finest of weapons.

Words were like lightning, swiftly crossing valleys, mountains, seas, bringing needed information as readily to monarchs as to vassals, creating hope or fear, establishing alliances, abolishing enemies, changing the course of events. Words were warriors, be they sacred warriors like the Lord Aguila, or simple mercenaries. As to their divine character, words transformed the empty space in the mouth into the center of Creation, repeating there the same act with which the universe had been made, by uniting the feminine and masculine principles into one.

Malinalli knew that if life was to thrive, and these two principles remain united, she had to position herself in a circular place to safeguard them, to blanket them, since circular forms were what best contained and protected all of creation. Sharp forms, on the other hand, broke things apart, separated them. The mouth, as a feminine principle, like empty space, as a cavity, was the best place for words to be engendered. And the tongue, as a masculine principle, sharp, pointed, phallic, was the one to introduce the created word, that universe of information, into other minds in order to be fertilized.

But what would fertilize it? That was the great unknown. Malinalli was convinced that there were only two possibilities: union or separation, creation or destruction, love or hatred, and that the outcome would be influenced by "The Tongue," that is, by herself. For she had the power with her words to include others in a common purpose, to clothe them, to shelter them. Or she could exclude them, making them into foes, separate beings with irreconcilable ideas; or into solitary beings who were isolated and destitute as she had been in her status as slave, feeling for so many years what it was like to live without a voice, without being taken into account and forbidden to make any decisions on her own.

But that past now seemed very far away. She, the slave who listened to orders in silence, who couldn't look directly into the eyes of men, now had a voice, and the men, staring into her eyes, would wait attentively to hear what her mouth uttered. She, who had so often been given away, who so many times had been gotten rid of, now was needed, valued, as much as if not more than cacao.

Unfortunately, this privileged position was unstable and could change at any moment. Even her life was in danger. Only a victory by the Spaniards would guarantee her freedom, for reasons that she had not been afraid to state on various occasions in veiled language, that the Spaniards truly had been sent by the Lord Quetzalcóatl, and not only that but that Cortés himself was the incarnation of the revered god.

Now it was she who could decide what was said and what went unsaid, what to confirm and what to deny, what would be made known and what kept secret. It was a grave dilemma, for it wasn't simply a matter of saying or not saying, or substituting one name for another, but that in doing so she ran the risk of changing the meaning of things. When translating, she could change what things meant and impose her own vision on events, and by doing so enter into direct competition with the gods, which horrified her. Because of her insolence, the gods could very well become annoyed with her and mete out their punishment, and this absolutely frightened her. She could avoid this fate by translating everything as closely to the meaning of the words as possible. But if the Mexicas were to question for a moment—as she herself had—whether the Spaniards had been sent by Quetzalcóatl, she would be destroyed along with them in the blink of an eye. So she found herself in a delicate position. Either she remained faithful to the gods and to the meaning that they had given to the world, or she followed her instincts, her most earthly and primary instincts, and made sure that each word and each action acquired the meaning that most suited her. The second choice was clearly a rebellion against the gods, and their eventual reaction filled her with fear and guilt, but she saw no other alternative.

Malinalli's feelings of fear and guilt were at the least as powerful as those of Montezuma. Weeping, trembling, filled with dread, he await-ed the punishment of the gods for how the Mexicas had destroyed Tula long before and in that sacred place dedicated to Quetzalcóatl, had engaged in human sacrifice. Before, in the Toltecan Tula, there had been no need for such practices. It was enough that Quetzalcóatl lit the new fire and accompanied the sun on its path through the celestial dome to maintain balance in the cosmos. Before the Mexicas, the Sun did not feed on human blood; it did not ask for it, did not demand it.

The great guilt that Montezuma bore on his shoulders made him certain that not only was it time to pay old debts but that the arrival of the Spaniards signaled the end of his empire. Malinalli could prevent this from happening. She could proclaim that the Spaniards had not been sent by Quetzalcóatl, and they would be destroyed in a moment—along with her, and she did not want to die a slave. She yearned to live in freedom, no longer to be given from one to another, no longer to lead such an errant life.

There was no going back, no way to come out unharmed. She knew too well Montezuma's cruelty, and she knew that if the Spanish were defeated in their venture, she would be condemned to death. Faced with this possibility, she understandably wanted the Spanish to triumph. And if to assure their victory she had to keep alive the idea that they were gods come from the sea, she would do so, although by now she wasn't very convinced of the idea. The hope that one day she would be able to do whatever she wanted, marry whom she wanted, and have children without the fear that they might be taken into slavery or destined as sacrifices, was enough to make her take a step back. What she most wanted was a piece of earth that belonged to her and where she could plant her grains of corn, the ones that she always carried with her and that had come from her grandmother's cornfield. If the Spaniards could make sure that her dreams would crystallize, then it was worthwhile helping them.

Of course, this didn't assuage her guilt or make clear to her what she should say and what she should keep silent about. What kind of a life is worth defending with lies? And who could confirm that they were lies? Perhaps she was being too harsh. Perhaps the Spaniards had been sent by Quetzalcóatl and it was her duty to collaborate with them until she died, sharing with them privileged information that had come directly from the mouth of a woman in Cholula. This woman had loved Malinalli's confident personality, her beauty, and her physical strength, and she wanted her as a wife for her son. With the intent of saving Malinalli's life, she had confided in her, warning her that in Cholula they were preparing an ambush against the Spanish. The plan was to arrest them, wrap them up in hammocks, and take them to Tenochtitlán alive. The woman suggested that Malinalli leave the city before this happened and that afterward she could marry her son.

Malinalli now had the burden of deciding whether to share this information with the Spaniards. Cholula was a sacred place. One of Quetzalcóatl's temples was situated there. The defense or attack of Cholula meant the defense or attack of Quetzalcóatl. Malinalli was more confused than ever. The only thing she was sure of was that she needed silence to clear her mind.

She implored the gods for silence. What most tormented her, aside from the external noises, were the noises within, the voices in her mind that told her not to say anything, not to give the Spaniards any valuable information that might save their lives, for something was wrong. Perhaps the foreigners were not who she thought they were, not the envoys of Quetzalcóatl. Certainly, their recent behavior did not conform to the ideal model that she had devised. She felt disillusioned.

For one thing, there was a total incongruity between the meaning of the name Cortés (courteous) and the man himself. To be cortés was to be sensitive and respectful, and she didn't think the man possessed either of these attributes nor did the men that he had brought with him. She couldn't believe that god's emissaries would behave in such a manner, that they would be so rough, so rude, so ill spoken, even insulting their own god when they were angry. Compared to the gentleness and lyricism of the Náhuatl, Spanish was a bit aggressive.

There was one thing, though, that was worse than the unpleasant manner with which the Spanish gave orders, and that was the odor that emanated from them. She never expected that the emissaries of Quetzalcóatl would smell so bad. Cleanliness was a common practice among the natives. The Spaniards, on the other hand, did not bathe, their clothes reeked, and neither water nor the sun could rid them of their stench. No matter how much she scrubbed and scrubbed the

clothes in the river, she wasn't able to wash from them the smell of
rotted iron, of metallic sweat, of rusted armor.

Moreover, the interest that the Spanish and Cortés, in particular,
expressed for gold did not seem right to her. If they in fact were gods,
they would be concerned with the earth, with the planting, with making sure that men were nourished, but that was not the case. Never
had she seen them interested in the cornfields, only in eating. Hadn't
Quetzalcóatl stolen the grain of corn from the Mount of Our Sus-
tenance to give it to mankind? Didn't the Spanish care how the gift
had affected men? Weren't they curious to know whether they were
reminded of its divine origin when they ate it? Whether they protected it and venerated it as something sacred? Did they care about
what would happen if man stopped planting it? Didn't they know that
if man stopped planting corn, it would die out? That the ear of corn
needs man's intervention to strip it of the leaves that cover it, so that
the seed may be free to reproduce? That there is no way for corn to
live without man, nor man to live without corn? The fact that corn
needed man to reproduce was proof that it was a gift from the gods
to mankind, for without mankind there would have been no need for
the gods to give away corn, and mankind, on the other hand, would
not have been able to survive on the earth without corn. Didn't the
Spaniards know that we are the earth, from earth we were born, that
the earth consumes us, and when the earth comes to its end, when the
earth is exhausted, when corn no longer sprouts, when Mother Earth
no longer opens her heart, it will be our end as well? Then what was
the point of accumulating gold without corn? How was it possible that
the first word Cortés learned in Náhuatl was precisely the one for gold
and not corn?

Gold, known as teocuitlatl, was considered to be the excrement of
the gods, waste matter and nothing else, so she didn't understand the
desire to accumulate it. She thought that when the day came that the
grain of corn was not revered and valued as something sacred, human
beings would be in grave danger. And if she—who was a mere mortal—knew this, how was it possible that the emissaries of Quetzalcóatl,

who came in his name, though under a different guise, who communicated with him, did not know it? Was it possible that these men were more likely emissaries of Tezcatlipoca than Quetzalcóatl?

Quetzalcóatl's brother had once deceived him with a black mirror, and that is what it seemed the Spaniards were doing with the natives, but this time with resplendent mirrors. Tezcatlipoca, the god who sought to overthrow his brother, was a magician. Showing off his talents, he sent a black mirror to Quetzalcóatl in which Quetzalcóatl saw the mask of his false holiness, his dark side. In response to such a vision, Quetzalcóatl got so drunk that he even fornicated with his own sister. Full of shame, the following day he left Tula to find himself again, to recover his light, promising to return one day.

The great mystery was whether indeed he had returned. What was most troubling for Malinalli, independent of whether the Spaniards achieved victory over Montezuma, was that her life and liberty were at risk. All this had begun months earlier when Cortés had accidentally found out that she spoke Náhuatl. Since Aguilar—who in all the years that they had spent in these lands had only learned Mayan—couldn't help Cortés in understanding Montezuma's messengers, Cortés asked Malinalli to help him translate and in exchange he would grant her her liberty. From that moment on, events followed one after another with extraordinary speed, and now Malinalli found herself trapped in a whirlpool that allowed no escape. Images of moments that had sealed her destiny, going back to the days when the Spaniards had first landed, appeared and disappeared in her mind.

Foremost was the day when the chief of Tabasco had gathered her along with the nineteen other women to tell them that they would be given away as spoils of war to those who had recently arrived since the foreigners had battled and defeated the people of Cintla.

She remembered in detail the conversation that had taken place among the women on the journey to the Spanish camp. Almost in secret, they mentioned the possibility that there might be a connection between the men that arrived from the sea and Quetzalcóatl. The current year was One Sugarcane year which, according to the Mexica calendar, was the year of Quetzalcóatl, who had been born during One Sugarcane year and died after a cycle of fifty-two years, also a One Sugarcane. It was said that the coincidence of the Spaniards having arrived during One Sugarcane year was too powerful to ignore. One of the women said that she had heard that One Sugarcane years were disastrous for kings. If something bad happened during One Lizard year, the evil befell men, women, and the old. If it happened during a One Jaguar, One Deer, or One Flower year, it befell children, but if it happened during One Sugarcane year, it befell kings. This had been made evident by the fact that the foreigners had battled triumphantly against the citizens of Cintla and would likewise triumph if they confronted Montezuma. This was a sign that they had come to conquer and to reinstate the kingdom of Quetzalcóatl. And so Malinalli accepted it in her heart; on listening to these words, she was filled with joy and hope and illusion, with a longing for change. To know that the kingdom that permitted human sacrifices and slavery was in peril made her feel at peace with herself.

Far from there, in the palace of Montezuma, the same conversation had taken place but between Montezuma, his brother Cuitláhuac and his cousin Cuauhtémoc. Cuitláhuac and Cuauhtémoc thought that Cortés and his men, rather than gods arrived from the sea, were a simple band of plunderers. Montezuma, on the other hand, decided that whether or not they were gods, he would give them preferential treatment, since it was considered that even plunderers were protected by Quetzalcóatl. So he sent off his principal envoy with the following message: "Go with haste, make reverence to our Lord, saying that his deputy Montezuma has sent you in honor of their arrival."

Maybe Montezuma was not aware of the great uncertainty that his actions caused among his people, for when they heard that the emperor himself had paid respect to the foreigners, and not just that, but that he put himself at their service, they saw themselves obliged to behave likewise. The preferential treatment toward the Spaniards signified to everyone that the Spaniards were superior to the emperor Montezuma.

But in the light of certain recent events, Malinalli was no longer sure this was so. From the first instance that he had made contact with the messengers from Montezuma, Cortés betrayed his insatiable desire for gold. He wasn't impressed by the feathered arts, or the beauty of the cloths and jewels with which they paid him respect, but with gold. Cortés had forbidden the members of his party from trading gold privately, and he set up a table near the camp so that the natives made their trades officially. Every day Totonacans, as well as Mexicas, came with offers of gold for Cortés that he traded through his servants for pieces of glass and mirrors, for needles and scissors.

Malinalli herself was given a necklace made with pieces of glass and mirror. She very much liked the reflections it produced. She understood mirrors well. When she washed clothes in the river she examined herself in the water and her reflected image spoke to her of fear. She did not like seeing it, for it bothered her, sickened her. She remembered that once as a girl, when she was ill, they had made her watch her image reflected in a pail of water and she had gotten better. She asked the river to speak to her, to heal her, to tell her if she was doing the proper thing, whether she was making a mistake. She knew the waters spoke in all receptacles. Her grandmother had told her that in the Anáhuac region there was an enormous visionary lake, where images of what was to come were reflected on the waters, and in that place, the holy men had seen an eagle devouring a serpent. The river where she was washing the clothes, however, did not speak to her, said nothing to her, and she could see nothing in it but the filth from the clothes of the Spaniards arrived from the sea.

The sea was a vast expanse of reflections. The lakes and the rivers, as well. In them were contained the sun and the god of the waters. Malinalli knew that she could find something of herself behind each reflection, like the sun reflected in the moon, as well as in the waters, on the stones, in the eyes of others. When using resplendent stones or objects, one is reflected in the cosmos as in a game of mirrors. The sun doesn't realize that it shines, for it cannot see itself. It would have to see itself reflected in order to understand its greatness. That is why we need mirrors, to understand ourselves. That is why Tula, Quetzal-cóatl's city, was created to be a mirror of the sky, and that is why Mali-nalli liked to use shiny objects as mirrors where Quetzalcóatl could be amply reflected. Her necklaces were her most beautiful mirrors.

Taking from her sack the necklace that Cortés had given her, she fastened it around her neck with the intention of being seen by the god. Of meeting him in the reflections. She looked at herself again in the river, and this time the water revealed to her a series of small images, one after the other, in an undulating line. Immediately, it re-minded her of the silvery snake that the Spanish soldiers made when they marched one behind the other, the sun reflecting off their armor. She also connected it to the soldiers of Tula, who marched one behind the other, seeing their reflection in the mirror that the one before them carried on his back.

Although Malinalli wasn't aware of it, Hernán Cortés was only a few steps away from her. Taking advantage of the clear day, he had decided to rest for a moment near the river. A while earlier, he had left off drawing wheels of fortune in his notebooks. Whenever he wanted to relax and clear his mind he would begin drawing wheels of fortune.

Doing so, he would enter a state of deep relaxation, pleased by the concept of a circular time that would cause one to be at the bottom one moment and then, just like that, at the top. But that day a new idea came into his mind and forced him to put aside pen and paper. On drawing the part of the wheel hitting the bottom, he felt as if that moment was the most important in the endless process of the turning: the moment that the wheel spins around to the bottom, that instant of bonding with the earth, all the rest is in the air, floating, where neither the future nor the present exists. This new understanding made him lift his eyes and regard his surroundings with fresh eyes.

Immediately he was in a much more agreeable mood. These new

lands, which until now had seemed so strange, so dangerous and inhospitable, where the heat and the giant flies, the humidity and the poisonous plants, had terrorized his heart, suddenly changed their appearance, and he found all his surroundings warm and friendly. He felt as if this land was his, that it belonged to him and that, rather than having voyaged there, he had always been there. With great peace in his heart—something foreign to him—he decided to take a swim in the river. When he got to the shore, he discovered that Malinalli was doing the same thing. She had shed her lovely huipil in order to go in.

Cortés caught sight of her naked body, observing her back, her hips, her thighs, and her hair, and was aroused as never before. Feeling his presence, Malinalli turned, and then Cortés could see her adolescent breasts, firm, enormous, the nipples prominent and pointing directly at his heart. He felt a magnificent erection and with it a huge longing to possess her, but knew he shouldn't, so he waded waist-deep into the cold water to see if it would cool his erection a bit. As he approached her, he tried to begin a conversation that would distract him from his thoughts.

"What are you doing?"

"Immersing myself in the god Tláloc, the God of Water."

In the water, facing each other, Cortés and Malinalli looked into each other's eyes and found their destiny and their inevitable union. Cortés understood that Malinalli was his true conquest, that there, in the depths of her black eyes, were the gems he had been searching for all this time. Malinalli, for her part, felt that on Cortés's lips, in his saliva, there was a taste of the divine, a piece of eternity, and she wanted to savor it and guard it with her lips. The clouds in the sky began to move with extraordinary swiftness. The air became laden with humidity, moistening the feathers of birds and the leaves of trees, as well as Malinalli's vagina. The gray clouds, like Cortés's member, made a great effort to contain their waters, to hold back, not to let them fall, so that their precious liquid would not be released. Cortés barely had time to ask, before throwing himself on her, "And what is that god?"

Malinalli still had time to respond before being taken. "Eternal, the same as yours, but his eternity is not invisible like yours. Our god evaporates, makes designs in the sky, moves whimsically through the clouds, shouts out his presence, spills his consciousness, and quenches our thirst and our fear."

Cortés, his eyes burning with longing, put his hand on Malinalli's breast, interrupting her. "Are you afraid?"

Malinalli shook her head. Cortés then caressed her slowly with his wet hand. He took hold of the girl-woman's nipple with his fingertips. Malinalli trembled. Cortés ordered her to continue speaking about her god. He thought that he would assuage his desire a little, but nothing more. He did not want to break the pact, that all men who were part of this undertaking would respect the native women. Malinalli continued with her speech as best she could, for Cortés had already put her nipple in his mouth and passed his tongue over it lustfully.

"Our God gives us eternal life.... That is why our god is water. Hidden in the water, in its invisible parts, is the truth, but we do not come to know it unless we weep or die forever."

Cortés's ambitious mind could not stand it any longer, and he wanted to possess Malinalli and her god at the same time. In his head, there was an explosion of pleasure, and the fire of his heart wanted to evaporate forever that god called Tláloc, that god of water. He lifted Malinalli out of the water and carried her to the shore, where he forcefully penetrated her. At that moment, the sky also exploded and let its rain fall over them.

Cortés did not notice the lightning. The only thing that he was aware of was the warmth at the core of Malinalli's body and the way that his member pushed and opened the tight walls of the girl's vagina. He did not care if his passion and force hurt Malinalli. He did not care if lightning struck nearby. All he cared about was going in and out of that body.

Malinalli remained silent and her black eyes, more beautiful than ever, became watery, holding in tears. With each thrust, Malinalli felt the pleasure of Cortés's naked, hairy torso brushing up against her breasts. This was her answer to her uncertainty regarding what she would feel when she touched hairy skin. In spite of the violence done to her body, in her delirium, Malinalli remembered what her grandmother had told her in such a sweet voice—as if the birds, all of them, had imparted their spirits in her throat—on the day before her death.

"There are tears that are the healing and blessing of the Lord of All Things. For water is also a language whose liquid voice sings at the breaking of the light; it is the essence of our God who brings together extremes and reconciles the irreconcilable."

For a few minutes—which seemed an eternity—Cortés penetrated her time and again, like a savage, as if all the power of nature were contained in his being. Meanwhile, it was raining so hard that his passion and his orgasm were drowned in the rains, as were Malinalli's tears. She had for the time being ceased to be "The Tongue" to become simply a woman, silent, voiceless, a mere woman who did not bear on her shoulders the enormous responsibility of building the conquest with her words. A woman who, contrary to what would be expected, felt relief in reclaiming her condition of submission, for it was a much more familiar sensation to be an object at the service of men than to be a creator of destiny.

It seemed as if no one else but God had been witness to that outburst of lustful anger, of passionate vengeance, of loving hate, but this wasn't so. Jaramillo, a captain in Cortés's army, had seen them. And the figure of Malinalli became engraved in his consciousness and he was attracted, as never before, to this woman whom Cortés, his chief, had possessed.

The Virgin of Guadalupe, saint and cultural icon, first appeared to an Indian peasant in 1531 at the Hill of Tepeyac in Mexico City. The Virgin has been a malleable symbol for centuries, but her image as the patroness of revolutionaries and others who fight oppression has become especially powerful since the War of Mexican Independence and the Mexican Revolution.

Virgin of Guadalupe

VIRGILIO P. ELIZONDO

In referring to "all her children" she is including everyone—Spaniards, Indians, and their mestizo children.

A REVOLUTIONARY IS A PERSON WHOSE ACTIONS, WORDS, IDEAS, OR INVEN-tions bring about profound, long-lasting, and irreversible change. Thus, the most powerful revolutionaries have not been violent ones. The love and teachings of nonviolent revolutionaries have enormously impacted people and societies. In this sense, I propose that Our Lady of Guadalupe, La Virgen de Guadalupe, is the first and the greatest revolutionary of the New World.

According to the memory of the people, the first apparitions of La Virgen took place in Tepeyac on December 12, 1531, just ten years after the defeat of the Aztecs by Cortés. The years following the conquest were the most brutal and cruel of all time. Spilled blood colored the canals red, rotting corpses filled the city, all while people wandered through the city. Temples were destroyed, families were broken apart, men forced into harsh labor, and children roamed the streets. It was a time of chaos.

Were the apparitions historical? Historians argue and will continue arguing this question. Yet, in the minds and hearts of the people, as in the collective memory of the Mexican people, there is no doubt whatsoever that the apparitions occurred. In a discussion about the authenticity of the apparitions with a friend of mine, an elderly lady asked: "Why do you doubt, don't you see that she [La Virgen] stayed with us and is still here today?" Does this constitute proof? Probably not to those who have doubts, but for the growing numbers of faithful in Mexico and beyond, there is no doubt. As she said: "Se quedo" (she remains).

With the Spanish conquest, everything of value to the Indians had been crushed and destroyed. These proud and skilled builders of one of the world's greatest cities, Tenochtitlán, had been defeated, humiliated, and reduced to serfdom. We know of their feelings from the ancient songs of lamentation composed by the people in their conversations with the Spaniards: "You have killed our warriors, destroyed our temples, raped our women, and now you tell us our gods are not true, if this is so, why live, just let us die."

It is true that after the apparitions, deaths continued to rise because of epidemics, starvation, and overwork. But the inner spirit of the indigenous people started to change as news of the apparition of La Virgen at Tepeyac continued to spread, inspiring a will to live. The very narrative of her encounters with Juan Diego Cuauhtlatoatzin brings this out clearly. Juan Diego leaves his home while it is still dark and arrives at Tepeyac when it is beginning to dawn.

This constant "while it was still dark…Beginning to dawn" has a profound threefold signification as it refers to the passage "unto the new life." The first signification refers to the darkness of the soul of a person. Juan Diego shared in the painful collective trauma of his people in which everything had gone wrong and there appeared to be no hope. It seemed that even their gods had abandoned them. There was nothing but darkness in their souls.

Spiritual writers have written about this as the "dark night of the soul." This was the state of mind of Juan Diego and of his people. Nothing made sense anymore, everything was confusing, and no future appeared possible. Old and beloved ways of their ancestors had been discredited, and the new ways did not make sense to them. Their whole way of life had come to an apocalyptic end. Yet at Tepeyac, new possibilities began to dawn. In the narrative of the encounters, Juan Diego passes from a timid and fearful Indian to a joyful and assured messenger of La Virgen de Guadalupe, the mother of God. Furthermore, he passes from a deep sense of inferiority and unworthiness to a healthy sense of dignity and human worth.

The second signification is that of historical time. The defeat of the Aztecs by Cortés in August 1521 marked an end. In Aztec minds, their time had come to an end! For them, time was not linear, and the conquest ended their cycle of time. Chaos and confusion were accompanied by pestilence, sadness, and depression. The narrative indicates this with the phrase "the inhabitants of the land had put down their arrows and their shields." In Nahua thought, life consisted of a constant struggle to nourish the sun so that humanity could survive.

In their system of logic, plants nourish insects, insects nourish animals, animals nourish humans, and so, humans must nourish the gods, especially the Aztec sun god Huitzilopochtli. Hence their divine mission was to engage in warfare where captives were offered to the gods as nourishment. So the term "put down their arrows and their shields" indicated they had given up. The builders of one of the greatest civilizations the world had ever known had now been reduced to servitude. There was no reason to struggle, for their great nation had come to an end.

At Tepeyac, a new nation began to dawn when La Virgen asked for a home for all the inhabitants of this land. She announced something far beyond the conquest, far beyond what anyone could have imagined, a land without borders where all her children could be at home. In referring to "all her children" she is including everyone—Spaniards, Indians, and their mestizo children. By including everyone, she is beginning a

new history for all. In and through her, a new historical time begins
to dawn—from the darkness of the end of a cycle to the dawn of a new
cycle where new life will emerge. It will not be just a continuity of the
previous life, but a coming together of forces to create a new life—the
mestizo life of this hemisphere.

But there was a third signification, one of cosmic proportions. In
Nahua thought, the phrase "while it was still dark...Beginning to
dawn" marks two moments of creation. The first one refers to the final
moments of the deliberation of the gods, and the second marks the
creation of the new mestizo humanity in the hemisphere. It is clear
from the narrative that it is not speaking of a mere change or adjust-
ment but of a new creation. What had appeared to be a tragic end was
converted into a powerful and beautiful new beginning. So we are here
at an event as powerful as the moment of creation itself!

The Guadalupe story is a creation narrative as certainly as are the
biblical stories in Genesis. Yet it could also be called a resurrection
narrative since it brings forth new life out of apparent death. This is
precisely why La Virgen de Guadalupe celebrations on December 12
take place early in the morning before the first rays of sunlight appear—it is the beginning of the new day, the dawning of a new age.
This marks the dramatic beginning in the Americas, humanity that
will break through all the barriers of separation that marked the Old
World. This new beginning was announced by the beautiful singing of
the birds and confirmed by the imprint of the miraculous image of the
Lady of Guadalupe on the tilma of Juan Diego. She is truly the mother
of the new creation that is gradually developing and evolving into the
multiethnic, multiracial *mestizaje* of our Western Hemisphere, a truly
new world.

Beyond these significations, La Virgen revolutionizes how we
describe religious figures. The usual religious discourse is absolute,
doctrinal, moralistic, and legalistic. Throughout history, most of the
religious language used terms like *hell, fire,* and *damnation.* It is truly
a joy to read her discourse with Juan Diego. It is full of tenderness like

"my poor but dignified Juan" or "Juanito, Juan Dieguito." Her religious language is not abstract but rather is a conversation among friends. It uses the language of the beautiful singing of the birds. There are no threats of punishment or hell but only the offer of love, care, protection, and compassion. It is a very simple narrative that can be easily reenacted by children while theologians and religious thinkers will continue to explore the depth of its meaning. Yet the core message that has inspired millions of people for hundreds of years is: "You have nothing to fear, am I not here, I who am your mother." Thus, she introduces a new style of religious language.

She is truly a revolutionary with a vision for the survival of our planet. Until now, religions seem to always have existed in opposition to one another. Some of the worst and most cruel wars have been fought in the name of religion. Religion can bring about heroic acts of virtue and goodness, but it can equally pit people against one another in the most violent ways. The Christian religion seemed to be totally opposed to indigenous religions. Both the Spaniards and the Indians were religious people deeply committed to their ways and convictions. The Spanish–Indian encounter and subsequent conquest seemed to have been a battle of the gods, and the Spanish god appeared to have triumphed. It was the role of the Spanish missionaries to eradicate every trace of the ancient religions. It was the way of radical opposition— as has often been the relationship between religions.

There was no way the Indians could abandon the religion of their ancestors. This would be the worst perversion ever. There seemed to be no way of accepting the new religion without betraying the beloved ancestors. Our Lady of Guadalupe offered a refreshing and revolutionary alternative. She broke through the either/or and offered unity. She borrows from each of the religions and offers something new. In this narrative, she introduces herself as the mother of the indigenous gods, but not of the ones who demanded human sacrifice. She equally introduces herself as the mother of the Christian God without mentioning punishment.

In her mestizo image, she appears as both an Indian princess and a Madonna. Her image tells the viewer that she is greater than the sun and the moon gods, but she does not destroy them. She shares in divinity because she is draped with the turquoise that represents divinity, while she is earthly because she is dressed in the brownish-reddish color of earth. She is a virgin because her hair is combed in the style of a young virgin, yet she is a mother because she wears the dark band around her waist indicating pregnancy. Over her womb is a four-leaf clover indicating her pregnancy with the firstborn of the new creation, whom Juan Diego will identify as "our savior Jesus Christ." This miracle unites the two religions that will not be opposed but will come together to form something new and beautiful. This is a totally new way of bringing different religions together and, I am convinced, a model for the enrichment and survival of our planet.

Another revolutionary aspect of Our Lady of Guadalupe is her transformation of social space from an insignificant and barren hill to the most sacred and beautiful hill of the hemisphere. Tepeyac becomes the Mt. Sinai of the new world where the tablets of the new law of compassionate inclusiveness will be given in the form of the miraculous image of La Virgen de Guadalupe. It becomes the Mt. Tabor of the transfiguration where the ultimate truth of the Indian and every human being will be manifested—not as inferior and undignified human beings as seen by the dominant power but as equal and dignified as created by God. Tepeyac likewise becomes the Mount of the Beatitudes of the New World where the blessedness of the poor, the mourning, the meek, the peacemakers, and the builders of the New World of compassion will be experienced in the presence of the beloved mother. Tepeyac is the revolutionary place where continuity with the past will be ensured while opening the way for transformation into a new and future life. This is revolutionary because normally people see social, cultural, and religious transformation as a separation from the past.

Our Lady of Guadalupe changed this. The sign that she offered to represent her was beautiful roses that were not from Spain but grew out of the sacred ground of the ancient sanctuary dedicated to Tonantzin, the beloved mother goddess of the ancient indigenous world. Something new and beautiful grew out of the ancient traditions and marked new humanity arising in the New World.

Sor Juana Inés de la Cruz (b. Mexico City, Mexico, 1648; d. Mexico City, 1695), colonial Mexico's luminary intellectual and poet, resisted church censorship of her writings. This was exceedingly difficult because the Catholic Church in colonial Mexico, through the auspices of the Holy Office of the Inquisition, had discretion over every aspect of religious life and any matter pertaining to morals. Even as Sor Juana gave evidence of complying with the Inquisition as a cloistered nun, she actively resisted its efforts to control her spirituality and intellectual creativity.

Sor Juana Inés de la Cruz

ALICIA GASPAR DE ALBA

Literacy for criolla girls was tolerable, even admired in some circles; but genius in women was akin to heresy.

UNLIKE MY COUSINS GROWING UP ON THE MEXICAN SIDE OF THE EL PASO/ Juárez border, I did not learn about Sor Juana in my English-only Catholic elementary schools, much less memorize her famous political poem (*"hombres necios que acusaís / a la mujer, sin razón"*). My cousins, my uncles and their wives, my father and grandfather, even my grandmother with her second-grade education—everyone seemed to know this poem by heart. As a budding organic feminist, I was fascinated that a seventeenth-century nun could write such a strong critique of patriarchy and its double standards. Who was this nun? What had happened in her life to lead her to pen those brazen lines blaming men for the faults and sins they themselves solicited from women?

Permit me to introduce you to Sor Juana Inés de la Cruz, in the different identities she occupied in her lifetime, many of them inimical to the gender codes of her sex and vocation: the girl-scholar, or *marisabia*, who became the talk of the town because of her erudition;

the astute lady-in-waiting at the viceregal court who was known as "the beloved of the vicereine"; the recalcitrant "bride of Christ" who entered the Order of Saint Jerome at age twenty and spent the rest of her days wrestling between her vows, her reason, and her passion; *la décima musa*, or muse of the ten-line poetic stanza, now considered the greatest female poet of the Spanish Golden Age; and the defeated "worst of women," the target of persistent religious persecution whose widening celebrity brought her face-to-face with the Inquisition at the end of her life.

MARISABIA

Sor Juana Inés de la Cruz was born in 1648,[1] in the small town of San Miguel de Nepantla just on the outskirts of Mexico City, in the shadow of the two volcanoes that rim the city to the south. Registered as an *hija de la iglesia*, or daughter of the church, a euphemism for illegitimacy, she was the third "natural" daughter of Dõna Isabel Ramirez and was baptized as Juana Ramírez de Asbaje. Her two older sisters were also daughters of the church and of the same absent Basque man who had fathered Juana Inés. From her earliest years, she was attracted to learning. At the age of three, she convinced her sisters' teacher to give her reading lessons. As she relates in her famous intellectual autobiography, *La Respuesta a Sor Filotea* (1691), she renounced cheese, which she had heard slowed the mind. At six or seven, "having learned to read and write, along with all of the other skills of needlework and household arts that girls learn,"[2] she was ready for higher education. She asked her mother to dress her in boy's clothing and send her to live with relatives in Mexico City so that she could attend the University of Mexico.

Her mother was not amused by her daughter's precocity, but her grandfather, Pedro Ramírez de Santillana, whose hacienda they lived in, indulged his clever granddaughter's hunger for learning. To her mother's displeasure, he allowed young Juana to roam freely among his library, perusing whatever books she liked, and so began the future scholar's autodidactic education.

Octavio Paz, author of the definitive (though not the first) biography, *Sor Juana; or, The Traps of Faith* (1982), writes that Sor Juana's maternal family *"era criolla por los cuatro costados"* (was creole on all four sides).[3] Although she is sometimes mistaken as a mestiza, of mixed Spanish and indigenous blood, Sor Juana was a criolla, or descendant of Spaniards born in Mexico.[4] Juana's maternal grandparents were of Andalusian origin, so more than likely there was some Moorish ancestry in their lineage, and possibly in Sor Juana's as well. After Juana's grandmother died, management of the household fell to Juana's mother, Isabel, who was an excellent administrator and yet illiterate.

Juana Inés was only eight when her grandfather died. That same year she experienced a trifecta of emotional upheavals that would not only change her life, but also set her on the path to fame and glory. Not only had the champion of her inquiring mind passed away; her mother had also taken another lover, gotten pregnant with her fourth "natural" child, and sent Juana Inés to live in Mexico City with her mother's sister, Tía María, who was married to a wealthy merchant, Don Juan de Mata.

During the eight years that Juana lived with her extended family in Mexico City, she made a name for herself as the *marisabia*, or "girl-scholar," of New Spain.[5] She frequented bookstores on her own and continued to read voraciously and offer opinions on what she read; she also participated in poetry competitions, one of which she won. She learned Latin grammar in twenty lessons, denying herself the pleasure of long hair until she had learned whatever she had set as her goal. If she did not meet her goal, she would cut her hair anew, for she saw "no cause for a head to be adorned with hair and naked of learning."[6] Juana Inés had a male tutor for these lessons, hired by her uncle, one Don Martín de Olivas, an undergraduate at the University of Mexico.[7]

Despite Juana Inés's gratitude for Don Martín's tutelage, expressed in a poem she wrote in his honor some years later, I wonder if she was perhaps alluding to him in *La Respuesta* when she wrote about the "notorious peril" that it was dangerous for young girls to have "the

immediacy of contact and the intimacy born from the passage of time"
with male teachers.

LADY-IN-WAITING

In 1664, during Juana Inés's sixteenth year, a new viceroy and vicereine
arrived in Mexico City from Spain. Rumors of Juana Inés's erudition
had already spread throughout the city, and the vicereine, Leonor
Carreto, Marquesa de Mancera, lost no time in extending an invitation
to Juana Inés's uncle to present the famous girl-scholar at court. With
her beauty and intelligence, she impressed the royal couple immensely
and was invited on the spot to serve as lady-in-waiting to the vicereine.
To circumvent her lack of paternity and noble standing, Juana Inés was
given the title *la muy querida de la virreina*,[8] the beloved of the vicereine, much to the chagrin of the other ladies-in-waiting, who could not
hope to compete with Juana Inés's wit and erudition, their noble blood
notwithstanding.

One of the most popular stories from her four-year stay at the viceregal court recounts the time the viceroy sponsored a tournament to
test their *marisabia's* autodidactic education. He called together forty scholars from the University of Mexico, among them historians,
mathematicians, theologians, philosophers, poets, and scholars of law
and music. I call it her dissertation defense in the liberal arts, which
she passed with distinction. Afterward the viceroy observed that, "in
the manner that a royal galleon might fend off the bothersome arrows
of a few canoes, so did Juana extricate herself from the questions, arguments, and objections these many men, each in his specialty, directed
to her."[9]

Not everyone was pleased with the tournament's outcome. The professors were humiliated by this arrogant marisabia. The court's father
confessor, Padre Antonio Nuñez de Miranda, scandalized by the pro-
digious display of vanity he had witnessed from the court's favorite,
feared for the girl's salvation if she were not immediately dispatched to
a marriage bed or a nunnery.

We must remember that these were dangerous times for an intelligent and independent woman. The spies of the Holy Inquisition lurked in every household. Padre Antonio himself was a censor for the Holy Office. Literacy for criolla girls was tolerable, even admired in some circles, but genius in women was akin to heresy. And heresy was the fodder of the Inquisition. For the sake of Juana's soul, Padre Antonio insisted that she be taken in hand and forced to curtail her studies and curb her popularity. Shortly after the tournament she spent three difficult months living with the Discalced Carmelites in the Convent of Saint Joseph, but she was unable to withstand the rigors of the Carmelite discipline, contracted an illness, and returned to the palace to recover.

BRIDE OF CHRIST

Eighteen months after the Carmelite fiasco, Juana at age twenty, entered another novitiate. With Padre Antonio's influence and her three-thousand-peso dowry paid for by a generous patron, Don Pedro Velásquez de la Cadena, she was accepted at the convent of Santa Paula of the Order of Saint Jerome. In February 1669 she signed her testament of faith under the name Sor Juana Inés de la Cruz. Because the convent of San Jerónimo was reserved for legitimate criollas (which implied wealthy families), either she or Padre Antonio told a white lie and listed her as the legitimate daughter of a deceased Basque father, Pedro de Asabje, and a criolla mother, Isabel Ramírez. "Irregularities" such as these, Octavio Paz tells us, were common in New Spain and revealed how *"si las reglas eran severas, las prácticas eran blandas."*[10] Indeed, the Hieronymite Order was "known for the mildness of its discipline."[11] Unlike the severe austerity she had encountered with the Carmelites, Sor Juana found that the Hieronymite nuns owned slaves, jewels, and property and were permitted to entertain their guests in the convent's *locutorio*, or sitting room, with their faces uncovered, and sometimes with no bars between them and their visitors.

The nuns' "cells" were two-story apartments, complete with kitchens, parlors, and bathrooms (literally small rooms with tiled basins where the nuns sat to be bathed by their servants). Unique among her sisters in many ways, Sor Juana had a substantial library that some scholars say was as large as four thousand volumes; others say even a library of four hundred would have been huge by convent standards. She collected musical and scientific instruments, many of them gifts from the vicereine and other friends, and an assortment of souvenirs given to her by visiting nobles. Like her mother and grandfather, Sor Juana had a head for business; she was elected treasurer of the convent for two terms (nine years) and served as archivist for one. She also owned her cell, had investments in convent property, and kept a slave—Juana de San José—whom her mother had transferred to her when she took her vows.[12]

Her work consisted of more than chanting prayers during the seven canonical hours in the upper choir of the convent's chapel. She also tutored the convent's boarders in music and theater, oversaw the renovation of the convent's more damaged structures, balanced the ledgers, and participated, against her will, in the political squabbles of her sister nuns. It is little wonder, then, that her time for study and contemplation was late at night, when the convent slept.

Convent life consisted of a number of rituals, most of which were "repugnant" to Sor Juana, as she confesses in La Respuesta. She disliked anything that interrupted her studies or interfered with the solitude necessary to concentrate on her writing. Although one school of sorjuanistas, or Sor Juana critics, argues that she joined the convent because of a deep devotion to Jesus Christ, she writes at the end of her life, in her final testament, that she "lived in Religion without Religion, worse than a pagan."[13] She chose the veil because marriage was the only other "decent" alternative for a young woman of her caste, and because she felt a total aversion to surrendering her free will to a husband and her daily life to a family (a condition of relentless servitude that would prevent her from opening a book). Thus the convent was a more "decent" place to "insure [her] salvation,"[14] which I interpret to mean escaping the attentions of men and the consequences of their desires.

Four years after Sor Juana had professed and taken the name Sor Juana Inés de la Cruz, the viceroy and vicereine were recalled to Spain. La Marquesa fell ill and passed away en route to Veracruz, where they were to board a ship bound for Spain. Sor Juana mourned the death of her first patroness for years and wrote three heartfelt requiems for her beloved marquesa, who had shown her the love, acceptance, and encouragement she had only received from her grandfather.

The new viceroy also died suddenly, after only twenty-six days in his position, so the king of Spain appointed Fray Payo Enríquez de Ribera, the archbishop of Mexico, to serve as the vice-regent. Fray Payo, the archbishop, had been a good friend of the Manceras and an admirer of Sor Juana's intelligence and poetic talents, so he gladly took on the role of her protector. As the archbishop-viceroy, he was doubly empowered to quell the petty tyranny perpetrated against Juana by jealous sisters in the convent and mother superiors resentful of her continued favoritism by the powers that be. One funny story relates how a mother superior of San Jerónimo complained to the archbishop that Sor Juana had called her "stupid." His response was for the Mother Superior to "prove the opposite" and he would seek justice.[15]

LA DÉCIMA MUSA

In November 1680 the new viceroy—Don Tomás Antonio de la Cerda, Marqués de la Laguna—and his wife, María Luisa Manrique de Lara y Gonzaga, Condesa de Paredes, made their official entrance into New Spain. All the cloistered nuns of the city watched the ceremonious event, full of pomp and circumstance, from the rooftops of their convents. Sor Juana had been commissioned to design the triumphal arch for the church council to welcome the sovereigns to their new home, and it was with that triple-arched triumphal structure and the allegorical richness of its conceits and images that she won the royal couple's immediate approval. That same year what we now call Halley's Comet blazed over the Novohispanic sky for more than two weeks, and a new archbishop joined the leadership of New Spain—the flagrant misogynist and tyrannical zealot Don Francisco de Aguiar y Seijas, who would be the driving force in the spiritual cleansing of New Spain.

The Marqués de la Laguna's eight-year reign in New Spain corresponded to the happiest and most productive years of Sor Juana's life. The couple took Sor Juana under their wing, and a very close, particular friendship developed between Juana and la Condesa. I argue in my novel *Sor Juana's Second Dream* (1999) that she stirred in Juana something she had never known—an emotional and intellectual connection that felt both sexual and spiritual, a desire surpassing logic and the laws of the church, a devotion that exceeded the rosary and the habit. I know that Octavio Paz, like many of his fellow sorjuanistas, would disagree with my radically feminist interpretation of Sor Juana's feelings for la Condesa, a relationship he labels a "platonic love-friendship" marked by "an excessive libido" that "had no outlet in the opposite sex."[16]

Clearly Paz is not concerned with la Condesa's sex life; it is Sor Juana's closeted libido that intrigues him. Perhaps she joined the convent because of a doomed love affair with a courtier from her days as lady-in-waiting. If there had been a man at court she could have satisfied her sexual needs with, perhaps her passion for la Condesa would have been less "excessive." Indeed, if there had been a legitimate father figure in her life, perhaps she would not have developed such masculine tendencies: her drive to learn, to write, to excel. Paz does not deny that the two women loved each other, but he assures us that their love was "chaste."[17] Despite Sor Juana's own primary evidence to the contrary, some people (aka homophobes) cannot stomach the idea that *la décima musa* might have been a lesbian, as if somehow that would diminish her wisdom or tarnish her significance in history. She certainly wouldn't be the first lesbian in history, nor the first lesbian nun,[18] nor even the first tenth muse, as Plato called Sappho, the bisexual poet from the Greek island of Lesbos, millennia earlier.[19]

Paz asserts that "it is futile to try to learn what her true sexual feelings were. She herself did not know."[20] And yet, omniscient patriarch that he is, Paz knows what Sor Juana herself could never have known.

I am convinced, however, that Sor Juana knew very well the contours of her desire. Just as she knew she had an aversion to marriage and a "black inclination" for learning,[21] she knew she loved la Condesa "the way air loves space / the way fire loves matter…[is] the way I love you, Filis." She knew that openly loving another woman in a carnal way would be seen as apostasy, and so she used the courtly metaphors and poetic conventions of the day to hide her feelings in open sight, as we see in her sonnets, her ballads, her décimas, and her letters. In "Romance 19," cited above, Sor Juana exalts la Condesa to the status of a divinity to be worshipped from afar, a goddess names Filis/Phyllis for whom Sor Juana felt not "indecencias" (indecency or sexual desire) but "pure love." She called this love a "holocaust," a religious "sacrifice" of the soul that burns within her in "adoration and silence." Nina Scott finds that "Sor Juana's many love poems to her protectoress, the Countess of Paredes, comprise[s] a full 15 percent of her personal lyric." Despite Paz's admonition that there are no "documents" to prove her "Sapphic tendencies,"[22] Sor Juana offers us ample evidence of her desires, not just for learning, writing, and participating in public discourse but for loving and being loved by another woman.

By 1690 two volumes of her collected works and a second edition of each volume were circulating in Spain and New Spain. Sor Juana's celebrity was more widespread than ever, and yet she was also more vulnerable, more persecuted by her convent sisters and Archbishop Aguiar y Seijas. She had lost her powerful protectors in the viceregal court; la Condesa and her husband had returned to Spain in 1688. Her close friend Don Carlos de Sigüenza y Góngora had transferred his loyalty to the archbishop, and the new viceroy, the Count de Galve, and his wife, Doña Elvira, had more of a diplomatic relationship with her rather than a real friendship.

THE WORST OF WOMEN

It was during the last five years of her life that Sor Juana was finally overthrown by church patriarchs. Prodded by Manuel Fernández de

Santa Cruz y Sahagún, the bishop of Puebla, Sor Juana wrote a rebuttal of a Portuguese Jesuit priest's analysis of Christ's "Sermon on the Mount" that she called "Crisis de un sermón," a critique of Christian doxology that unleashed a huge crisis in her life. That she had committed an unforgivable faux pas in the hierarchy of the Roman Catholic Church gave her detractors the ammunition they needed to close in on her defeat.

Although he had been an admirer of Sor Juana's and a frequent participant in the gatherings that took place in her *locutorio*, the bishop of Puebla betrayed her trust, publishing her critique without her knowledge or consent under the ironic title *Carta atenagórica*, or "Letter Worthy of Athena." Adopting the persona of a fictitious cross-dressed nun named Sor Filotea de la Cruz, the bishop included a prologue to the "Carta" with an ominous warning about Sor Juana's salvation if she continued to preoccupy herself with worldly matters rather than with reading Scripture.

Sor Juana's rebuttal incensed Aguiar y Seijas, who, aided and abetted by the bishop of Puebla and her old father confessor, Padre Antonio Nuñez de Miranda, who felt personally slighted by her temerity to contradict the wisdom of this priest from his own Jesuit order, just wanted to see the arrogant *décima musa* brought down from the pedestal of her fame and influence. Her sorority of enemies in the convent, and this trinity of priests, reminiscent of the three witches in *Macbeth*, laid out what Paz calls "the traps of faith" to ensnare Sor Juana in the final controversy that would bring about her definitive downfall.

One year after publication of the *Carta atenagórica*, she wrote her response, the autobiographical *La Respuesta a Sor Filotea*, defending her right to discourse with theological doctrine. Although published posthumously, *La Respuesta* scandalized the clerical community more than her rebuttal of the Jesuit priest. It is perhaps her most important work for those interested in the more private details of her life and her scholarly formation and rhetorical mastery. But it was also the catalyst for her fall from the scaffold of celebrity she had been building with every breath of her life.

La Respuesta was the epitome of Sor Juana's defense of a woman's right to an education and a life of the mind, a comparative analysis between her own life and that of a long list of learned and holy women from antiquity and the Old Testament who, like her, practiced the cultivation of knowledge as the highest expression of their souls. Here we see her rebelliousness as a child, her true feelings about marriage and why she chose to take vows, her displeasure with the other nuns who envied and persecuted her for her studies, her indulgence in books and writing at the expense of the other labors and obligations of her vocation, and, finally, what we could call her feminism, her denouncement of the church's gender inequalities and double standards when Christianity was full of examples of other learned women, many of whose stories were to be found in the Bible and in whose wake she followed.

The following year, drought struck Mexico City, killing crops and animals. A famine ensued, which brought more people to the city, and deaths multiplied by the day. As more and more died of starvation and illness, a great upheaval rose up from among *las castas*, or the lower social castes, who demanded grain from the city's stores. There were riots and protests, looting of the viceregal palace, the burning of the city's granaries, the destruction of books. While the city devolved outside the walls of San Jerónimo, Sor Juana's world inside the convent and within the church started to implode.

In 1694 Sor Juana underwent her mandatory silver jubilee—her twenty-fifth anniversary as a Hieronymite nun—in which she was expected to renew her vows to the church, offer a public confession of her sins, and sign another testament of faith to the Order of Saint Jerome. This was the perfect opportunity for the trinity of patriarchs and their veiled minions to bring the church's full vindictive wrath upon *la décima musa*. Sor Juana wrote three documents attesting to her sincere desire to remain a Hieronymite nun and her acute penitence for all the ways in which she had offended God and her superiors. To substantiate the truth of her words, she signed her name in the Book of Professions in her own blood, calling herself "*la peor del mundo*" (the worst woman in the world) and *"la peor que ha habido"* (the worst woman who ever lived).[23]

Sentenced to silence, Sor Juana was forced to abandon her writing, sell her books, renounce her worldly possessions, increase her self-flagellations, and dedicate herself to the care of the sick sisters of her convent, which had been hit by another unidentified plague. At four o'clock in the morning on April 17, 1695, Sor Juana Inés de la Cruz died of the epidemic that killed nine of every ten sisters in the convent. She had spent almost twenty-seven of her forty-six years cloistered in the convent, separated from the world, writing, reading, learning, fighting for her rights, and hiding what her critics and biographers have called everything but a spade: her lesbianism.

REBEL WITH A CAUSE

In my book *[Un]Framing the "Bad Woman": Sor Juana, Malinche, Coyolxauhqui, and Other Rebels with a Cause* (2014), I use Sor Juana as a primordial example of the "bad woman" stereotype—the woman who disobeys, who does not follow protocol, who resists patriarchal prescriptions of her sex and gender, who flaunts her attributes, and who persists in her rebellious ways against all odds and all forms of censure and punishment. "World, why do you insist / on persecuting me?" she asks in a poem. "How do I offend, / when all I seek is to put beauty in my mind, / and not my mind on beauty?"[24] For Sor Juana, beauty was the cultivation of the mind and the spirit through poetry, music, art, and especially writing, learning, and producing knowledge. The superficial notions of beauty did not interest her, for these included not just aesthetic concerns but also the qualities that a society ruled by men had deemed beautiful, and therefore desirable, in women: purity, modesty, humility, maternity, and passivity, to which had to be added the poverty, chastity, and docility demanded of nuns in the church if they expected redemption from their sins. Because she defied every one of those traditional norms of a "good bride of Christ," because she "refused to comply with those social [expectations] by which 'good girls' and 'good women' were constructed,"[25] she did everything in her power to resist her erasure from history, and she persisted in her lifelong quest for equality and emancipation.

Sor Juana left a legacy of decolonial feminist thought three hundred years before the feminist revolution. This is why, in 1925, Dorothy Schons, a Latin Americanist scholar at the University of Texas, gave her the epithet "the First Feminist in the New World."[26] This is why, in 1689, la Condesa de Paredes, the vicereine with whom Sor Juana shared her mind, her heart, and her body, called her the tenth muse in the title of her first book, which la Condesa herself edited and had published in Spain. This is why, in 1999, I published a radical Chicana lesbian feminist interpretation of her life and work, a quantum history, if you will, composed of her own words and invented pages of her Sapphic diary and letters that together signify the possibility of the Second Dream. Seventeen years later, the Netflix series, *Juana Inés*, portrayed her in exactly the same way. This is why, in our lifetime, we must recognize Sor Juana Inés de la Cruz as a mighty "rebel with a cause," one of our earliest queer Latinx revolutionary sisters.

Jane McManus Storm Cazneau (b. Troy, New York, 1807; d. at sea, 1878), diplomat and adventurer, was the first woman appointed to the U.S. foreign service. She served during the Mexican-American War in the 1840s and conducted secret negotiations with the Mexican government. She also served as a war correspondent from Mexico and the Dominican Republic. Years earlier, though, she had thrown herself into the War of Texas Independence, giving money and weapons to the Texan cause.

Jane McManus Storm Cazneau

LINDA HUDSON

With her pen, Cazneau did more for Texas in her
days than any other person.

HENRY WATTERSON, THE PULITZER PRIZE—WINNING EDITOR OF THE
Louisville Courier, learned the newspaper business from Jane McManus Storm Cazneau. Watterson credited his knowledge of journalism to Jane's teaching him when he was a cub reporter at the *Daily States* in Washington, D.C. He claimed "a braver, more intellectual woman never lived" and called her "a born insurrecto and a terror with her pen." Watterson was correct: there were few revolutionary causes that Jane did not promote between 1830 and 1878.[1] By choice, and by sheer determination, she can be found, front and center, in one political upheaval and revolution after another. This is her story.

Jane was a prolific writer. She published in six metropolitan newspapers and three national journals, wrote fifteen or more books and pamphlets, and edited five or more newspapers and journals during her career. Many of her publications were unsigned, but she used several pen names until the late 1840s, when she became best known as

Cora Montgomery. The central theme of her life work was that the United States had a "Manifest Destiny to fulfill," and that was to spread republican government throughout the world. Although she is virtually unknown today, her quest for the spread of democracy illustrates the influence that one woman of the press had on nineteenth-century U.S. foreign policy.[2]

Born, reared, and educated in New York, Jane came to Mexican Texas in the 1830s to start a colony of freed slaves and German immigrants. She supported the Texas Revolution, and beginning in the 1840s she made her living in the male profession of journalism. She knew more about the revolutionary politics and the diplomacy of Mexico and the Caribbean than officials who asked her advice during the Polk, Taylor, and Fillmore administrations. She was banished from New York for aiding Cuban revolutionaries in 1850 and later corresponded with William L. Marcy, secretary of war; Jefferson Davis, secretary of state; President James Buchanan; and various cabinet members of Presidents Abraham Lincoln, Andrew Johnson, and Ulysses S. Grant in support of revolutionary activity in Mexico, the Dominican Republic, Nicaragua, and Cuba.[3]

Revolution was in Jane's blood. Her family fought in the American Revolution, and she had family connections to powerful men. Aaron Burr was her family's attorney. Jane served as her father's secretary and, when he was elected to the U.S. House of Representatives (1825–27), went with him to Washington. There she met politicians whom she later corresponded with, such as Sam Houston, James Buchanan, and others who were sources when she wrote for New York and Washington newspapers.[4]

Jane tried to have a conventional life and married Allen B. Storm in 1825; their son, William, was born the following year. Within a few years, Jane was working in New York, without her husband. She supported herself as a German translator of pamphlets that Burr used to promote Texas land in Germany. She also worked as a bookkeeper for the Galveston Bay and Texas Land Company owned by wealthy New York investors.[5] This work would bring her into the world of U.S.-Texas-Mexico politics and revolution.

In 1832 Jane and her brother Robert McManus, who was a surveyor, came to Texas and made the first of several attempts to purchase land in Texas from Mexico and to establish a colony. In 1834 she and her father came to Texas with a ship of immigrants and freed slaves who temporarily settled in Matagorda. There she first met William Leslie Cazneau, a Boston cotton buyer. Jane filed a claim for six leagues of land near Matagorda, and she filed a homestead claim as head of household. She and her father returned to Troy, where he died shortly thereafter.[6]

After gaining independence in 1836, the Texas government refused to recognize eleven-league grants, one of which was claimed by Jane. Before Jane could leave New York for Texas to press her claim, she was inadvertently drawn into Aaron Burr's divorce proceedings. After Burr's death, she sued to clear her name, eventually traveling to Texas in 1837, but her reputation had been ruined by the Burr divorce scandal. Jane could do nothing further in Texas and left Cazneau to keep her land claims active in the courts. She returned to New York in 1838, leaving her son, William, with her brother Robert's family on their land on the Trinity River near Liberty. While traveling internationally, Jane wrote articles for Horace Greeley's *New-Yorker Magazine*. Anonymous articles in her distinctive writing style also appeared in the *U.S. Magazine and Democratic Review*. Jane wrote favorably of the Mexican revolt of northern states that proclaimed the Republic of the Rio Grande in 1840.[7]

In 1843, when Texas began its drive for annexation to the United States, Jane published letters in the *New York Sun* promoting Texas. When Texas again made its bid for statehood in 1844–45, Jane, writing as C. Montgomery, published "The Presidents of Texas" in the *U.S. Magazine and Democratic Review*. As Corinne Montgomery, Jane published her first book, also the first history published of Texas, *Texas and Her Presidents with a Glance at her Climate and Agricultural Capabilities* (1845).[8]

With Congress voting to annex Texas in February 1845 and her publishers taking credit for the positive publicity that had influenced congressional votes, Jane turned to women's revolutionary issues. To aid working women in New York, Jane helped organize the Female Industrial Association with fellow authors who agreed to write stories about the difficulties of working women. While Horace Greeley of the *Tribune* urged women to withhold their labor to raise wages, Jane advised women to educate themselves, improve their skills, and enter professions that paid more money. She wrote that as clerks and bookkeepers, women would hardly be taking "a real man's job" and added, "Surely women can sell lace and ribbons." Greeley urged women to go west and find husbands, and Jane organized a boycott of Fifth Avenue stores until they hired women clerks for women customers. On May 1, 1845, she wrote in the *Sun* that New York stores would hire young women to sell ribbons, lace, and other notions to women customers. Thus began honorable professions and acceptance of women in the public workplace; another revolutionary idea at the time.[9]

In 1845 Jane contributed several articles on Texas annexation and Mexico to the *U.S. Magazine and Democratic Review*. Textual analysis strongly suggests that it was Jane who wrote the now famous July–August 1845 article "Annexation" that contained the famous words it was "our Manifest Destiny to overspread the continent." She gave name to the expansionist feeling that had existed since the country's founding. Analysis shows her known signed writing as 93 percent compatible with the article and O'Sullivan's having only 41 percent similarity. Nevertheless, since the 1950s the phrase has been attributed erroneously to O'Sullivan, who was in England at the time and returned later in the year to find he had been fired as editor. At this time, Thomas Richie, editor of the *Washington Union*, offered Jane a position as staff writer, but she declined. As she explained to ex-Texas president Mirabeau B. Lamar, she preferred the independent press, which gave her the "free[dom] to write" as she had for "the *U.S. Magazine*." In late 1845 Jane began contributing two columns on politics each week to the *New York Sun* under the nongendered byline MONTGOMERY.[10]

In 1846, when the Rio Grande border dispute between Mexico and the United States grew more intense, Jane wrote a series of articles in the *Sun* explaining the area was never part of Texas on Spanish maps and urged diplomacy to settle the issue. She wrote that the Polk administration represented shipping and canal interests that wanted to expand into Lower Mexico, Oregon, Cuba, and California. After war began, military defeats and several changes in the Mexican government made policy unclear. Acting on behalf of President James K. Polk, and with a British passport secured in Havana, Cuba, Jane and her publisher, Moses Beach, and his daughter Drusilla traveled to Mexico City in an attempt to negotiate with moderate Mexicans who wanted peace. They traveled with Catholic priests from Saint Louis who arranged talks with like-minded Mexican bishops. Beach hoped to found a bank in Mexico City for United States investors.[11]

Everything went wrong with Jane's revolutionary plan for Mexico when General Winfield Scott did not land his troops in Vera Cruz as expected. The Woman's Revolt, or "Revolt of the Polkos" as it is sometimes called, failed awaiting invasion by the Americans that would bring an excuse for overthrow of the government. Jane traveled back to Vera Cruz to see what happened. Beach and his daughter escaped to Tampico with a price on his head, and he lost the $50,000 taken without stockholder approval from the New Jersey bank where he was chairman of the board.[12]

When confronted about his delay, Scott refused to believe Jane about her mission. When Beach later explained, the general complained, "Never send messages of such importance by a plenipotentiary in petticoats." Jane labeled Scott "old fuss and feathers" in the columns sent to New York by diplomatic courier. Before she returned to New York, the forty-year-old Jane traveled back through enemy lines with messages for Mexican officials.[13]

WAR, POLITICS, AND DIPLOMACY: NO PLACE FOR A WOMAN?

Jane's Mexico experiences published in the *Sun* earned her international fame when Horace Greeley, hoping to discredit the *Sun*, revealed that MONTGOMERY was a woman writing about war, politics, and diplomacy— another revolutionary experience for women. Missouri senator Thomas

H. Benton condemned her as a "female... with a masculine stomach for war and politics." Jane supported the creation of three republics of the Rio Grande, Vera Cruz, and Yucatán, which Benton opposed. Because of her vivid descriptions of the war while she was with the *Sun*, it reached its largest circulation of 55,000 copies per daily issue with a weekly London edition. In May 1848, when the New York Associated Press Association, consisting of the *Tribune, Herald, Express, Journal of Commerce,* and *Sun* met to form a common wire service, Jane was selected the first Washington correspondent of the Associated Press.[14]

In 1848 Jane published pamphlets in support of the Cuban revolutionaries and their independence from Spain. Operating out of New York, Cora Montgomery edited a Cuban revolutionary paper, *La Verdad* (The Truth), written both in Spanish and English. In addition, Jane wrote two pro-Cuban pamphlets, *King of Rivers* and *Queen of the Seas*, advocating gradual emancipation with removal of slaves from the United States to Cuba. In 1849 Jane was such a vocal leader of Cuban independence that she was threatened with prosecution and prison for breaking U.S. neutrality laws. Several invasions of Cuba from the United States failed, and a large contingent of U.S. citizens and Cubans were seized by the U.S. navy in September when they departed ports from Boston, New York, Philadelphia, Baltimore, and New Orleans. The anti-expansionist administration of Zachary Taylor clamped down on Cuban rebel activity based in the United States.[15]

Threatened with prison for promoting revolution in Cuba, Jane married her old friend and ally William Cazneau in September 1849 and left the country. The couple first sailed from Boston to Morocco and brought back camels that Cazneau took across the Isthmus of Panama for use in the California desert. Jane published *The Camel Hunt* (1851) about that adventure and *A Story of Life on the Isthmus* (1853) about the California-bound immigrants. Jane next joined Cazneau in Texas where, in her words, she hid herself in a dugout on the banks of the Rio Grande at Eagle Pass, a city Cazneau helped found on the lower California Trail near Fort Duncan. Jane soon discovered Mexicans living along the river who had fled their homeland because of peonage. Greeley published her letters on peonage in the *Tribune*, and U.S. senator William Seward from New York read from them on the Senate floor when congress debated allowing peonage to continue in the New Mexico territory.[16]

In *Eagle Pass; or, Life on the Border* (1852), about her Rio Grande experiences, Jane predicted that the Mexican people would revolt against their oppressors, just as they later did in the Mexican Revolution (1910) that ended debt peonage. The 1850 U.S. Census shows Jane, Cazneau, and the Mexican workers living as she described them. While in Eagle Pass, rebels in northern Mexico again raised militias and, under General José Carbajal, along with Seminole Indians and U.S. volunteers, fought the Mexican government for independence of the region.[17]

While at Eagle Pass, Cazneau made yet another ill-fated trade expedition into Mexico. He led a hundred wagons from Indianola through Eagle Pass to Mazatlán, Mexico, on the Pacific Coast in an attempt to create the shortest trade route from the Atlantic to the Pacific Ocean. Somewhere in Mexico, Cazneau was arrested by authorities and, after months of bargaining, lost all his trade goods. The Cazneaus next moved back to Washington, D.C., in 1852 with the election of Franklin Pierce who proclaimed himself the Manifest Destiny president. Cazneau filed claims for the loss of the trade goods, and Pierce named Cazneau a secret agent to the Dominican Republic. He was to access its bays for a coaling station and as a possible colony for freed slaves. Critics wrote that Jane was the real agent and called Cazneau "Mr. Cora Montgomery." When Jane traveled to the Dominican Republic, she brought freed Virginia slaves and settled them near her home, an abandoned plantation near the capital of Santo Domingo.[18]

After a near-fatal illness when a former slave nursed her back to health, Jane dedicated her life to improving conditions for blacks. She urged African Americans to come to the Dominican Republic, where they would escape the prejudice of the United States. In anticipation of a mass migration of freed slaves financed by the federal government, Jane and her husband invested in land and port facilities.[19]

On November 6, 1860, Jane wrote Attorney General Jeremiah Black about the "narrow-minded senators [that] had cast Cuba and Mexico overboard" as safety valves for slavery transported from the States. Upon the election of Republican Abraham Lincoln, the southern states began leaving the Union, and with the chaos, Spain declared the Dominican Republic a colony once more. William H. Seward became secretary of state and, in March 1861, hired Jane to return to New York and write in support of preserving the union. He paid $750 for Jane's travel and office expenses and an additional $1,300 for her services ending July 1, 1861. No records explain the fifty-four-year-old woman's assignment, but editorials in the *New York Sun* and the Seward memo "Thoughts for the President's Consideration" reflected her thinking and writing style.[20]

Although her name does not appear in its columns or masthead, Jane's distinctive writing style again appeared in the *Sun* beginning in February 1861. The *Sun* stated that secession was impossible while other New York papers recognized the South's right to secede. Jane's presence is evident on February 15, with her "Opinions of the Press," a summary of other paper's editorials as she had done at the *Sun* years before. The next day's editorial praised Lincoln as a "man of the people" and a cool-headed moderate. By March, she focused on the southern states. "No secession ordinance can separate us," she claimed. "We are one people by blood, by interest, and by historic achievements."[21]

The *Sun* began featuring news of the Dominican Republic and its re-colonization by Spain. By May, Jane mimicked the *New Orleans Crescent*, which had declared that a line had been drawn between two nationalities: "If the Southern journals would only tell the truth—if the Southern people were truly informed regarding Northern sentiment, the disastrous rebellion into which they have been so blindly led, would soon be at an end." As Lincoln hesitated and Congress acted bewildered, she prodded: "The freemen of the Union ask nothing of their leaders but to do their duty, and in that they will follow them loyally, with all they possess, to death and beggary, if need be, to save a country for their children." Her object was "to arouse our rulers to the full measure of their power as the proper leaders of the greatest military force, and the noblest movement for liberty, that ever was embodied and embattled on this globe." She began a regular column called "Spirit of the People," which outlined the formation of volunteer military units, parades, and other patriotic activities. As Confederate raiders began taking their toll on merchant ships, in June a regular news feature became reports of seized prizes. By July, and with New York's newspapers united in solidarity to defend the United States, Jane's editorial duties ended. She returned to the former Dominican Republic and resumed caring for her extended family of dependents and colonists. Cazneau reported to Seward that Dominicans were carrying out a guerilla war from the hills against Spain.[22]

Almost as soon as the American Civil War began, former slaves in Union-held territory became an issue. Whigs and Democrats who had worked for relocation of blacks before the war continued their efforts. Jane wrote that "St. Domingo" was the "happy solution to the great problem of races." She anticipated a "large emigration from the ruined cotton states." Before she left New York, Jane editorialized about the *Dred Scott* Supreme Court decision that declared slaves property. As property, they could be declared contrabands of war. By the end of 1861, because of the loss of southern commerce and trade, almost 10,000 New York businesses had failed, and 11,500 New Yorkers were on public assistance. As conditions worsened, the unemployed took out their frustration on the contrabands. Lincoln proposed assistance to blacks who would emigrate. Frederick Douglass advised immigration to the Dominican Republic because of the "prejudice of the white race."[23]

About the time Union and Confederate forces met at Antietam in September 1862, Jane suggested "How We Live in San Domingo" as a title for the immigrant guide she prepared for the West Indies Company relocation effort. Spain welcomed the former slaves because they could grow cotton, then in high demand because of the blockade of Confederate ports. On December 12, 1862, Congress abolished slavery in Washington, D.C., and appropriated $100,000 to aid in colonization of former slaves. The American West Indies Company was only one such project. With $600,000, the Chiriqui Improvement Company also formed to establish the Colony of Linconia in Panama.[24]

After the Emancipation Proclamation, the war became one fought by the poor whites to free the slaves who were used as strikebreakers against them. Government officials advocated colonization to ease the racial violence that was growing more intense. In all, five editions of Jane's guidebook, *In the Tropics by a Settler in Santo Domingo* (1863), were published anonymously in New York and London. In Jane's next publication, *The Prince of Kashna* (1866), she was identified as the author of both books.[25]

After 1861, General Cazneau's career overshadowed that of his wife, Jane, who became responsible for her son, William, who was manic-depressive, and her granddaughter Cora. In Santo Domingo, Jane was hampered by conditions of war and a progressive loss of eyesight that hindered her activities. Even so, between 1863 and 1878, she wrote four books promoting expansion into the tropics, composed three essays read before the American Geographical and Statistical Society, and wrote for the *New York Sun*, the *New York Herald*, and two Dominican newspapers.[26]

Like *Eagle Pass*, *In the Tropics* was an example of people who made a choice not to be trapped by their environment and who gained control over their lives. Shortly after Union victories at Gettysburg and Vicksburg, Santo Domingo erupted into full-scale civil war. Spanish officials accused the Cazneaus of inciting the revolt and burned their home. The Cazneaus fled with their settlers to the British consulate for protection.[27]

The Cazneaus next traveled to Jamaica with their settlers and leased a bankrupt plantation in the mountains of Saint Catherine Parish. Always a voracious reader, Jane read every book in the plantation house, including the handwritten journal of the former tenant, which resulted in *The Prince of Kashna*. The book was meant for former slaves as a beginning reader, and it had a moral about honesty, loyalty, hard work, and education.[28]

With the end of the American Civil War, Secretary Seward warned Spain against its challenge to the Monroe Doctrine, and Spain, holding only the capital city and fearful of the largest military force in the world, withdrew in July 1865. Cazneau resumed his work at developing Samana Bay as a port, and in August 1865 Jane was in New York to arrange publication of *The Prince of Kashna* and encouraged the ongoing Cuban independence movement.[29]

With slavery ended, Jane, like Seward, expected territorial expansion to resume. "I handled the preliminaries of the Texas Annexation movement and the *Sun* not only had the press on that subject but ran up its own circulation at the same time," she wrote the *Sun* editor. "I would like to do the same with the new affair of the Antilles now looming....If you are inclined...allow me to work it up." From New York in September 1865, Jane wrote Secretary of the Interior James Harlan about her plans. She asked that he forward her letter to Secretary Seward. Harlan, whose family was involved in the steamboat business, contacted Seward, who wanted a coaling station in the Caribbean. Former slaves, then under the care of Harlan's Freedmen's Bureau, as colonists would help increase an American presence in the Dominican Republic.[30]

At the last Johnson cabinet meeting of December 1865, Seward announced he would tour the Caribbean. While in Santo Domingo, Jane was hostess and interpreter at informal meetings held with Seward and Dominican officials. Seward saw the United States stretching out through colonies and trade while Jane preferred the term "American System" for a "great circle of republics." At that time Seward was negotiating for the purchase of the Danish Virgin Islands, Russian Alaska, Spanish Puerto Rico, Guam, Midway, and British Hawaii as coaling stations for U.S. merchant ships.[31]

In Washington, in January 1866, President Johnson urged recognition of the Dominican Republic. Johnson appointed Cazneau minister in residence—a position that did not require Senate confirmation. In September the Johnson Administration recognized the government of the Dominican Republic. In exchange, the United States had the use of the coal mines at Samana Bay for a coal and naval depot. The Cazneaus served as interpreters during more negotiations as U.S. business penetrated the once-exclusive European trade zone. Colonization of freed slaves failed with the death of Thaddeus Stevens, the chief proponent of providing freed slaves with land, farm implements, and supplies, either in the United States or some other location.[32]

In her pamphlets, *To the American Press* (1870), *Our Winter Eden* (1878), and in her letters published in the *Herald,* Jane promoted Samana Bay as a free port. In 1869 the United States Geological and Mineralogy Survey Company formed, and its investors wanted annexation to stabilize the Santo Domingo government. The American Geographical and Statistical Society of New York published *Resources of Santo Domingo* (1869). It was the same type of material Jane had once produced for Texas annexation, with subheadings on history, geography, climate, soil, agricultural products, mineral resources, and inducements for colonization.[33]

In March 1869 President Grant saw annexation as a step in making "America for the Americans," once the slogan of young Americans who promoted Manifest Destiny. During the Civil War, British-built Confederate raiders destroyed U.S. shipping. Few American deepwater shipping companies survived the Civil War. Foreign trade carried by American ships dropped from 73.7 percent of the world's trade in 1858 to 25 percent during the war. For twenty-five years, Jane advocated territorial and commercial expansion and a steam-powered navy and merchant marine. Samana Bay would assist in regaining the lost trade and commerce with the West Indies, South America, and beyond.[34]

President Grant sent naval vessels to Santo Domingo to protect U.S. shipping. The mercantile house of Spofford and Tileston, once the largest deepwater shipping firm in the United States, began regular service and chartered the National Bank of Santo Domingo to stabilize the Dominican currency. Grant sent General Orville Babcock to examine Samana Bay as a naval port. Jane wrote of the meeting in the *Herald* in August 1869, in which the Cazneaus again served as hosts and interpreters for a party of about thirty Dominican and U.S.

officials who met at their rebuilt cottage, their discussions blending foreign policy and business.

The Santo Domingo situation was complicated by President Grant's support of the Cuban war for independence. The Cubans declared independence and freed their slaves in September 1868. President Grant paid Santo Domingo $100,000 for the annual lease of Samana Bay with secret service funds, and the United States flag was raised over Samana Bay. Grant demanded that Congress approve the annexation treaty. He believed the bay would "go far toward restoring to us our lost merchant marine." Grant saw annexation as a matter of national security by rebuilding the U.S. deepwater merchant marine.[35]

In June 1870 the Senate voted against the annexation of the Dominican Republic, but Grant did not give up on a naval base. He appointed a commission that urged annexation, but with the Senate's rejection in June 1871, Grant had no funds to pay for lease of the bay. In 1874 the Dominican Republic erupted into war with pro-American Reds fighting against the European-backed Blues. The British would make peace if the United States left Samana Bay. Without trade, Spofford and Tileston closed their wharves and coal depot and went bankrupt. It would be two years before Richard Henry Dana, the editor of the *Sun*, revealed how railroad interests backed by the British and French corrupted Congress and prevented the restoration of U.S. merchant shipping.[36]

For twenty years, General and Mrs. Cazneau invested their lives, their fortunes, and their reputations to extend U.S. trade and republican ideals into the Caribbean. While the general tried to salvage their investments in the Dominican Republic, Jane returned to Keith Hall Plantation and opened it as a residential hotel for winter tourists. From Spanish Town, tourists climbed by buggies through Bog Walk Gorge, lunched at Keith Hall atop the gorge, then went across the mountains to the north shore where they continued their cruise.[37]

While Jane supervised Cazneau School and reared her granddaughter, Cora, she also entertained hotel guests—and still found a way to keep her hand in revolutionary politics in Cuba. In 1865 Jane claimed,

"By an odd set of coincidences I have been better informed than the state department itself." New York Cubans issued a pamphlet, *Voice of America*, perhaps written by Jane. By 1874, the Cazneaus, now in their late sixties, could offer the Cubans little more than moral support. They had little money, Jane was almost blind, and the general had malaria. Their only wealth was Keith Hall, undeveloped land in the war-torn Dominican Republic, and unrecorded land deeds along the Rio Grande in Texas. The Cazneaus made plans to return to Texas and reclaim their Eagle Pass property.

In June 1875 William Cazneau was negotiating the sale of their Jamaican property and thereafter would proceed to Texas, but the general died on January 8, 1876. His obituary in the *San Antonio Herald* on March 22, 1876, states: "He leaves a wife, now old and blind, who with her pen did more for Texas in her days of trial, than any other person." In 1878 Jane returned to New York and published *Our Winter Eden: Pen Pictures of the Tropics* (1878), sketches of people and places in the Dominican Republic. Jane and her daughter-in-law booked passage to Jamaica on the *Souder*, the last remaining U.S. deepwater merchant ship. She was to return to Texas with Cazneau's remains for burial in the state cemetery, but, on December 31, 1878, the *New York Tribune* publicized the ship's most famous passenger as front-page news when the ship went down at sea: "A SKETCH OF MRS. CAZNEAU THE REMARKABLE CAREER OF ONE OF THE PASSENGERS OF THE SOUDER." In closing, the article offered a tribute: "Few women leave a record more desirable," and she "commanded the admiration of all who knew her."[38]

Jane's influence was apparent when editors, senators, diplomats, political leaders, and foreign dignitaries singled her out as a source of information, and for special favors or criticism. She advised presidents and cabinet members from the Polk to the Grant administrations. Jane's life presents a better understanding of professional women in the nineteenth century. She was accepted as an intellectual equal by editor-colleagues. She has been ignored by women activists because she did not support women's suffrage. However, she was an avid supporter of equal pay for equal work and the expansion of employment for women.[39]

Jane was one of the more influential women of her generation. Many policies that she advocated eventually succeeded. For example, she promoted the need for a steam navy and merchant marine fifty years before Alfred T. Mahan, and she wrote about the problems of the working class sixty years before it became a Progressive crusade. She advocated agrarian reform fifty years before Populists took up the cause, and she assisted republican revolutionaries in Cuba and Central America years before the United States recognized the need for justice in sister-republics of the Western Hemisphere. More than anything, Jane defies the stereotype of a nineteenth-century woman who stayed out of politics and out of public life. Without hesitation, without regret, and without any mind to social expectations, Jane put herself in the middle of one revolution after another and used her voice, and her pen, to shape their outcomes.

Teresa Urrea (b. Ocoroni, Sinaloa, Mexico, 1873; d. Clifton, Arizona, 1906), a healer and later a patroness of Indians in northern Mexico, is an icon of borderlands culture. She became a reluctant revolutionary when Indians fighting Porfirio Díaz came to believe that she would protect them from death or injury in battle. Because insurgents called her their saint, Díaz blamed her for inciting rebellion, exiled her, and tried to have her killed. In the century since her death, her image as a political and cultural revolutionary has been fashioned under many guises.

Teresa Urrea

SANDRA CISNEROS

Saints don't make good housewives.

THERE WAS ONCE A MEXICAN GIRL SO FAMOUS SHE FRIGHTENED THE PRESident of the republic and had to be exiled. It doesn't seem so outrageous in our times for someone to terrorize a head of state now that we are living in the age of *puro susto* when plenty of people get deported or worse, but it's hard to imagine a woman, a teenager, a *mexicana* capable of such power then or now. Her name was Teresa Urrea, and she was known in her lifetime as Teresita, the Saint of Cabora, a village in northern Mexico.

Teresita lived and died before the Mexican Revolution began, yet she was certainly part of its volcanic rumblings that warned of the end of the old world order. Her story is extraordinary because she was a woman of color with no formal education who rose to power and fame as a mystic healer in Mexico and in the United States.

Teresita was mixed race, a mestiza when class and color differences were more pronounced than even now. Her mother, Cayetana Chávez, was an indigenous woman, and her father, Tomás Urrea, was a light-skinned Mexican of Spanish descent. He owned all the lands and ranch where Teresita was born and where Cayetana was employed. Teresita was his natural daughter, but when she was in her midteens he recognized her as his offspring and invited her to live with him and his second (common-law) family.

Before this, Teresa had lived in a *ramada*, a house made of sticks and mud, with her mother's relations. She was said to have been an excellent horsewoman, and she knew how to play the guitar and sing—all this the vaqueros had taught her. She must have been a remarkable child to have caught her father's attention. Girls were not valued, especially those who were illegitimate and indigenous, and certainly not by a wealthy man like Tomás Urrea. But Teresita was tall and beautiful, as we can see for ourselves from her photographs, as well as charming and clever by all accounts. Maybe her father recognized some part of himself in her and was proud to claim her as his. Only God knows. But by her midteens, she was living the plot of a Latin American telenovela by moving under her father's care and protection and moving up in class and color.

It was in her father's house that she met an indigenous elder who would lead her on her life path. The woman was known as Huila, and she was a *curandera*, a healer and midwife who knew the powers of native plants. Teresa began working as Huila's apprentice, and Huila shared all her skills since the girl showed aptitude. But something happened that would change Teresita's life forever and give her powers that surpassed her mentor.

They say that Teresita suffered a seizure as a result of a terrible *susto* in her midteens. Some say she was sexually assaulted or that there was an attempted assault. Some believe she suffered from epilepsy. It isn't certain what happened exactly, but it was something powerful enough to cause Teresita to go into a coma for several months, with her pulse and breathing so imperceptible that a mirror had to be held to her nose to make sure she was still alive. Over time Teresita's pulse grew weaker and finally dimmed completely until her family had to admit death had claimed her.

Teresita's wake was held in the family home as was the custom in those times. Tomás Urrea ordered a coffin built for Teresita, and Huila bound the girl's wrists together with a ribbon. It was during her *velorio* when the community had gathered to pray the rosary over her body that Teresita's first two miracles occurred. First, she rose from the dead, or at least from her temporary death, and second, she announced that they need not remove the coffin as it would be needed in three days. Her prediction proved true; her teacher Huila passed away and was buried in the coffin intended for Teresita.

Teresita was reborn, but she was visibly altered, and her life would never be the same. She spoke of having visited the Virgin Mary while she was away, and lived distracted for several weeks, unable to even feed or dress. When she finally came back to herself one morning, she could not remember anything that had happened since she fell ill. It was as if she had been alive but not alive, as if she were paying attention only to things inside her own heart.

Other strange events occurred. After her rebirth, Teresita exhibited extraordinary powers of healing and vision. Teresita claimed she could look inside her patients and see their illness clearly as if she were looking into a window. Sometimes she was able to cure them just by placing her hands on them, and those she was unable to cure, she was at least able to comfort and give temporary relief.

Word spread across the region that a young girl could cure miraculously. Thousands of sick people, rich and poor, came to seek her out. Her father's ranch was soon transformed into a carnival. Although Tomás Urrea tried to dissuade his daughter from doing her work, in the end, her piety and dedication won him over. "I believe God has placed me here as one of his instruments to do good." She was fulfilling an obligation.

And so the Urrea family made huge sacrifices on Teresita's behalf. The world as they once knew it turned upside down. Teresita was installed in her own building where she might receive her patients, and those who could afford to pay for food were charged, and those who could not were fed for free. In the way of a true healer, Teresita did not charge, however, for her healing services.

Teresita's family loved and supported her, but they never claimed she was a saint. Whenever Teresita cured someone successfully, it was the crowd who called out, "Miracle!" and "Santa Teresa!"

Teresa did not want to be a saint. Who would want to be a saint? Would you? But sainthood is conferred by others, not by the saint, isn't that so? Savvy businessmen out to make a living printed holy cards with Teresita's image with angels floating about her, and these sold very well and were popular among her followers, especially among the indigenous tribes who claimed her as their patron and who wore them on their hats to protect themselves from harm.

"I'm not a saint," Teresita insisted in an interview. Teresita admitted her body was like any other person's, but she knew that her soul was different. Teresita's family also denied Teresita's sainthood, though they had to admit Teresita had certain gifts even they could not explain. For example, when she wanted to, she could make herself so heavy that not even her strong half-brothers could pick her up, but when she willed it, her slender best friend could pick her up in her arms. Even more amazing was her ability to invite her best friend to travel together with her while they dreamed the same dream at night. They could go to Mexico City and walk about there, and then travel back to their bodies and remember the journey the next morning.

A great many theories abound as to how exactly Teresita accomplished what she did. Was it magnetism, hypnotism, spiritualism? Well, what exactly? Not even Teresita herself knew except she knew she was doing God's work, and later in life she even expressed an interest in going to Europe or to India for an explanation of her own mystical gifts.

Throughout her life, Teresita defended the rights of indigenous communities, perhaps because she was half-indigenous and had lived in their world. Then, as now, *los indios* were the poorest of the poor and suffered greatly. Teresita always spoke on their behalf and criticized the abuses inflicted by the government and the church. She encouraged the people to pray directly to God without the intercession of the priests or costly sacraments. Needless to say, the Mexican church did not look kindly on Teresita's power over the multitudes and denounced her as a fraud.

Eventually, Teresita's popularity among the Mayo, Tarahumara, and Tomochic communities caused her to become involved in politics and ultimately exiled from the country. It so happened that the indigenous communities held Teresita in high regard as they recognized in her a person of great spiritual integrity and power. Porfirio Díaz, the dictator/ruler of Mexico, felt she was inciting them to rise against him and had her escorted to the U.S.–Mexico border where she was booted out of the country. Her father accompanied Teresita and protected her during her exodus; eventually they established a home in Arizona and later in El Paso, Texas. While Teresita was exiled, several indigenous communities did indeed organize themselves in strikes and uprisings. And though she was no longer a Mexican resident, Teresita was often implicated in these events because her followers carried her image on them. This caused Porfirio Díaz to fear she was even more powerful than imagined. Maybe the Mexican president believed the stories of Teresita's ability to appear in more than one place at the same time. At any rate, he purportedly sent agents across the border to kidnap Teresita or to assassinate her.

It is with good reason that the Urreas feared for Teresita's safety, and so they were advised to move inland, away from the border and its volatile environment. Tomás sent for his wife and children and settled his family finally in Clifton, Arizona, a beautiful mining town tucked in the cleft between two bluffs. Here he established successful dairy and firewood businesses. But it was also here that he and his daughter would experience heartache.

It seems that Teresita fell in love with a Mexican miner from a neighboring town. His name was Guadalupe Rodríguez, and he was tall and handsome, like her father. Maybe she saw in him a man who could protect her, and she felt safe with him. And after knowing him eight months she married him, though her father did not approve of the match. She was twenty-seven years old when she met Lupe. Did he see in Teresita a beautiful young woman and not a saint? Perhaps this was something altogether new for Teresita, and though her father cursed her choice in love, women are always brave in the face of love even if it means defying fathers.

Lupe had to steal Teresita from her father's house. He came with his rifle and took her away, but not against her will. Maybe she had planned the confrontation, and she willingly went away with him. They were married in the neighboring town of Metcalf where he lived. But by morning her husband began to act strangely. Many Mexican men act strangely after their wedding night. Maybe he'd been drinking. Maybe he suspected Teresita was not such a saint, and this made him angry. Maybe she had been violated that day when she went into a coma, and this may have made Lupe feel he was cheated and getting damaged goods. Maybe he was hired by Porfirio Díaz. Or maybe he was simply *un loco*. We can only imagine, because we don't know what happened to trigger such strange actions in Teresita's new husband. He went into a rage, Teresita reported, and tore up her things. He made her pack her clothes in a bundle, and then, carrying it over his shoulder, ordered his new bride to follow him.

Witnesses watched Teresita follow this madman. Was he shouting? Did he beat her? What did he do that folks came out and warned her not to follow him? Maybe they knew he was a crazy man all along. Guadalupe Rodríguez walked on the railroad track, and Teresita was forced to follow him. Then he broke into a run, and she ran after him. He turned around and started to shoot at her. And only then did the bystanders come after him and carry him off to the authorities. They brought him back to Clifton and put him in a jail that had been created from a cave in a mountain, and there he behaved like a wild creature pacing his cage.

I want to imagine the things Lupe shouted about his bride for all to hear. I want to imagine her pain and sadness. It couldn't have been more humiliating to have gone against her father's wishes and then return the next day knowing he was right. Her husband, frothing in jail, spewing out words against her. Now was she a saint?

And what does her father say? And what does Teresita say to him?

What do they not say to each other, and what do they think? And if she could see into people's hearts and into the future, why was she not able to see through love, the townsfolk ask? If you ever have lived such a scene in your life, you can fill in the blanks. Perhaps love makes fools of us all.

At the right moment, a Mrs. C. P. Rosencrans arrives and invites Teresita to California to heal her child, and perhaps because of her disastrous marriage, Teresita accepts and leaves Clifton, because she too is sick and needs to heal her own heart.

More than five hundred citizens go to the train station to see Teresita off. I think one person is not there. I think her father refuses to go and goes to work that day and pretends he is too busy with his dairy, with his firewood business. This is how I imagine a man too proud, too hurt, dealing with his sadness. Or perhaps he is there. Does he join the crowd in waving a handkerchief, or does he stand as hard and still as a mountain?

Teresita is lost to him. Her father is lost to her. How powerless her father must've felt when she married, and now when she moves away, does a part of him die too?

And what about her? What must she feel to accept a trip to California that will take her far away? I think of her father sitting, watching the sunset in Arizona. I think of Teresita watching that same sunset in California. Each thinking about the other.

Is this the beginning of the saint's loss of her powers? In California, a medical company will hire Teresita and promise her thousands of dollars to go on a curing crusade, and they will tell her she can travel and heal many people. But they don't tell her they will charge her patients, and because she will be healing Anglos, she will have difficulties because she doesn't speak English. And so Teresita begins a career in Los Angeles, which then takes her to Saint Louis and on to New York. And because she can't find an adequate translator now that she is serving an Anglo audience, she sends a letter to her good friend, her *comadre* Juana Van Order in Arizona, a Mexican woman who has married an Anglo and has two bilingual boys. The older son is sent to

New York to assist Teresita in her work. His name is John Van Order, and he will become the father of Teresa's two daughters.

How could love not develop between a nineteen-year-old boy and a woman of twenty-seven who has very little experience in love? Maybe he tells her things he believes with all his heart, but his heart is the heart of a child. But her heart is the heart of a girl. And though they cannot marry, because she is still legally married to Lupe, they promise to love each other as if they were married and to marry when they can. I can't imagine it any other way, because Teresita lived and spoke always by way of her heart.

She cannot know that she and John will have very little to say to each other in a few years.

They have little in common. Even though she will seek out the divorce in Los Angeles, by then John will have outgrown his love with the girl/saint. Saints don't make good housewives.

It's when she's expecting her child in New York that she hears her father is ill, and finally that he has died. Teresita with life in her belly and with a contract that is keeping her in New York, what is she thinking now?

How is it that Teresita finally becomes aware of the duplicity of her employers and hires a lawyer to cancel her contract with the medical company? She is exhausted. She wants to go home. And she does go home, with her two girls, but not with their father. She has given up being a saint.

With her savings from her touring, she is able to open a small hospital in Clifton, and here she lives until she contracts tuberculosis in her thirty-third year and dies. During Teresita's short but extraordinary life, doors opened for her wherever she went, even though she was Mexican. She never forgot her indigenous roots and always allied herself with the poor, with the oppressed, even in the United States. While living in Los Angeles, it is said she supported the Mexicans organizing a union. She was a bridge between conflicting communities, and this in a time when Mexicans were even more oppressed than now.

Teresita Urrea was not a writer, so we don't know how she felt about the things that happened to her. We have accounts by witnesses. We have newspaper interviews, but these were translations of her words. We don't have her words directly; we have to trust those who put words in her mouth. And it seems as if everyone has put their own thoughts, their own politics, their own spin on how they see her, including this writer.

But perhaps that is the mystery and power of Teresita Urrea, a woman from both sides of the border. Activists, revolutionaries, historians, writers, indigenous communities, kin, friends, and enemies alike have used her to carry their own words, their own stories. Over a century after her death, she continues to inspire and haunt us.

Nahui Olin (b. Mexico City, Mexico, 1893; d. Mexico City, 1978), an artist and writer, used her talent in the 1920s to express her intellect and her sexuality and to break down gender barriers at a time when Mexican women were severely constrained by law and social custom. A painter and photographer who organized her own shows, Olin invaded an artistic realm dominated by men. In allowing herself to be depicted nude by sculptors and photographers, she took charge of her sexuality and made it possible for other women, like Frida Kahlo, to publicly do the same.

Nahui Olin

TERESA VAN HOY

Her mother's coercion succeeded in forcing her to marry, but her family's refusal to endorse divorce could not confine her to marriage.

NAHUI OLIN AS "OTHERWORLDLY FLAME," "SACRED SPARK," "WOMAN OF THE Sun," "a rose opening to the sun," "luscious ripened fruit of cactus pear," "the most beautiful woman in postrevolutionary Mexico." She was the daughter of General Manuel Mondragón, wife of Manuel Rodríguez Lozano, lover of Dr. Atl, model and muse of Edward Weston, Antonio Garduño, Diego Rivera, and Charlot. Through these two gazes, Olin figures as a great beauty and the intimate of Great Men.

Unstated in these accolades is their short duration. Originally feted, she was eventually forgotten. Nahui Olin died in 1978 without an obituary. From great heights in the 1920s, Olin fell from grace. Her most recent biographer traces her trajectory poignantly, writing that "she was in the 1920s the most beautiful woman in Mexico City. And there she died, in misery, walking around San Juan de Letrán and selling nude photographs of her youthful beauty at whatever price in order to feed herself and her cats."[1]

The insults grew ever harsher as she aged, culminating in the 1970s: "the Powdered Woman," "the Lunatic," "the Phantom of the Post Office," "the Cat Lady." The harshest referred to her alleged nymphomania and accused this woman in her eighties of accosting young men: "the Bitch," "the Long Arm," even "the Rapist."[2] Her contemporaries and biographers concur that she went from center to margin, from beauty to hag.

Etymologically, the word *hag* derives originally from "wise" or "holy" woman—whence Hagia Sofia and hagiography. Likewise, Olin has been recently rescued from ignominy and redefined as worthy. Her biographers Tomás Zurian, Adriana Malvido, Elena Poniatowska, and others have, moreover, broadened public appreciation and critical acclaim beyond merely honoring her as muse or beauty. Thanks to their great dedication and judiciousness, Olin once again wins accolades from the cultural elite.

Scholars and artists now acknowledge Olin as a central figure in the Renacimiento mexicano, the intellectual and artistic "renaissance" emerging in the 1920s after the Mexican Revolution. Gerardo Estrada Rodríguez, the general director of the National Institute of Fine Arts, wrote that an exhibit of her work in 2000 was an homage to "a period and a group of Mexican artists who beyond scandal and particular circumstances left a profound mark on the profile of modern Mexico." Olin found herself included in a group of notables the likes of Diego Rivera, Tina Modotti, Xavier Guerrero, Edward Weston, and Rodríguez Lozano, who are credited with bridging "the most authentic expressions of Mexican tradition and folklore, the incipient urban popular culture, and universal culture."[3] Américo Sánchez Hernández, director of the Museo Mural de Diego Rivera, set an exhibit of her work in the context of the Renacimiento mexicano, broadening the definition of artistic creativity to include events, declarations, and other projects of that period and underscoring her mural painting as the axis on which an entire interpretive mechanism had been erected.

Olin's biographers focus on her rather than on her relationships, and in any case they define her relationships beyond the narrow context of 1920s Mexico City, as is evident in the titles of their biographies: "a woman of her time," "a woman of modern times," "Woman of the Sun," "a Mystery."[4] Whereas her contemporaries tended to see her fall as her fault (due to her madness or meanness), Olin's biographers tend to see it as their fault. Whereas her contemporaries link her rise to her intimacy with great men, her biographers champion her work on its own merits. If her contemporaries condemned her, her biographers redeem her, not because she would have cared but because we should. Her invisibility impoverishes our vision no less than it denies Olin her due.

A trove of rediscovered Olin works has yielded such inquiry into her history: her paintings, caricatures, feminism, philosophy, poetry, sexuality, animal defense, daily shamanistic ritual, aesthetics and connoisseurship, even music. For example, sundry pieces—a prologue to her book *Energía cósmica*, a Guggenheim fellowship application she prepared in the 1940s, letters from Atl and other sources—point to Olin as a musical performer and composer.[5] Critics have reaffirmed her artistic talent, moving beyond the dismissive categorization of her work as "naive."[6] Tomás Zurian recasts the logic that prompted her to pose naked and exhibit the nudes, underscoring that she "doesn't show her body for perversion, lightness, or frivolity. Far from that, she does it as an act of generosity, of expansion of her radiant energy, to bestow on humanity a little of the exuberance of her body."[7] She has been called "one of the first feminists without placards who, with the sole force of her acts, generates an aperture for the feminine condition."[8]

Olin has also gained admiration for her sexual liberation. Mexican writer Elena Poniatowska says she is considered a precursor of women who claim their own instincts. By likening Nahui's nudes to an amphora, Poniatowska deepens the historicity of Nahui's sculpture-of-self. Yet, according to Poniatowska, it cost her dearly. "Living her sexuality without prejudices ended up destroying her," she writes. The best portrait of Olin as revolutionary woman emerges, then, from the chiaroscuro of all three perspectives—hers, her contemporaries', and her biographers'.

Thanks to the nearly two decades of commitment from her earliest biographers, subsequent scholars can risk untethering Olin from her time and place, from postrevolutionary Mexico of the 1920s. A volume on revolutionary women invites a revolutionary approach: to take her own vision as normative and to examine her life and art in terms of it. This essay interprets Olin in terms of the Nahua cosmology to which she explicitly linked herself.

In reference to Nahua cosmology, Olin distinguishes herself by a cyclical constancy. She refuses to hew to the linear "rise-and-fall" pattern often attributed to her by those who focus first on her "beau monde" credentials as artist or artists' muse in the 1920s, only to trace her tragic "descent" into old age, grotesquerie, frailness, madness, and marginality.[9] Nor does she fit well the conventional rise-and-fall narrative common to ordinary people: launching from childhood (portrayed as immature or neophyte), climbing to "prime" adulthood (maximum productivity, strength, fertility), then sliding into the deterioration of old age. Instead, Olin exhibits a rare cyclical constancy of powerful creation, of sustaining life, contradicting the rise-and-fall narrative. She said late in life that she had had a good childhood, good adulthood, and good old age.

If we can presume to attempt a reading of Olin that privileges her own vision, then two motifs register most prominently: creation and light as linked to destruction and dark. Most of her contemporaries note "the dark, destructive side" of Olin without glimpsing its generative power—as though the phenomenon (or the artist herself) could be dichotomized. Consequently, biographers have been obliged to reckon with her contemporaries' negative interpretations, almost to the point of defensiveness given the harshness of some detractors.

If many contemporaries damned Nahui's ersatz darkness and destructiveness, others exalted it. Dr. Atl led with it. No sooner had he met her, in July 1921, than he rushed home to write in his journal that an "abyss green like the sea: the eyes of a woman" had opened before him, and he "fell into that abyss, instantaneously, like a man who slides from a rock and plunges into the ocean." In the next paragraph,

he extols her beauty further, reiterating the drama of her eyes and con-
cluding, "Pobre de mí!"[10] So his first response after he first met Olin
portrayed her as devouring and himself as doomed. His last response,
published some thirty-eight years later, near the end of his life, continued in the same vein.[11] His early poem, "Carmen," opens with the lines:
"Mythological serpent, sinister and plumed, twisted 'round the tree of
Good and Evil; from branch to branch you entice toward your abys-
mal maw, my terrible animal instincts, my conscience without eyes,
and the remnants of my will."[12] Likewise, in his opening dedicatory
poem published in her volume *Óptica cerebral*, Atl speaks of Olin as
fire, death, abyss, chaos, desire, illumination, humanity, and renovating power; he spoke of himself as enthralled.[13] Detractors likewise attributed "dark," destructive qualities to her, but they condemned them.

Such projections do enjoy considerable appeal. Indeed, it may be
impossible to imagine order without the disorder, and certainly disorder has been most often defined as darkness. Historically, cosmogonies
have ascribed roles to darkness and light, ranging along a "spectrum"
from a dualism that damns darkness and reveres light to a holistic
embrace of both. Certainly the Nahua, or Aztec, creation story Olin
identified with celebrates deities such as the god Tezcatlipoca and the
goddess Tlaltecuhtli, both of which exercise simultaneous powers of
creation and destruction. Olin explicitly recognizes the regenerative
powers of destruction.

In her signature poem "Insatiable Seed," it is above all her spirit that
is insatiably thirsty "to create, possess, and destroy with another creation of greater magnitude than the one it destroyed."[14] Five times in
this short poem she reiterates her act of creating "new worlds" without
ceasing; once she mentions the destruction of a world.

Such holistic models notwithstanding, the dualistic model predom-
inates. The tragic legacy of this model is that darkness and destruction
have become erroneously associated with evil. Their powers of generation and regeneration have been denied. Olin's personal history has
suffered from similarly crude misperceptions of "darkness," ironically
from critics and admirers alike. Though the facts are much disputed,

her critics' claims conform perfectly to classic misogynist "evil wom-an" archetypes: woman as baby killer;[15] woman as woman hater (Atl reported her as being so jealous that he once soaked her with water, bound her up, and left her alone all day as punishment); woman as unstable and chaotic; woman as lunatic; woman as destroyer of her mates (Atl later claimed she threatened to shoot him); woman as sex-ually impure (she wrote about desire even as a child, "I know that plea-sure comes from a desire to let a little of our infinity emerge through our skin").[16] As an adult Olin scandalized the public by hosting an exhibit in September 1927 of Antonio Garduño's photos of her in the nude; she was perhaps the first woman in Mexico to display pubic hair in public as art. The inscription on her photo exhorted Atl to "wet the eyes of your beloved with the semen of your life."[17] Poniatowska writes that Olin received guests naked, serving them elixirs of fertility, and that into her eighties she grabbed at young strangers on public transportation.[18]

Not only did Olin embody the many archetypes of the Evil Woman; she failed to embody the few archetypes of female decency. She did not conform to the narrow standards of innocent girl, nor virtuous wife and mother, nor dignified crone. If piety might have redeemed Olin for her failings as girl, wife and mother, or crone, she was not pious either. Though atheism defined the majority of Mexico's postrevolutionary elite, Olin's rejection of conventional religiosity was her own, long predating the anticlerical political posturing that polarized Mexico in the 1920s. Unlike her contemporaries, the artists and intellectuals for whom radical secularism became a badge of revolutionary zeal, Olin defined herself independently from the church while still a child.

If the external perceptions of her contemporaries are of Olin as Evil Woman, then the obvious first task is to counter these. And her biog-raphers have performed that task well. Rather than let the proponents of the "rise-and-fall" paradigm dictate the parameters of Olin's history, this essay privileges her own words (those she published). Fortunate-ly, her published work covers an unusual range given that some of her childhood writings also reached print. For her youth, we have *Caline-*

ment je suis dedans and *A dix ans sur mon pupitre*; for her adulthood, *Óptica cerebral* and *Energía cósmica*. Further research would include her letters and other sources.

Fundamental to Olin's art, thought, and life is the paradigm of creation without end. The name she took in the early 1920s and kept until her death in 1978 derives from the "Nahui Ollin" of Aztec cosmogony, which translates as "Four Movements," the regenerating life force of the Fifth Sun.[19] Embedded in the macrocosm of Life was the microcosm of her own life, conceived likewise as eternally regenerating, without beginning or end. On the subject of her name, boundlessness, and the tension between the one and the many, Olin wrote:

> My name is like that of all other things:
> without beginning or end,
> and nonetheless without isolating myself from the totality
> by my distinct evolution within this infinite set,
> the words that most closely name me
> are Nahui Olin.[20]

To that extent, the paradigm is one of constancy rather than "rise and fall." If we recast normativity as "Nahui Ollin" rather than the linear progression exalted by modernity, fluid constancy becomes the normative paradigm. Olin discredits stability as antithetical to Nahui Ollin and condemns predictable progress, stagnation, or paralysis. "You became gangrenous in your stability," she chastises, and the "fluidity of beauty-color that things and people have is nothing if not the vibration of instability."[21]

The episode that most resembles a deviation from Olin's norm of fluidity is her marriage. Indeed, her stint as the wife of Manuel Rodríguez Lozano may be the closest thing to a fall that we might identify by her terms. Ironically, her period of greatest conformity to convention—complete with white bridal gown and veil, anonymity, and few known works—corresponds to the nine years of her stable, unhappy marriage. Neither childhood nor dotage silenced her so effectively. According to third parties, she balked, first at the prospect of her imminent wedding, and later at the prospect of remaining wedded. Her mother's coercion succeeded in forcing her to marry, but her family's refusal to endorse divorce could not confine her to marriage.

If marriage silenced Olin in her early twenties, certainly her writings before and after loudly denounce patriarchy. They challenge not only the patriarchal control exercised by fathers and husbands but also the laws, religions, and governments that exercise patriarchal power outside the household. As a child of ten, she chafed at "being destined to be sold as slaves formerly were to a husband. I protest despite my age for being under my parents' tutelage."[22] Twenty years later, she dedicates two of the short essays in *Óptica cerebral* to a feminist challenge. The second, "El cáncer que nos roba la vida" (The cancer that robs us of life) denounces that cancer as one "with which we are born—the stigma of womanhood." She contrasts women who have been dwarfed by sexist laws and mores with those "of tremendous spirit and virile strength" who likewise have been subject to similar constraints but who fight to free themselves.[23]

The first essay also speaks to the entrapment and seething tension of women subjected to sexism, yet it treats women as one rather than ranking those who resist as superior to those who conform. The piece likens women to Mexico's volcano, anthropomorphized as the Aztec princess Iztatzihuatl, beautiful yet buried by a "deathly inertia" that they long to overthrow. Olin writes, "Under the death-grip of human laws sleeps the world mass of women, in eternal silence, in deathly inertia...but underneath exists a dynamic force that accumulates from instant to instant, a tremendous power of rebellion that will activate their soul trapped in perpetual snows, in human laws of ferocious tyranny."[24]

"Insaciable sed," Olin's best-known poem, expresses her "crazy thirst" to create ceaselessly. In it, she also reconciles antitheses. By recognizing the simultaneous oneness and multiplicity of reality, and by acknowledging that thirst springs from both the body and the spirit collaborating in creation, Olin rejects false dichotomies. Accorded pride of place as first in her volume, this poem is arguably her manifesto. She concludes it by underscoring the constant cyclical creation she is committed to despite the risk of being consumed:

And from this admirable thirst is born the power of creation—
and it is a fire that my body cannot resist, that in continuous
renovation of the youth of flesh and spirit, is
one and thousands because it is insatiable thirst.
And my spirit and my body always have crazy thirst...

In his introduction to an exhibition of thirty centuries of art in Mexico, Octavio Paz defined the quintessential artist's commitment as a "will to form." Surveying three thousand years, his definition grounds art as an act of transforming matter from unformed to formed. But perhaps this view privileges positivist, even phallic, presumptions. It certainly ignores the totality central to indigenous art/life, the indivisibility of the cycle: creation—destruction—regeneration. Olin defines herself within indigenous cosmology. Long after *indigenismo*, popular in the 1920s, had fallen from fashion, Olin continued to see herself as daily guide and guardian of the sun, which, in turn, accompanies her. Throughout her life, from childhood on, her writings and life choices affirm the cyclical, keenly aware of dissolution of form as intimately linked to the emergence of form. Cognizant of Olin's openness to the power of dissolution, some observers fetishized it in her. But by ignoring it as part of a totality, they projected an exaggerated expression of it on her—portraying her as a festering rawness, an abyss, a volcano, a dangerous, destructive power. She did give full expression to the "dark side," but to limit her to that is to ignore the wholeness of the cycle that defined her vision, life, and art.

Olin insisted in equal measure on giving unfettered expression to the creative, sustaining part of life-as-cycle. The most explicit example of the life-affirming expression in her art is the painting in which Agosín's head protrudes through the "concha" of San Sebastián as though the Earth Mother were birthing him from the bay-as-womb through the narrow portal into the wide sea. Less conventional examples of her "will to form" include preserving the corpses of her animals, head and all, in the form of a blanket.[25] That is to say, Olin insisted on expressing (in art and life) both dissolution and will to form. Therein lies the power of Olin's art and especially her life-as-art. Because she always embraced the full cycle, her creative expression remained unsullied by the chaos-kampf agenda that tainted much postrevolutionary art (by essentializing peasants, for example).

Olin's will to form found wide-ranging expression, though it was not always conventional. Much of that expression could be tolerated, even admired, by art circles then and now. Her first exhibition in Mexico, soon after her return from exile in Spain, featured caricatures. Zurian recently curated a major retrospective to bring this work to the public. Her paintings, though they did not conform to the didactic agenda of revolutionary art and have been dismissed as naive, now easily find an appreciative audience. But much of her will to form is not counted as legitimate artistic expression. Transgressing the boundaries of what counts as art is the love poem to Atl that she scrawled hugely on a brick wall, the Agosín wall hanging that served her as a blanket and dead lovers' embrace, and her nudity. In three masterpieces of body-as-art, Olin blurred the boundary between form and formlessness: unadorned in the sea, in the desert, in stark light where the shadow has more substance than flesh. Olin commands the cameras and the viewers to reckon with a nude so naked as to be newborn—reborn. Like all artists, Olin dares. She ventures beyond in a cyclical conception that requires a "return" as the full completion of "forward" progress. At those thresholds where she moved ahead of us, her audience balks...or budges.

For all the power of cyclical creation/destruction that she claims for herself, Olin does not presume to claim exclusive power to create and destroy. On the contrary, that power belongs to the natural order. In her twenties, Olin wrote, "Time in unconscious evolution, destroys and fertilizes marvels and in its multiple potential as regenerative and destructive element, devours what it has in its claws, and sublimely remakes each time a world better than the one it entombed."[26] Her writings suggest that humans can gain this power of nature by "thirsting" or otherwise struggling for it. It is said that by her seventies, Olin exercised still greater powers of creation and destruction. She claimed to bring the sun up in the morning and put it down at night.[27] Whether she said it is open to debate, given that detractors can prove unreliable sources. If she said it, then her intention also merits consideration given that she might have been performing the "local" or witch to amuse or alarm her audience. If, indeed, she came to see herself as controlling the sun, then she saw herself as exercising the supreme power, according to the theory she expanded in *Energía cósmica*. In her piece "On Duration and the Difference in Beings, Elements, and Things," she wrote that the very duration of the existence of *"los seres"* is determined by the intensity of the force of the electric movement that formed them, which itself derives from the sun.[28]

There is much to celebrate about Olin if we define a revolutionary woman in familiar terms as a woman of modern times, one ahead of her time; an original artistic vision and expression, one of uncompromising authenticity; or a woman of great influence on revolutionary figures and historical developments. But if these celebrations succeed mostly in championing the gaze of others, then we do well to reverse the gaze: Olin looking out, in, and beyond. She painted everyone's eyes like her own, always yoni-shaped. Of the mouth as a universal orifice (also painted alike for male and female), of the public pubis. She who experienced the quotidian and the material as a hierophany. Our Trinity of Openings—eyes, mouth, yoni—that we seek to close, control, and conceal. Not Olin. She opened them all. She refused to conceal and control them. Not only when she was in her so-called prime, when it is at least somewhat permitted for a woman to project herself through these orifices, to delight in the give and take through these portals. No, she opened them and herself, before and after it was permitted—as a child and as a crone. Nor did she limit them to the sanctioned purpose of wife and mother. Hers was a rare and raw human sensibility, open to the festering fecundity, the Nahui Ollin, the life force that cyclically and eternally creates, reabsorbs, and re-creates the world. She was a figure akin to the Tlaltecuhtli recently uncovered in the Templo Mayor precinct. Sundown to sundown, birth to death, conquest to conquest, age to age, evolution to revolution.

Olin's use of space also reflects her motif of cyclical constancy. Open spaces recur in her work and life: *la plaza, la azotea, la calle, el mar*. Rounded spaces figure in her work: conch-shaped bays, bullrings, hamlets encircled by water and hills. Her space was layered in that the background and foreground were rarely empty, rarely serving as a frame for a single central object. Her movement through space had a wayfaring quality, out and back, like a pilgrimage or a labyrinth. From San Sebastián in her proper married days she returned with Agosín; from Paris to as close as she could get, a French restaurant in Mexico City every two weeks. The ultimate cyclical constancy: Nahui Olin died in the same house where she was born.

Late in life, Atl tried to deny Olin her Náhuatl name, though he preserved his own. In a book published only five years before his death, he referred to her as Carmen and to himself as Dr. Atl, a name given to him by Leopoldo Lugones in Italy some sixty years earlier. He gave his assumed name prominence by titling the volume *Poemas del Dr. Atl*. Published in 1959, some thirty-eight years after he fell into the abyss of her eyes, the book begins with a single word in the middle of the first page: Carmen. If he fancied he could rebaptize or infantilize her, he was mistaken. Olin never reclaimed her original name yet never denied her original self.

According to her writings, "Nahui Olin" signified the power that produced light and life. As a child, she found life full of marvels, including light that resonated with her spirit. As a crone, she devoted herself to the Nahua role of guide and companion to the sun and stars.[29] Throughout her life, she gave artistic expression to everything that attracted her attention—yes, everything. "Sí, de todo," she wrote at age ten, "I long to create sensations of beauty…from everything that attracts my attention. Yes, everything. Everything that reaches my spirit resounds and responds."[30] Thirty years later, her vision had grown complex enough to embrace the destructive powers required also as part of creation. In her pieces "Totality" and "*Matemáticas*," she theorized that everything was connected but that the balance operative on earth could be threatened in the realm of the universe, that "relativity of space … permits all matter of any species to evolve distinctly but always within the enormous and terrible totality which crushes and nullifies us."[31]

Nahui Olin (née Carmen Mondragón), she who renamed herself after the creative force of the Nahua universe, is also well defined by the Nahua concept of light. The intricate meanings and derivations of Tlahuiztli—light, brightness, glow—merit full treatment here as a fitting conclusion to an interpretation of Olin as revolutionary woman. Aztecs idealized the concept of Tlahuiztli to the point of using it to accord high status. Its multiple permutations represent Nahui's legacy well: Tlahui, "to give off light as the stars do"; Tlahuilia, "to illuminate others, to educate, to shed light on new or strange ideas." A related concept, Tlamacaz, resonates with the trajectory of Olin's life in which her vision as elder drew from her vision as a child. Tlamacaz means "perfected human being, someone who deeply understands life and acts with rectitude," "one who assimilates the sufferings of the world"; Tlamacazqui means "youthfulness—whose experience is filled with Tlamahizolli" (marvels, miracles, and the supernatural). With proper training, it leads to Tlamatiliztli, "wisdom," embodied in the Tlamatini, the wise person who guards the tradition and gathers knowledge and transmits it to future generations. In the closing poem in *Óptica cerebral*, Olin illuminated the complex relationship between life and death, exhorting that the following epitaph be carved (all in capital letters) into the tombstones of herself and all others "of Asia, Africa, America, y Europe" who chose to live freely and fully:

INDEPENDIENTE FUI, PARA NO PERMITIR PUDRIRME SIN RENOVARME;

HOY, INDEPENDIENTE, PUDRIÉNDOME ME RENUEVO PARA VIVIR.

INDEPENDENT I WAS, SO AS NOT TO PERMIT MYSELF TO ROT WITHOUT RENOVATING

MYSELF; NOW, INDEPENDENT AND ROTTING, I RENEW MYSELF IN ORDER TO LIVE.[32]

Alice Dickerson Montemayor (b. Laredo, Texas, 1904; d. Laredo, 1989) was a
LULAC (League of United Latin American Citizens) activist and social worker. In
her twenties she attacked LULAC's machismo culture and gender discrimination,
initiating a revolution that broke down its barriers to female leadership. As
a social worker in 1930s and 1940s South Texas, she took on racial and ethnic
discrimination. When sheriffs and judges in Cotulla prevented Mexican American
families from applying for services they were entitled to, she set up her operation
on the courthouse lawn with a bodyguard supplied by the state. Her efficiency and
determination won over local officials, who became her allies in providing equal
access to state services.

Alice Dickerson Montemayor

CYNTHIA OROZCO

Women also had common sense and were "able to
see at a glance and penetrate into in a second what
most men would not see with a searchlight or a
telescope in an eternity."

THE HISTORY OF MEXICAN-ORIGIN WOMEN IN VOLUNTARY ORGANIZATIONS
is a history largely untold. As a result, scholars have overlooked the
ways in which those women organized and worked successfully for
major political change. In her book *The Grounding of Modern Feminism,* historian Nancy Cott refers to "those activities" outside of elec-
toral politics in which women participated as "voluntarist politics."[1] By
taking a new look at the League of United Latin American Citizens
(LULAC), we can better discern the significance of one woman's influence on the oldest Mexican American civil rights organization in the
United States. Mexican American men founded the league in 1929 in
Corpus Christi, Texas. By 1940, LULAC had expanded nationwide.
Comparable to the National Association for the Advancement of Colored People, LULAC is a middle-class organization that has diligently
protected the civil rights of Mexican Americans in the United States.

In the 1930s, LULAC men filed the first class-action lawsuit against segregated public schools. They were also responsible for changing the classification of La Raza from "Mexican" to "white" in the 1940 U.S. Census. At the local level, LULAC desegregated schools, pools, theaters, housing, and real estate.[2]

In 1930 LULAC extended full membership privileges to women through gender-segregated councils, called "Ladies LULAC." Ladies LULAC councils became particularly important in Texas and New Mexico. The first ladies council was formed in 1933 in Alice, Texas. In 1934 LULAC created the office of ladies organizer general to organize women's chapters. By 1940 these chapters numbered twenty-six while men's chapters totaled one hundred. In the 1990s, women constituted more than 50 percent of LULAC's membership; they helped elect the organization's first female national president in 1994.

Through analyzing the gender politics of LULAC in the 1930s, this essay assesses patriarchal ideology as related to the family as well as addressing female participation within LULAC. It focuses on LULAC feminist Alice Dickerson Montemayor. At the time of her activism she was a wife, mother, worker, and middle-class businesswoman. She was also a freethinking, assertive, independent feminist who belonged to LULAC when patriarchal ideology was especially strong.[3]

Many view LULAC as a men's organization because its leadership has been overwhelmingly male. Others believe that all women in LULAC were in ladies auxiliaries, which were thought to be composed of wives.[4] Still others either believe all women participated in a sex-segregated Ladies LULAC or contend that, for women, LULAC was merely "a social gathering...to go drink coffee and get together."[5] In sum, historians have hardly addressed Ladies LULAC.

Independent women like Montemayor filled the ranks of LULAC with feminist inclinations. The league's own newsletters show what she was up against. Member J. Reynolds Flores expressed the typical sentiment about women's place in his 1932 essay "How to Educate Our Girls": "The foundation of society rests on the homes. The success of our homes rests on the wives. Therefore, first of all, teach our girls how to be successful wives.... Train them to do small things well and to delight in helping others, and instill constantly into their minds the necessity for sacrifice for others' pleasure as a means of soul development."[6] In the essay "La Mujer," which appeared in *Alma Latina,* a short-lived LULAC publication for parents, the author viewed women *"como madres, como esposas, como hijas, o como hermanas"* (as mothers, as wives, as daughters, or as sisters), basing this description on Catholic doctrine and particularly the story of Adam and Eve; Adam represented *fuerza* (strength) and Eve *amor* (love).[7]

Montemayor followed Adela Sloss as a critic of LULAC's family ideology.[8] A committed member, Montemayor was a woman of many "firsts" and promoted the interests of middle-class Mexican American women, girls, and youth during her LULAC tenure, from 1936 to around 1940. In 1937 she was the first woman elected to the position of second vice president general, the third-highest post in the organization.[9] She was also the first woman to serve as an associate editor of *LULAC News* and the first person to charter a Junior LULAC chapter. She was an ardent advocate for the inclusion of youth, including girls, and she was an avid supporter of more Ladies LULAC chapters.

Born and raised in Laredo, Texas, on the Texas–Mexico border, Montemayor grew up with a Mexico-Tejano identity. Through her maternal grandmother, she was descended from one of the twenty-eight families who settled Laredo in the 1750s; her Irish father was a native of New Orleans.[10] Her command of the English language gave her an advantage over other Mexico-Tejanos, but her middle-class status distinguished her from most of La Raza in Laredo. Her mixed heritage also privileged her.[11]

Montemayor's private secondary education made her an exception in the Mexican-origin community in Texas, especially for women. Barriers created by race and gender limited her schooling, despite her desire for higher education. Southwest Teachers College in San Marcos accepted her, but she was unable to leave home because her father died two days after her high school graduation, and she was "forced to earn her livelihood in order to support herself and her mother."[12] At her first full-time job, as a desk clerk for Western Union, she met Francisco Montemayor of Nuevo Laredo, a bookkeeper at Banco Longoria, and they married in 1927 when Alice was twenty-two.

In 1933 she became a social worker, a position that broadened her horizons—and also opened her eyes to race discrimination when she went to work in Cotulla, in the next county over from Laredo. When she arrived in Cotulla, the white county judge refused to give her a key to her county courthouse office because she was Mexican American. She set up shop on apple crates in front of the courthouse until he finally conceded. Even her clients discriminated against her; poor whites refused to reveal their financial circumstances to a "Mexican."[13]

During her fifteen-month stay in Cotulla, Montemayor challenged white privilege. She helped desegregate the county courthouse, which prohibited "Mexicans" on the second floor, personally escorting the first group to her upstairs office. While in Cotulla, she also questioned the practice of segregated masses at the Catholic church, which had one mass for "Mexicans" and another for "whites."[14] Much later in life, Montemayor reflected that she had experienced the greatest job satisfaction with her work in Cotulla, where she "had to fight."[15]

Montemayor joined civic life around 1937 when Ladies organizer general Ester Machuca, a member of El Paso Ladies LULAC, contacted her. They and other women helped charter a council in Laredo.[16] Members had to be recommended, and most had a high school education. Most were married homemakers, while others worked as secretaries for the city and county. By the 1930s, Laredo Ladies LULAC was one of the most active councils. *LULAC News* noted: "What council in the League has shown the most activity since the beginning of the present fiscal year and has obtained results? Without hesitation we answer the Laredo Ladies Council No. 15."[17] The chapter encouraged women to vote, held citizenship classes, and urged members "to have aspirations to work away from home." The educational committee helped the mother of a second-grader obtain justice for her son, whose teacher had "severely whipped" him. The council also sponsored benefits for the Laredo orphanage, raised $250 for flood survivors, bought school supplies for Mexican-origin children, sponsored a column in Laredo's major newspaper, and published an edition of *LULAC News*.

Delegates traveled out of town to LULAC's annual national conventions and sponsored Junior LULAC councils. *LULAC News* reports indicate that the Ladies LULAC largely worked independently of the Laredo men's council. It was definitely not an auxiliary. Montemayor was the first secretary of the Laredo council and was president from 1938 to 1939.[18] As secretary, she reported the chapter's activities to the *LULAC News* column "Around the Shield," which focused on local councils. She wrote, "We have always said and we still maintain that at the back of progress and success the ladies take a leading hand."[19]

Montemayor soon garnered national attention. She was one of two Laredo Ladies council delegates to the national 1937 Houston and 1938 El Paso conventions. At the Houston convention, she was the only woman on the five-member finance committee. In 1937 the nominating committee, which consisted of one delegate from each council and was overwhelmingly male, named her to a national post. Montemayor was a member of the nominating committee but recalled being out of the room when Albert Redwine of the El Paso men's council nominated her and she was appointed; she was completely surprised. The news of her sudden rise in LULAC began to spread.[20] Between 1937 and 1940, Montemayor held three national positions—second national vice president general, associate editor of *LULAC News*, and director general of Junior LULAC.

Montemayor used her three positions to advocate for women and youth. As second vice president she promoted the establishment of more ladies councils in her columns, speeches, and letters.[21] As associate editor of *LULAC News*, she also advocated for women, penning a stinging unsigned editorial in response to two sexist incidents. The first occurred when an unidentified male member of LULAC, in a clear expression of fear that Montemayor would become the organization's national president, had written to a national officer: "I hope that President Ramon Longoria will get well soon. There are those of us who hate to be under a woman."[22] The second incident also involved a national officer, presumably President Ramon Longoria of Harlingen, who ignored three letters from El Paso Ladies LULAC, which eventually prompted the group to withdraw from the league.

According to Montemayor, the national office's inaction could be attributed to men who "are cowardly and unfair, ignorant and narrow minded." In her written critique of the incident, she appealed to the LULAC and U.S. constitutions and asked any member to step forward and write an article favoring the suppression of ladies councils and their denial of equal rights.[23] The third national position Montemayor held was director general of Junior LULAC. In 1937 Mrs. Charles Ramirez of San Antonio's Ladies LULAC developed the idea for Junior LULACs and sponsored a resolution to create the youth chapters. Ramirez and Mrs. Santos Herrera organized the first chapter, but Montemayor was the primary force behind the chapters. In August 1938 Montemayor began writing a series of essays in *LULAC News* encouraging senior councils to organize the youth. Besides serving as a local sponsor, she penned several essays to foster their organization after she was no longer an associate editor or an official youth organizer, and she wrote the first charter for a youth chapter.[24]

Around March 1937 Montemayor organized the second junior council at her house, and it proved to be the most active chapter. Montemayor recruited both girls and boys for Junior LULAC so that "by the time they are ready to join the Senior Councils they will abandon the egotism and petty jealousies so common today among our Ladies' and Men's councils." Her son Francisco echoed his mother's sentiments, writing for the *LULAC News*: "We have heard that there is a Junior Council of 'just girls.' Heck, we don't like that. We [would] rather have a mixed group like we have in Laredo, because we feel like there is nothing like our SISTERS." He warned against a majority of girls and rallied the boys to prevent this.[25] Montemayor believed that leadership training was necessary to the formation of good citizens and future LULAC senior members. From Junior LULAC would come "good Americans" who would be capable public servants, skillful debaters, knowledgeable citizens, and literate, independent thinkers.

Montemayor taught the juniors debate and acting skills every Sunday. She also took five junior officers to the El Paso national convention.[26]

Montemayor's feminism even affected the youth group. In 1938 Laredo Junior LULAC member Leonor Montes rallied for a girl president. She wrote: "Now that the publicity chairman is of the 'nervier' sex but HOW ABOUT A GIRL PRESIDENT this coming term? We want a girl president! We want a girl president! RAH! RAH! RAH! BOOM!" Montemayor's son called Montes "the little Monty of the Juniors," for "she too is always wanting for the girls to outshine the boys."[27]

In addition to encouraging women and children to challenge the patriarchal nature of LULAC's political mobilization, Montemayor also challenged patriarchal ideology through her essays. She wrote more articles for the *News* than any other woman in LULAC's history.[28] Among youth and adults, Montemayor stressed independent thinking. She wrote, "Having the ability to think for oneself and forming an opinion of your own is a necessity in our organization." She asked LULAC to recall the 1938 national LULAC election: "Did we not have a hard time to think for ourselves about the candidates? Did not some of us have the desire to influence our fellow members to vote our own way?"[29]

Her first essay, "We Need More Ladies Councils," pointed to many inactive LULAC councils and asked women to come to the rescue. "Sister LULACs," she wrote, "our brothers need a good big dose of competition." She noted that there were seventy-one men's and fifteen women's chapters, but only twenty-six and four, respectively, had been represented at the annual convention.

Competition with men became a rallying point for Montemayor: "Now that our brothers have given the women a chance to show them what we can do, let all the Ladies Councils that are active now try and revive the Dormant Ladies Councils, and the Ladies Organizers and Governors try and get more Ladies Council [sic] to join our League so that we may prove to our brothers that we can accomplish more than they can."[30] She believed men engendered this competition through their allegations of superiority over women.

But Montemayor believed in the fundamental superiority of women. In "A Message from Our Second Vice-President General," she asked women to join the "LULAC family." Women, she believed, had intuition: "Women wish to mother men just because it is their natural instinct and because they see into the men's helplessness." Women also had common sense and were "able to see at a glance and penetrate into in a second what most men would not see with a searchlight or a telescope in an eternity." She added, "Women are the possessors of a super logic. They hang to the truth and work with more tenacity than our brothers." She concluded that LULAC would not flourish until the women got involved to help the men.[31]

Montemayor also penned "Women's Opportunity in LULAC," which proclaimed: "The idea that 'the women's place is in the home' passed out of the picture with hoop skirts and bustles, and now it is recognized that women hold as high a position in all walks of life as do the men." She noted that among the Greeks and Romans "the girl was not trained for public life, as that was left for the boys and men. She occupied no place in the activities of her country." She added that "no thought was given to the girls in anything other than the keeping of the homes." Rather, she defined women's place to be "in that position where she can do the most for the furthering of her fellow women." She called on "women LULACs" to "realize that it is now time to get into our League, and stay in it."[32]

In her March 1938 editorial "Son Muy Hombres (?)" Montemayor did not doubt that machismo attitudes were prevalent in LULAC, despite the question mark. But she had faith in men's ability to change. She noted that there "has been some talk about suppressing the Ladies Councils of our League or at least to relegate them to the category of auxiliaries." She attributed this reaction to the "aggressive attitude which some of our women members have adopted." She noted that men "fear that our women will take a leading role in the evolution of our League; that our women might make a name for themselves in their activities; that our MUY HOMBRES (?) might be shouldered from their position as arbiters of our League."[33] Montemayor also noticed that gender lines were drawn on these issues: "What surprises us mostly is the attitude assumed by some of our General Officers and members. While some of them may not be in complete accord with the move, at least they countenance it. Others are noncommittal and remain painfully silent."[34] Male bonding and collusion were in effect, and *LULAC News* includes no articles written in support of Montemayor.

"When...and Then Only," another of Montemayor's articles, emphasized the importance of organizing women and youth. "God gave Eve to Adam, because Adam was lonesome and needed a mate," she wrote. "Back of the success of any man, there is a woman," she said, and "women are God's MOST PRECIOUS GIFT to MEN, therefore let's organize more Ladies Councils. Ladies, let's organize more Junior LULAC Councils, let's train our children." For Montemayor, God commanded heterosexuality; thus, women were to assist their mates and bear and raise children.[35] Competition and conflict could sometimes characterize relations between men's and women's councils. The February 1937 *News* hinted at a conflict when it mentioned that the Laredo chapter had "weathered a storm" of local character, but the article did not provide details "since such things happen in the best regulated families."[36]

In a 1984 interview, Montemayor recalled that Laredo LULAC men "had no use for us...they didn't want us." In fact, she said, they "just hated" her, especially Ezequiel Salinas of Laredo, the organization's national president from 1939 to 1940. The men, she claimed, refused to vote for her at the national conventions.[37] Still, she believed she had the respect of some men's councils.[38] Indeed, she must have had their support because in 1937 she participated in the Corpus Christi ceremony honoring the deceased Ben Garza, LULAC's first president. And she optimistically believed she had the support of men throughout Texas. She could count among her allies J. C. Machuca, San Antonio attorney Alonso S. Perales, Brownsville attorney J. T. Canales, and Austin educator Dr. Carlos Castaneda. She also corresponded with San Antonio attorney Gus Garcia. These supporters, however, were atypical LULAC members, all college graduates and well traveled.[39] LULAC's dismal record of gender politics suggests that typical male sentiment reflected the attitudes of Laredo men.

The league witnessed growth and expansion in the 1930s, but World War II proved disruptive to organizing efforts. Like men's councils, Ladies LULACs declined. The national LULAC reorganized in 1945, and ten men's councils attended the annual convention that year, yet only Albuquerque represented women.[40] After April 1940, Montemayor's name is absent from *LULAC News*, but she nevertheless left her mark.

As early as June 1937 the *LULAC News* wrote, "No wonder she has been cussed and discussed, talked about, lied about, lied to, boycotted, and almost hung, but she claims she has stayed in there, first because she is a LULACker, and next because she wanted to see what the heck would happen next."[41] A Junior LULAC member said she seemed like a "hard-boiled supervisor" but was really "the swellest dame."[42] LULAC's method of political mobilization, its theory of political empowerment, and its familial ideology were patriarchal. Montemayor's activism and ideology challenged male privilege. She argued for LULAC to mobilize women and children to empower La Raza and defined women's place as extending outside the home and helping other women.

Her radical voice, however, proved a lonely one, and her local chapter did not promote her vision, refusing to directly challenge male privilege or battle gender segregation. Montemayor may have influenced Laredo women and women in the national organization, but there is no evidence she attempted to garner their support for a united front. According to her son Aurelio, she was highly individualistic. By her own accounts, she was "very independent. Nobody tells me what to do. [But] I can always take advice from people I think are intelligent."[43]

What were the limitations of Montemayor's vision? She attacked male privilege and power but did not question the family, marriage, or religion as oppressive institutions. Nor did she question separate councils for men and women in LULAC, although she insisted on integrated youth councils. Segregated councils allowed her—and other women—to thrive in a distinctive female political culture where they learned to organize, deal with issues deemed important, and socialize with other women in a safe, nonsexist environment. LULAC was "as much a vital organ to the Latin American women, as it is to the Latin American men," she said, and, to the end, she considered LULAC the most important organization she had ever been involved in.[44]

As seen through articles in *LULAC News*, Montemayor introduced progressive ideas to LULAC, decrying women's oppression decades before the Chicana feminist movement. She challenged the notion of women's place in the home and personally demonstrated the diligent work women were capable of in public and political life. She identified machismo in action and fought to eradicate it through informed feminist reasoning.

While she exhibited a feminist consciousness, Montemayor also embodied a female consciousness in her concern for children and family. She actively disproved assumptions about women in LULAC, about wives, and about members of Ladies LULAC councils. She was an anomaly in the history of LULAC—and even a revolutionary. Openly feminist long before other Chicana feminists, Montemayor continually questioned the myth of male superiority and argued that women were as competent as men, if not superior. Moreover, she opened the door to women's involvement, women's influence, women's claim to civil rights, and women's leadership at the highest level in one of the most influential Hispanic civil rights organizations in the United States.

THREE

The Legacy: Women Revolutionaries of the Postrevolutionary Era

Frida Kahlo (b. Coyoacán, Mexico City, Mexico, 1907; d. Coyoacán, 1954) initiated an artistic revolution in both subject matter and expressions of the body and suffering. She profoundly identified with the Mexican Revolution for the ways it had disrupted the nation. Painting became a vehicle for expressing the magnitude of suffering that both Kahlo and the nation endured—the nation from conquest and the violence of war, and herself from polio and a catastrophic accident. It was also a means of bringing together Mexico's broken pieces in art.

Frida Kahlo

AMALIA MESA-BAINS

**Kahlo is radical in her treatment of her body in
images that integrate the medical conditions she
faced, her sexuality and self-image, and her political
and cultural identity.**

MY JOURNEY WITH FRIDA KAHLO BEGAN THIRTY-SIX YEARS AGO DURING THE
Chicana/o movement, during which she became a role model for the
place of women within a struggle for cultural identity and social justice. The Chicano movement, or *movimiento*, begun in the late 1960s,
was a widespread national movement composed of smaller regional
collectives committed to civil and cultural rights and a collective struggle for social justice and self-determination. It was a time of community *centros* or *galerías* and *museos*, which constituted a widespread
network connecting Chicana/o communities across the southwestern
and western United States.

The artistic purpose of this period was focused on cultural reclamation, and many artists and cultural workers sought to find political and
cultural models in Mexican history. We began to look at other periods
of revolutionary change and at the artists and cultural workers who
fomented this change in Mexico.

The Mexican Revolution of 1910 produced in its aftermath the Mexicanidad movement beginning in the 1920s and 1930s. The Mexican renaissance, referred to as the Mexicanidad movement, was concerned with providing a new movement in education and the arts. It focused on the affirmation of the indigenous and placed the Mexican national emphasis on the country's cultural identity with its ancient, indigenous heritage. Reformers like José Vasconcelos, the minister of education, and writers and artists like Diego Rivera, Frida Kahlo, Manuel Alvarez Bravo, Jean Charlot, and David Alfaro Siqueiros led the movement. We can see links some forty years later between Mexicanidad in Mexico and the Chicano movement. Mexicanidad served as a potential model for the political and cultural goals of the Chicano movement. Its focus on *indigenismo* gave artists and intellectuals a role in a new national identity and were inspirations for the Chicanidad era, in which concepts like Aztlán, the original land, the value of the indigenous, and the role of cultural workers were dominant organizing principles.

For Chicana/os in the late 1960s and early 1970s, the roles of Mexican artists and intellectuals were an inspiration. Los Tres Grandes (José Clemente Orozco, David Alfaro Siqueiros, and Diego Rivera) were already a powerful artistic influence for Chicano painters and muralists. By the 1970s, Chicanas in search of their own cultural identity had discovered Frida Kahlo. Her biculturalism resonated with the Chicana dualities and negotiation within the dominant North American culture.

Beginning in 1969, my mentor Yolanda Garfias Woo, a Tehuana teacher and artist living in San Francisco, introduced me to the traditions of the Day of the Dead and to Frida Kahlo. I encountered Kahlo's life and work on a 1975 trip to Mexico, where I had traveled to see the Blue House and museum. I was struck by the warm familial feeling in the house and grounds, and I began to understand Kahlo as a woman, a revolutionary in her age, political in her perspectives and profound in her artistic expression. In a journal and drawing book I kept during that time, I noted:

Her studio was filled with large wooden tables and her brushes and boxes of watercolor paints that were to be used for her diaries. It was just as though she had just left the room. It was a place to record each pain, each pleasure, to color the world to her vision. Light all around, glass, looking out to the garden...all of Diego's books, notes, her diaries, the gifts of the paintings for her alone, the admiration from friends for her alone. In this moment I felt the combination of all I strive for...the dream, the real, the symbol, the word, the spirit of individuation...the process we all live for. I see it here in Frida's life. She cannot give birth to the person...therefore only to the dream, the vision. Can only pain and tolerance create such an individual?

There was a major emphasis during this time on Mexican women artists, in conjunction with the First World Conference on the International Women's Year sponsored by the United Nations. The exhibition at Bellas Artes in Mexico City included painters Frida Kahlo, Maria Izquierdo, Remedios Varos, Leonora Carrington, and others. For the first time I was able to see the legacy of Mexican women's artwork that rivaled the Tres Grandes. The work provided many women of my generation a sense of gendered artistic, political, and cultural genealogy.

Frida Kahlo's life was revolutionary in its historical framework and political dimension, and Kahlo's personal, sexual, social, and cultural life was also radical in its time. Born into one of the most profound revolutionary periods in the Americas, Kahlo showed a desire and propensity for breaking barriers from the beginning. Kahlo, who was a child of two cultural backgrounds (European and indigenous Mexican heritage), found her identity marked by the historical period of the Mexican revolution and the complexities of her dual cultural upbringing.

She was born in 1907, during the early struggles of the Mexican Revolution, an epic period that framed her sense of history—so much so that she mythologized her birth to coincide with the actual date of the revolution in 1910. It is a telling revelation of her political and historical disposition and a sign of the cultural stance she would take in the future. She took strength from a nation struggling to throw off the yoke of European dominance and colonial oligarchies. The 1910 revolution for land reform precipitated a rich period of reclamation of Mexico's Mesoamerican heritage and indigenous life. It was a period of turbulence and idealism as the people of Mexico struggled to build a new nationhood more equitable and more rooted in the continent. Kahlo began her life in this era as a daughter of the revolution in both spirit and social commitment.

Her own heritage was a complex mixture of her Mexican mestiza mother, Matilde Calderón, and her Hungarian/German Jewish father, Guillermo Kahlo. Born in Baden Baden in 1872 of purported Hungarian Jewish ancestry, Guillermo immigrated to Mexico in 1891 at age nineteen. He was a notable photographer whose melancholy disposition was expressed in the photographs of colonial Mexican architecture for which he became quite well recognized. He became a naturalized citizen and, in his last years, was active in the resistance against the Nazis. Frida was frequently in conflict with her mother, a religious zealot. Frida was devoted to her father and accompanied him on some of his photographic expeditions. Her origins reflect the tension that marked the remainder of her life. She prized her Mexican Indian roots but often struggled with her European ancestry as Mexican intellectuals came to see their European past as a colonial burden.

The most profound event in Kahlo's adolescent years was a bus accident, which caused severe pelvic injuries that injured her back and required her to be bedridden for a year. The injuries led to lifelong complications that kept her from having children, but the long recovery was alleviated by drawing with the help of a bed easel and mirror for self-portraits. Thus was born Kahlo's artistic career.

In looking at family photographs of Kahlo, particularly in her adolescence, one can see the emergence of her radical approach to gender. In a family portrait taken following her accident in 1926, she is dressed as a man amid her grandmother; her sister Adriana and Adriana's husband, Alberto; her mother; a cousin named Carlos; and Frida's sister Cristina. She clearly implies many issues in this pose that will arise as themes in her artwork and her life. The severity of her injuries had a damaging effect on her adolescent self-image, and much of what is known about her personal life has portrayed her as a suffering victim. For many Chicanas and Latinas, however, she can be more aptly viewed as a resilient and radical figure, living on her own terms despite her physical challenges and her deep attachment to Diego Rivera.

Kahlo's relationship with Rivera has played out in the scandals and myths of Mexico and perhaps more lyrically in her paintings. In the earliest one, a wedding portrait that Kahlo painted in 1931, two years after their wedding, she appears light, her feet barely touching the ground; he is large and weighted like a rooted tree. The painting belies the real role Frida played in Rivera's life as a companion, confidante, valued adviser, and psychological foundation. Despite their artistic temperaments, their scandals and love affairs, Rivera often said Kahlo's artistic capacity was superior to his because she was a woman who opened her soul. They shared a bond of artistry, love, and politics, and their greatest involvement was with Mexicanidad, the reclaiming of popular art forms, the indigenous and Mesoamerican past.

To write about Kahlo's revolutionary nature as an artist, we must examine her most productive years, from the 1930s to the late 1940s—a relatively brief period, even for an artist who died at age forty-seven. We must also consider the role of women and the arts in Mexico and internationally during this time; opportunities for exhibition and recognition were quite limited for women. Revolution in Mexico, Russia, and many Third World countries was afoot, as was the rise of Nazism and fascism. Through it all, Mexico was a nation undergoing change, and Kahlo's young life was transformed by these changes.

Her work has often been seen as an example of the personal as political, a rejection of male-dominated themes that exclude the personal and recognize the political nature of women's oppression and struggle. This model for understanding women's art places value on Kahlo's personal life in a developmental record of love, marriage, aging, and death. Her art centered on themes of the body and sexuality, and domestic life and family, with emphasis on her private emotions, her heritage, and the tempestuous love of Diego Rivera. Kahlo is radical in her treatment of her body in images that integrate the medical conditions she faced, her sexuality, her self-image, and her political and cultural identity. Through the emphasis on Mexicanidad, she integrated Mexico's folk art and ancient past into her painting narrative.

At several points in her paintings, she deals with her cultural identity and mixed heritage. In a period of intellectual and cultural emphasis on indigenous and Native identities in Mexico, she continued to struggle with her Mexican and European ancestry. Like her 1936 painting *My Grandparents, Parents and I*, the 1939 self-portrait *Dos Fridas* portrays two Fridas clearly separated but conjoined by a shared cardiovascular system. The painting, one of Kahlo's largest, is both biological and cultural; the Fridas are presented in the clothing of two selves, Victorian/European and indigenous/Mexican. Kahlo created the work during an intense period of separation from Rivera. In the image, her European heart is sliced open and her indigenous heart is whole. On her Victorian dress we see the snipped vein and falling drops of blood; indigenous Frida holds Diego in a locket connected to her wounded sexuality. In her Indian side we see the strength, which tells us of the conflict between the two aspects of her cultural ancestry. Perhaps the turbulent El Greco–like sky behind the two figures is the most telling of this deeper, more interior struggle, suggesting a new Mexico reclaimed through the Mexicanidad movement.

In the movement, so central to Kahlo and Rivera's cultural and artistic life, the affirmation of indigenous, ancient, and folk art traditions and history was critical. There was a return to popular Mexican culture and a casting off of European trappings. Day of the Dead traditions took on a special meaning for Kahlo in the aftermath of her near-death accident; *la muerte* became her constant companion and appeared frequently in her work. She continued to paint in the ex-voto retablo folk style, and this would be a dominant form in the years to come. It offered her the ability to depict extremity and salvation simultaneously, in a popular style that was accessible to the family and friends who were most often the recipients of her paintings.

In the same way that Kahlo and other artists borrowed from popular styles, they also pursued the reclamation of an ancient Mesoamerican past. As many of the first archaeological digs were taking place in Mexico in the 1920s and 1930s, often sponsored by universities in the United States and Europe, Rivera became an avid scholar and collector of ancient art. Kahlo, also exposed to the same moment of envisioning the roots of nationhood, was adept at blending in references from the pre-Hispanic heritage. In *My Nurse and I,* one of her most important self-portraits, she seems to be searching for her collective and personal roots through an Indian mother merged with an ancient mask. The wet nurse in the painting may be a reference to her own breastfeeding, as many Mexican women of her mother's class would have had a servant to breastfeed. The diminutive Frida baby has an adult head, which gives the scene, typically a tender image, a more sinister and psychological power. It is a pre-Christian Madonna with child, almost a pagan pietà; like the *My Birth* retablo, the scroll is unwritten. The absence of Kahlo's traditional ribbon dedication may be an indicator that the narrative cannot be fixed in time. The painting also reveals her deep biological disposition with drops of milk, dew, raindrops, veins, and mammary glands all fluid signs of the life sources and of metamorphosis or transformation. The complexity of Kahlo's imagery rests with her multiple, layered levels of meaning that are narrative and personal as well as collective and symbolic. Hers is a worldview that attests to her emblematic mythologies.

Artists, cultural workers, and educators connected to the Chicano cultural movement have embraced Kahlo as an activist who resonates with Chicana/o values. Her defiant struggle in face of incredible physical and social odds, and her reenergizing of popular cultural forms, has helped establish a link between the Mexicanidad and Chicano movements.

The Mexicanidad movement of the 1920s and 1930s, led by José Vasconcelos, was a mass literacy campaign, a reformation of the educational system, and a new movement of patronage of the arts. He brought Rivera and Siqueiros back from Europe to create a new Mexico founded on ancient past and a mixed-race future. In this context, the Chicano movement of the late 1960s and 1970s could look back to this Mexican renaissance as a model. Both Rivera and Kahlo were seminal to the renaissance and later became icons of the Chicana/o cultural and artistic movement.

While interest in Kahlo evolved in Chicano and Latino centers across the country, I can best share the story of Kahlo in the San Francisco Bay area, where she spent time with Rivera in the 1930s and 1940s after their first marriage and their remarriage. Their friendships with area artists left a lasting legacy, and we Chicana/os were fortunate to interview many of them before they passed away.

In the Bay Area there was a smaller system of community art centers, including the Galería de la Raza, founded in 1970 by an artists' collective, and the Mexican Museum, founded in 1975 by Peter Rodriguez, with a substantial colonial Mexican collection and an emerging Chicano art collection. Artists associated with the Galería de La Raza collective in San Francisco were working with the image of Kahlo as early as 1974 and 1975. After my first visit to the Blue House, we shared the catalog from Kahlo's museum and any other information we could find on her work and life. Her love of the popular arts was an influential connection to the Chicana drive for cultural reclamation. Her interest in and love of the folk forms, the ex-voto or retablo, the Judas figures, and her continual relationship with death were seminal to Kahlo's aesthetic. The Chicano/a engagement with a Mesoamerican worldview was a way for Chicana/os to assert their own identities as indigenous peoples.

It was critically important to Chicanas to find our artistic genealogy, and Kahlo served as a feminist icon. Beyond the historical parallels of Mexicanidad and Chicanidad are perhaps deeper cultural and psychological constructs linking her to contemporary Chicanas, including the notions of tension and invention. The concept of *rasquachismo*, making the most from the least, was a prevailing aesthetic. Women's version of rasquachismo emphasized the domestic arts in new and reinvented ways. Kahlo's love of folk art was an earlier manifestation of this *domesticana*.

The painting *Dos Fridas* best captures Kahlo's connection, contestation, loss, negotiation, and eventual reconciliation with her bicultural identity, which embodied aspects of the Chicana experience in the United States, and it was natural for Chicana artists to want to learn more about her. When we began our research, Hayden Herrera's biography had not yet been written, and we were able to access stories of Kahlo's younger years and critical moments of change. We also learned of Kahlo and Rivera's experiences in New York and Detroit through their friends and fellow artists, but we focused much of our work on enhancing the California Chicano community's understanding of Kahlo.

Kahlo's friendships with Lucienne Bloch Dimitroff, Emmy Lou Packard, and Ella Wolfe were critical to her time in the United States, and references to them helped Chicana/os in northern California create a deeper sense of connection to Kahlo. Progressive social movements often brought together artists like Packard with such Chicano printmakers as Rupert García, Ralph Maradiaga, and René Yañez, directors of the Galería de la Raza, and played a pivotal role in the development of interest in Kahlo. García was most responsible for the iconic approach to Kahlo's image through a series of prints and drawings and later an annotated bibliography of Kahlo. He developed these works in brilliant palettes and created images that could be disseminated inexpensively through *calendarios* based on Mexican *almanaques*, posters, and eventually pastel drawings. Maradiaga, a peer of my mentor Yolanda Garfias Woo, led the project to establish a history of Kahlo in San Francisco. We began by identifying individuals in the Bay Area who could help us, including Bloch, Packard, Pele de Lappe, and Imogen Cunningham.

De Lappe knew Kahlo in 1931, when the Riveras inhabited the Ralph Stackpole studio and Rivera developed public work in the United States, including the San Francisco Stock Exchange mural. Rivera worked on a mural of himself painting at the California School of Fine Arts (San Francisco Art Institute). De Lappe joined Ralph and Ginette Stackpole and other artists, including Rivera and Kahlo, in the collaborative game of exquisite corpse; the process of drawing body parts onto a folded paper brought out the ribald and humorous side of Kahlo. De Lappe found her to be quiet (she did not speak English), but she was also mordant and witty.

Conducting these interviews with Kahlo's friends was powerful and inspiring. Through Packard, whose progressive poster work was well known to the Galería de la Raza, we were able to meet De Lappe, Bloch Dimitroff, and even Ella Wolfe, wife of Bertram Wolfe, Rivera's biographer. Through their immense generosity, we gained insights into Kahlo the young artist and first-time visitor in the United States. Bloch Dimitroff shared her recollections of Kahlo's work on the ex-voto-style paintings on tin and Rivera's encouragement:

> Rivera loved to see Kahlo's paintings. He always encouraged her to paint. He thought she was great. So she started to paint. One of the first she did was to show the contrast between the United States and Mexico. There is one where she is standing between the U.S. and Mexico. Mexico has all the beauty of the primitive Maya and Aztec. She has a pale pink dress and is just standing there. Just absolutely marvelous!

Bloch Dimitroff, of course, was talking about *Self-portrait on the Borderline between Mexico and the United States, 1932.*

This early painting captures in a strangely symbolic way the inherent conflicts Chicanas were to experience some sixty years later as they tried to regain a Mexican identity in the United States. The border as a theme has come to be both a real and visionary element in the work of many contemporary Chicano/as. In this sense Kahlo was prophetic, a critical image-maker for the Chicano/a generation. The narratives of life-changing friendship and intimacy that Bloch Dimitroff, Packard, and others shared made it possible for us to know Kahlo in a different way. In the development of the book project, we gathered enough material to begin lectures at nearby universities, colleges, libraries, and community centers. Many of us came away with a life-changing attachment to Kahlo's life and work. For me personally, as a woman artist unable to have children, in a marriage with another artist, I gained a model and a sense of the possible. I began working with Kahlo's image for a window altar in 1975 for Frida's birthday in July and followed that with a large altar honoring Kahlo and Rivera in the legendary *Fifth Sun*, a Chicano/a exhibit at the University of California at Berkeley art museum in 1977.

As we continued gathering material, it became clear we needed to find a way for other artists to pay homage to Kahlo. In 1978 we reached out to artists interested in honoring her for the Day of the Dead. Carmen Lomas Garza, René Yañez, Rupert García, and other artists created artwork, which was featured in the *San Francisco Chronicle*. Central to the exhibition was a collective *ofrenda*, or altar, for the dead constructed and designed by Carmen Lomas Garza, curator of the exhibition at the Galería de la Raza; René Yañez, Galería codirector; and myself. Others could add objects and offerings to the altar, including pan dulce, sugar skulls, cempazuchitl flowers, candles, food, and drink.

Imogen Cunningham donated the beautiful photograph she had taken of a young Kahlo, which was placed in the central shrine. Ironically, on the exhibit opening night, Hayden Herrera accidentally broke the Rivera sugar skull on Kahlo's *ofrenda*. We have wondered many times since if this was an omen of the different approach Herrera would take in interpreting Kahlo's life. While Herrera's work has brilliantly captured Kahlo's paintings, it seems to have given less consideration to Mexico's cultural and historical legacy in a period of change.

As the years have passed and Kahlo's commercialization has increased, we have tried in the larger Chicano community to hold true to her profound political and cultural values. In 1987 the Galería de la Raza presented an Evening with Frida Kahlo in which we re-created her kitchen from the Blue House. We hosted her many friends, including De Lappe, Wolfe, Lucienne Bloch Dimitroff, and Steven Dimitroff. They sang songs they had learned from Kahlo and reminisced in a tender and loving way about the woman who marked their lives as artists.

Kahlo has been a guide, companion, model, and ancestor for my own creative work for more than thirty-five years. Beginning with my first *ofrenda* in 1976 at the Galería de la Raza, an Homage to Five Women, I have included her as an imagined ancestor in my extended family with the power to guide and inspire. In 1987 I created a small installation of a temple ruin for Kahlo at INTAR Gallery in New York. I referenced her imagery and values in several other works. She appeared as a fashion doll in a recreation of the 1940s French Théâtre de la Mode exhibit, which I made for El Fin del Siglo Latino World's Fair in 2000.

My 2001 work *Transparent Migration* featured a mirrored armoire with a baby dress hanging above a glass miniature scene of Tenochtitlán. My life with Frida came full circle in 2005, exactly thirty years after my first encounter at the Blue House in Coyoacán, when I was invited to participate in a symposium at the Tate Modern organized to coincide with Britain's first major Kahlo exhibition. The greatest joy was to be on a panel with Mexican scholar Carlos Monsiváis, whose book on Kahlo is the seminal text for a Mexican understanding of the artist. Touring the exhibition and seeing the massive lines of visitors waiting to see the work filled me with satisfaction; some part of the Frida I had come to know was present in this museum, and she would be forever recognized for her enormous contribution to world art.

Kahlo continues to occupy a central place in the Chicana worldview. Her imagery often locates itself between life and death in a spiritual *muertos* that recognizes traditional forms through innovation. Her emphasis on the domestic and private life is at the same time a feminist struggle and resiliency. Latinas and Chicanas embrace her in our ancestral genealogy through a community memory that also functions as a political strategy.

She was a revolutionary woman with the radical power to self-represent at a time when women in Mexico could rarely openly depict their bodies, their sexuality, and their politics. Kahlo's importance rests not just with her art but also with her struggle to balance her life, including the limitations of her physical health and the female biology of motherhood, birth, and loss. She painted the sorrow and torment of her love battles with Rivera, yet she maintained strength and *alegría* in her private life. Surely these qualities are valuable to women everywhere, but most especially to the contemporary Latina and Chicana.[1] The legacy of Frida Kahlo is the triumph over boundaries, the mending of the soul, and the gift of passion, love, and friendship.

In 1938 labor organizer **Emma Tenayuca** (b. San Antonio, Texas, 1916; d. San Antonio, 1989) led a successful strike of twelve thousand pecan shellers in San Antonio, nearly all of them Mexican American women and children. She was eventually forced to leave San Antonio for her work as a labor organizer and for Communist affiliations. She returned twenty years later to teach children basic skills like reading and to ensure that they continued on the path of social and political revolution for Mexican Americans in Texas.

Emma Tenayuca

CARMEN TAFOLLA

**Emma accompanied her grandfather to voting
booths and to political speeches and activities,
and every evening she sat in his lap while he read
the newspaper to her, pointing out articles relevant
to community impact and social justice.**

THE TINY GIRL WITH THE ALL-ABSORBING EYES WATCHED SAN ANTONIO OF
the 1920s and 1930s through the lens of politics and social justice.
Influenced by her grandfather's interest in politics and social issues
impacting the Mexican American population, she read the newspapers with a burning hunger to discover answers to the problems that
plagued her society: hunger, disease, exploitation of a cheap labor
force, ethnic prejudices, unfair employment practices, disempower-
ment of the poor and voiceless, and the constant struggle of the poorest workers for basic economic and physical survival. She grew up in
a time when San Antonio had the highest infant mortality rate and
the highest tuberculosis rate in the nation, and when the seasonal flu
would sweep through and wipe out entire families, while neighbors
watched the body bags carried out of their shacks and tents, counting
the number to see if any had remained. Often, none did.

Emma Tenayuca's mother's family, the Zepedas, had lived in San

Antonio for centuries, a long Tejano heritage that preceded the existence of the United States and three other governments in this area. Her father's family, the Teneyucas (spelled differently from Emma's name because a priest wrote it incorrectly at baptism and it was never corrected), traced their origins to the interior of Mexico and indigenous roots. Perhaps the priest was influenced by the spelling of the pre-Columbian Tenayuca Pyramid in central Mexico, or perhaps fate simply moved his hand, but her name remained Tenayuca and she would become one of a kind.

Because of the large family size, the three oldest children were sent to live with their grandparents, and this increased Tenayuca's exposure to political and academic literacy. She accompanied her grandfather to voting booths and to political speeches and activities, and every evening she sat in his lap while he read the newspaper to her, pointing out articles relevant to community impact and social justice. In the 1920s, many of these articles related to the Mexican Revolution. In addition, their weekly walks to La Plaza del Zacate exposed them to the speeches and open-air meetings held there. In this plaza (modern-day Milam Park, where the Texas State Historical Association posthumously honored Tenayuca with a bronze plaque), Francisco Madero, the Flores Magón brothers, and other revolutionary figures made speeches and entreated the people's support on sociopolitical issues. It was Tenayuca's early training ground for a career studded with fiery oratory and stunning eloquence, to such a degree that the FBI classified her as a-1 Most Dangerous for her ability to rouse a crowd.

Tenayuca was one of San Antonio's most brilliant organizers and civil rights activists in the 1930s and 1940s. She was a committed champion for the rights of the poor and an eloquent orator against the injustices Mexican American communities suffered in the city. Just sixteen when she took part in her first public protest, the Finck Cigar workers strike, she was jailed along with the striking workers. When she was twenty-two she led the city's twelve thousand pecan shellers in a two-month strike that has been called the first successful major political action in the Mexican American struggle for economic and political justice. The city's primary industry, pecan companies were furious at the workers' (and Tenayuca's) audacity in believing they should have a voice in company economic policies and practices. Also controversial was Tenayuca's belief in a society where workers had the right to unionize and the right to a weekend, healthy working conditions, and social security and unemployment benefits.

Her protests and organizing activities were the cause of many arrests, and on January 31, 1938, the San Antonio police department arrested her for her role as an organizer in the pecan shellers strike. She was held without any charges being filed. The police also raided the Workers Alliance hall, destroying the property. Tenayuca was released after many letters protesting her incarceration. As she became a popular folk hero and labor movement icon, she was hated by much of the business community and soon found herself blacklisted for jobs. The police department, under the direction of Chief Owen Kilday, used an obscure city ordinance to arrest thousands of sign-carrying strikers for not having a city permit to protest.

The height of violence and controversy occurred in August 1939 when Mayor Maury Maverick, a former New Deal congressman (from 1935 to 1938), granted Tenayuca a city permit to hold a meeting at the Municipal Auditorium. Maverick defended the ideal that everyone had the right to freedom of speech, but many groups complained loudly, including the American Legion, the Catholic Church, the Ku Klux Klan, veterans organizations, the Elks, the Texas Pioneers, and many of San Antonio's newspapers.

Thousands of angry protesters marched on the auditorium with rocks and bricks. Fearing violence, the mayor ordered police to create a crowd barrier. One reporter was hit with a flying brick, and firefighters wielding hoses were overcome as the mob broke windowpanes, crawled through windows, and ripped out auditorium seats. Police were forced to whisk Tenayuca and the two other speakers to safety through a secret tunnel. The mob's anger was seeking a target, and curtains and seats were slashed, toilets were ripped out of bathrooms, and finally the mayor was burned in effigy. Total damage to the auditorium was estimated at four thousand dollars in 1939 dollars.

The best-known image of Tenayuca, published in papers worldwide in the late 1930s, shows her on the steps of city hall speaking to workers, the Workers Alliance, and the Sociedad Social Mutualista de Texas. Today she is recognized as one of the pioneers in the civil rights movement for Mexican Americans. She has been inducted into the Texas Women's Hall of Fame and was named to the YWCA Outstanding Women of the Century list, among other honors. She was outspoken and unafraid in a time when neither women nor Mexican Americans were expected to have a voice. She stood up to the city's greatest powers and fought for justice and equality thirty years before the names of Martin Luther King Jr., César Chávez, and Dolores Huerta were even known.

Isabel Vargas Lizano (b. San Joaquín de Flores, Costa Rica, 1919; d. Cuernavaca, Mexico, 2012) is better known as the singer Chavela Vargas, who claimed Mexico as her artistic birthplace and upended strict gender norms in mid-twentieth-century Mexico by dressing as a man and singing her renditions of rancheras. Pedro Almodóvar called her *la voz aspera de la ternura*, or the rough voice of tenderness. The Latin Academy of Recording Arts and Sciences presented Vargas with a Latin Grammy and a Lifetime Achievement Award. Latin American music was greatly influenced by her interpretations of many traditional genres and songs.

Chavela Vargas

**In a Mexico City club, Vargas serenaded a couple.
Then she slipped off the man's tie, lassoed it
around his woman's neck, gave it a passionate yank,
and kissed her.**

ONCE, WHEN MEXICO WAS THE BELLY BUTTON OF THE UNIVERSE, ISABEL
Vargas Lizano ran away from home and resolved to make herself into
a Mexican singer. This was in the 1930s, when Europe was on fire, the
United States out of work, and Mexico busy giving birth to herself
after a revolution.

At fourteen, Isabel was busy birthing herself, too. Cast off from her
Costa Rican kin for being too strange, she would become Mexico's beloved Chavela Vargas.

It was the country's golden era. Visitors came from across the globe.
Sergei Eisenstein, Luis Buñuel, Leonora Carrington. Mexico was a
knockout, and everyone was crazy about her.

At first, Vargas made her living doing odd jobs: cooking, selling
children's clothes, chauffeuring an elderly lady. She was adopted by
artists and musicians and sang at their parties and favorite bars. When
she was not yet twenty-five, she was invited to the Blue House of Frida

Kahlo and Diego Rivera in Coyoacán. "Who's that girl, the one in the white shirt?" Kahlo asked. Kahlo summoned her over, and Vargas sat at her side the rest of the night. Because Vargas lived all the way up in the Condesa neighborhood, Rivera and Kahlo offered her lodging for the night. Rivera suggested she take to bed some of their Mexican hairless dogs. "Sleep with them," he told her. "They warm the bed and keep away rheumatism." Vargas had found her spiritual family.

Eventually Vargas apprenticed with Mexico's finest musicians: the composer Agustín Lara and Antonio Bribiesca and his weeping guitar. She fine-tuned her singing style listening to Toña La Negra and the Texas songbird Lydia Mendoza, among others. The songwriter José Alfredo Jiménez became her maestro with his songs that "expressed… the common pain of all who love," Vargas said. "And when I came out onstage they were mine, because I added my own pain, too."

With just a guitar and her voice, Vargas performed in a red poncho and pants at a time when Mexican women didn't wear pants. She sang with arms open wide like a priest celebrating mass, modeling her singing on the women of the Mexican Revolution. "A Mexicana is a very strong woman," Vargas said, "starting with la Adelita, la Valentina—*mujeres muy mujeres.*" Chavela Vargas belonged to this category of women-very-much-women.

Even when Vargas was young and her voice still as transparent as mezcal, she danced with her lyrics *tacuachito*-style, cheek to cheek, pounded them on the bar, made them jump like dice, spat and hissed and purred like the woman jaguar she claimed to be, and finished with a volley that entered the heart like a round of bullets from the pistol she stashed in her belt. "She was *chile verde*," remembers Elena Poniatowska, the grande dame of Mexican letters.

Vargas lived and sang *a lo macho*. She sang love songs written for men to sing without changing the pronouns.

Her big hit was "Macorina," Poniatowska said. "'*Put your hand here, Macorina,*' she sang with her hand like a great big seashell over her sex, long before Madonna."

In her autobiography, Vargas writes: "I always began with 'Macorina.'. . .And lots of times I finished with that song. So that folks would go home to their beds *calientitos*, nice and warm."

Because she immortalized popular rancheras, Vargas is often labeled a country singer. But she kidnapped romantic boleros and made them hers too. Her songs appealed to drinkers of pulque as well as of champagne.

The critic Tomás Ybarra-Frausto remembers the Vargas of the early 1960s. "I used to see her at La Cueva de Amparo Montes, a club frequented by the underground in downtown Mexico City. She dressed in black leather and would roar over on a motorcycle with a blonde gringa on her back."

Someone else told this story. In a Mexico City club, Vargas serenaded a couple. Then she slipped off the man's tie, lassoed it around his woman's neck, gave it a passionate yank, and kissed her.

She had a reputation as a *robaesposas*. Did she really have affairs with everyone's wives? A European queen? Ava Gardner? Frida? What was true, and what was *mitote*? You only have to look at Vargas's photos when she was young to know some of the rumors were true. In the town of Monclova, Coahuila, go ask the elders. They'll tell you: Vargas came to town and sang. And then ran off with the doctor's daughter. People still remember. Judy Garland, Grace Kelly, Bette Davis, Elizabeth Taylor. She was invited to their parties, danced with the wives of powerful *políticos*, claimed to have shared *un amor* with "the most famous woman in the world," but would not say more.

And then, somewhere in her sixties, Vargas disappeared. Some thought she had died, and in a way, she had.

"Sometimes I don't have any other alternative but to joke about my alcoholism as if it was just a one-night *parranda*," she said. "It was no joke. Those who lived it with me know it."

Before Pedro Almodóvar and Salma Hayek featured her in their films, there were friends who helped Vargas walk through fire and be reborn. The performers Jesusa Rodríguez and Liliana Felipe invited Vargas to make her 1991 comeback in their Mexico City theater, El Hábito.

"There were only a few minutes left before her entrance, and the place was packed," Rodríguez remembers. "All the hipsters of that era were waiting. No one could believe Chavela was returning to sing.

"She was very nervous. Well, she'd never appeared onstage without drinking. When we gave her the second call, she panicked and asked for a tequila. Liliana and I looked at one another, and then Liliana said, 'Chavela if you drink, it's better if we just cancel the show.' 'But how?' said Chavela. 'There's a full house.' 'Well, it doesn't matter,' we said. 'We'll just give everyone their money back, and that'll be that.'

"Chavela looked serious for a few moments, then she took a deep breath and said, 'Let's go!' We gave the third call, she climbed up on the stage, stood there like an ancient tree and sang for…years, without stopping, without drinking."

Her voice had become another voice. Ravaged but beautiful in a dark way, like glass charred into obsidian.

Vargas's specialty was *el amor y el desamor*, love and love lost, songs of loneliness and goodbyes in a voice as ethereal as the white smoke from copal, but as powerful as the Pacific. Songs that sucked you in, threatened to drown you; then, when you least expected it, pulled down your pants and slapped you on the behind. Audiences broke out into spontaneous *gritos*, that Mexican yodel barked from the belly and a lifetime of grief.

Mexican parties always end with everyone crying, the journalist Alma Guillermoprieto once noted. Vargas satisfied a national urge to weep. She embodied Mexico, that open wound unhealed since the conquest and, a century after a useless revolution, in need of tears now more than ever.

In summer 2012, at the age of ninety-three, Vargas returned to Mexico from Spain. She was sick. On August 5, death came at last and ran off with her.

Gloria Anzaldúa (b. Raymondville, Texas, 1942; d. Santa Cruz, California, 2004) was the child of farmworkers in South Texas and came to be a keen observer of social and cultural strife that touched race, ethnic, and gender relations in the world around her. First as a teacher and then as an academic and writer, she was one of the first openly lesbian Chicana writers. She articulated the compelling need to address sexual and ethnic multi-identities.

Gloria Anzaldúa

ELLEN RIOJAS CLARK

**Unlike me, Anzaldúa grew up speaking and being
in Spanish and English, in a combination of two
languages, two cultures, two histories; aware and
sure of her two-ness.**

I WAS BORN DIFFERENT—I WAS ALWAYS DIFFERENT, THAT IS, I SAW MYSELF
as different. One-eyed, thick, black braids, clunky corrective shoes, an
awkward stance, glasses, mannish voice, it seemed to me that everything about me was different. I was brown in a community of white,
quiet where everyone spoke, a reader instead of a contender. I never
looked up nor ever climbed up. Called many things: bookworm, poor
little thing, scaredy-cat, blind as a bat, shy, weird, whatever the word
was for nerd, and on and on. I always wondered what would have happened if I had had short hair, sunglasses, ballerina shoes, and if I had
been called musically sounding Maria Elena? Would I have looked
around at the world I lived in differently? Was I just a one-eyed girl
with three-pound braids that drew my face up where the sun hurt
my eye and who would hide her face in the fantasy world of an ever-
present book? Or was I someone other than who I was? Who was I?

Seems so long ago, and yet, when I read something that really de-

scribed me, it changed me. I am a wind-swayed bridge, a crossroads in-habited by whirlwinds....Do you say my name is ambivalence?...Think of me as Shiva, a many-armed and legged body with one foot on brown soil, one on white, one in straight society, one in the gay world, the man's world, the women's, one limb in the literary world, another in the work-ing class, the socialist, and the occult worlds....A sort of spider woman hanging by one thin strand of web....Who, me confused? Ambivalent? Not so. Only your labels split me.[1]

To read in Gloria Anzaldúa's work that it was others' perceptions of me that were lacking, I realized that their views were not really about me, the inner me. I could finally believe what my mother had always told me; I was unique, not different, I was fortunate not to be like ev-eryone else. She always said my one eye allowed me to concentrate on looking, and therefore I could see more, my one eye was like a camera, it focused on seeing. My transformation was beginning; from others seeing me as deficient and ugly because I was missing an eye, to now knowing I had other attributes. My spirits were lifted. I was strength incarnate, my many selves were more than monocultural beings, my many voices encompassed more than singular tongues, my multiplic-ity was to be envied for its potency, completeness, and even beauty.

I am visible—see this Indian face—yet I am invisible. I both blind them with my beak nose and am their blind spot. But I exist, we exist. They like to think I have melted in the pot. But I haven't, we haven't.[2]

What a provocative statement to read; it hit me in my most inner being. Anzaldúa's *This Bridge Called My Back: Writings by Radical Women of Color* (1981) changed my world. To finally be exposed to ideas and to analysis that dealt with my own experiences and thoughts was groundbreaking for me. That I am not so odd, that I am many things, is what her autobiographical essay showed me. Never before had I read work like this revolutionary collection of essays, letters, and poems.

To be exposed to the thoughts and conflicts associated with the painful process of struggle, denial, acceptance, revitalization, and vali-dation of self was world-shattering for me. To not only read someone's counter analysis to society's view of me, but also to see it as a valid theoretical framework and a philosophy, was radical. It required more of me than just a blanket assumption of her views. I had to review my socialization not just within the institutionalization of my family practices but from the white north-side community I grew up in, the schools I attended, my white friends, my English, my Methodist church, my life until then.

I remember how perplexed my father was when my younger brother chastised him with "Why didn't we live on the west side?" My bewildered father, who had never lived in the barrio, did not understand my brother's dilemma. In retrospect, my brother was speaking about his own ethnic identity, his lack of Spanish, his sense of understanding himself within the complexity of the borderlands, and in trying to integrate into two ethnic groups. I, on the other hand, was fortunate to read and be provoked by Anzaldúa's words and thoughts. The awakening of my inner self, to be able to work to understand and change those borders, created change.

The struggle is inner: Chicano, Indio, American Indian, mojado, Mexicano, immigrant Latino, Anglo in power, working-class Anglo, Black, Asian—our psyches resemble the border towns and are populated by the same people. The struggle has always been inner and is played out in outer terrains. Awareness of our situation must come before inner changes, which in turn come before changes in society. Nothing happens in the "real" world unless it first happens in the images in our heads.[3]

To understand that my sociocultural worlds were shifting and my inner being was strengthening and that I had to know who I was in order to be productive was the beginning of a conscious approach to my own empowerment. It was not happening just to my brother and me but to a whole community that was now undergoing cultural, linguistic, and ethnic self-acceptance to understanding Anzaldúa's statement: "ethnic identity is twin skin to linguistic identity."[4] It was the time of Chicano power.

My first exposure to Chicano literature had been in the early 1970s at Trinity University in a class with Dick Woods. It was fascinating literature; yes, it was great, but all by men. José Antonio Villarreal, Oscar Acosta, Raymond Barrio, Rudy Anaya, Alurista, Sabine Ulibarrí, Rudy Gonzales described some of my experiences but none of my thoughts. I don't remember readings by women except for some occasional poems in *Quinto Sol*.[5] But in the 1980s, women exploded on the literary scene, and among them a short, dark woman: Gloria Anzaldúa. A woman from Texas like me, born in the Rio Grande Valley of South Texas in 1942, a year younger than me. Unlike me, she grew up speaking and being in Spanish and English, in a combination of two languages, two cultures, two histories; aware and sure of her two-ness. She crossed over and back again many times, and this, I think, opened her to the dynamics of crossings and creating pathways.

These situational contexts, coupled with her descriptions and reflections, formed a valid framework for the revolutionary work she articulated that has continued to impact and challenge the premises for our thinking and our actions. Anzaldúa has become best known for *Borderlands / La Frontera: The New Mestiza*, her 1987 collection of poetry and prose, which was named one of the one hundred best books of the century. It is still recognized by scholars as one of the premier feminist texts, and certainly one of the first to deal with ethnic and sexuality issues. It was those initial works that stirred me into rethinking my own identity. The magnitude of Anzaldúa's writings continues to reshape my work and my worlds.

At some point, on our way to a new consciousness, we will have to leave the opposite bank, the split between the two mortal combatants somehow healed so that we are on both shores at once and, at once, see through serpent and eagle eyes. Or perhaps we will decide to disengage from the dominant culture, write it off altogether like a lost cause, and cross the border into wholly new and separate territory. Or we might go another route. The possibilities are numerous once we decide to act and not react.[6]

Anzaldúa and I also shared the pain, physical and emotional, hers from an early physical development that resulted in the subsequent removal of her female organs, and me from a tumored eye that also had to be removed. She had to hide her precocious sexual development under tight garments and rags her mother provided. As she remembers, "I'd take [the rags] out into this shed, wash them out, and hang them really low on a cactus so nobody would see them....My genitals...[were] always a smelly place that dripped blood and had to be hidden."[7]

And I, eye patches provided by doctors to hide my deformity so all could stare at the one-eyed girl. I did not trust doctors, for it meant pain as they washed out where my eye that could not see had been. My dad tells me that I could smell blood whenever it was time to be poked at, gouged at, or bandaged. When we went to the Medical Arts building on Houston and Alamo Streets, he would try many different things to disguise going to the doctor, taking me past the corner to a store to buy a toy, have the bus stop several corners before the actual stop, a taxi to behind the office. Nope, nothing would work. I would plunk my four-year-old bottom on the sidewalk and would not wail but scream, as my parents would try to entice me to the lollipop that awaited. No way in hell did that lure me. I learned early on that grown-ups could trick you, professionals would hurt you, several times around the block leads you to the same spot, and the lollipop did not taste as good afterward. That hiding something did not change it. Funny the things that drew me to connect with Anzaldúa's experiences and, subsequently, her work on the sameness and differences of identity. Those experiences shaped my perspectives.

As I continued my studies, in classes with Tomás Rivera where we explored terms such as *mestizo*, it was world-shattering to me to later read Anzaldúa's revelation of a *new mestiza*—what she called *mestizaje* theories, drawing connections between personal and systemic issues to social justice. That I should be aware of both my contentious and meshing identities and form a perspective for a new way of thinking of myself and for others to consider was revolutionary.

By creating a new mythos—that is, a change in the way we perceive reality, the way we see ourselves, and the ways we behave—la mestiza creates a new consciousness. The work of mestiza consciousness is to break down the subject/object duality that keeps her prisoner and to show in the flesh and through the images in her work how duality is transcended. The answer to the problem between the white race and the colored, between males and females, lies in healing the split that origi-

nates in the very foundation of our lives, our culture, our languages, our thoughts. A massive uprooting of dualistic thinking in the individual and collective consciousness is the beginning of a long struggle, but one that could, in our best hopes, bring us to the end of rape, of violence, of war.[8]

We had to "create new categories for those of us left out or pushed out of the existing ones," as Anzaldúa stated.[9] We had to take into account all those exogenous factors such as space, history, gender, politics, and culture that existed in our time of being. These sociocultural contexts differ for us based on where we grew up, when we grew up, and how we grew up. To think that it is not an either/or perspective but a totally new mestiza way of thinking, an in-depth look, a beyond the view of our selves was not only innovative but also radical. Her theoretical works revolutionized where I work, the academy. We had to go beyond what existed in the literature, to infuse it with this new way of thinking and seeing, one beyond traditional perspectives.

It was not easy to go against the culture of academia. For our research demonstrated not only the complexity of the changing boundaries of ethnic groups and individuals but also the challenges of cultural identity as affected by diverse settings, and it was cogent for new findings and theories, all influenced by Anzaldúa's work. This was a major contribution to the discussion of history, gender, sexuality, and identity when we were forced to analyze the past, the present, and all works and writings from this new way of thinking. This cannot be done by quantitative studies but only through ethnographic work, qualitative work, something that was not acceptable when I started my journey into academia. To go into the real world, to listen to people's stories, to examine different experiences was not seen as valid; only numbers counted in academic research. So we new academics began to change how the research was perceived. How else can one examine what Anzaldúa calls *nepantla, tierra entre media*? We have to dialogue with others to find out what drives thoughts and actions. And this is what now guides ethnographic research in my academic world.

Bringing Anzaldúa to my university in the 1980s to have informal dialogue with students and faculty was an eye-opener for many. To hear such a tiny woman voice provocative thoughts, revoke traditional views, and challenge us to do things differently was seen as threatening. This voice created unrest in how we perceive our work and yet stimulated us to know that we were on a valid quest.

Bridges are thresholds to other realities, archetypal, primal symbols of shifting consciousness. They are passageways, conduits, and connectors that connote transitioning, crossing borders, and changing perspectives. Bridges span liminal (threshold) spaces between worlds, spaces I call nepantla, *a Nahuatl word meaning* tierra entre medio. *Transformations occur in this in-between space, an unstable, unpredictable, precarious, always-in-transition space lacking clear boundaries.* Nepantla es tierra desconocida, *and living in this liminal zone means being in a constant state of displacement—an uncomfortable, even alarming feeling. Most of us dwell in nepantla so much of the time it's become a sort of "home." Though this state links us to other ideas, people, and worlds, we feel threatened by these new connections and the change they engender.*[10]

Though Anzaldúa did not become part of the tenured world of academia, she has impacted many disciplines I've chosen to work in, including American studies, interdisciplinary studies, cultural studies, ethnic studies, Latino studies, feminism/feminist theory, literary studies, women's studies, and queer theory.[11] Not too many professors can claim such an impact.

With students, I continue discussion based on Anzaldúa's concepts so that they can understand how their own identity production is co-constructed in social practice. That is what happened to me after reading Anzaldúa's work and happens with my students as we discuss her works in relationship to who they are. Power and positionality are inextricably linked to the forming of our identities. These conflicting voices in combination with continual repositioning can result in new ways of thinking and action in our imagined world and discourses.

Knowing that the production of identities is always in process helps us develop our potential. To change one's subjectivity, have a strong sense of self, transform one's identity, have cognitive self-respect, and respond to the esoteric question of who one is lead to the creation of pathways that speak to the metamorphic power of Anzaldúa's work. These explorations have led my colleague Belinda Flores and me to examine the development of identity as the basis for positive teacher efficacy with bicultural, bilingual students. In our work, we have expressed the need for teachers to understand that the sociocultural, historical, and political context acts as a mediator for their students' identities. We deem it important for individuals to have a sense of equality based on equity rights and believe that ethnic identity leading to ethnic solidarity is the conduit for social esteem and equity. We feel that this goes beyond self-reflection. It requires an examination of one's social, cultural, ethnic, linguistic, and economic positioning in society.

As early as in 1996, I began to develop a metamorphic model based on the process of struggle, denial, acceptance, revitalization, and validation of self so that teachers can develop a salient ethnic and cultural identity that can then affect all of their students' ethnic identities and pathways to success. The idea of metamorphosis is not only a biological process and a physical change; it also constitutes psychological transformation. My goal then is to use this notion of metamorphosis to transform the identity of teachers so they can become change agents in their classrooms, schools, and communities and not function as perpetrators of the status quo.

I am an act of kneading, of uniting and joining that not only has produced both a creature of darkness and a creature of light, but also a creature that questions the definitions of light and dark and gives them new meanings.[12]

In our work, we use exploration leading to cultural identity as a way of seeing self and others, and the basis for this is Anzaldúa's framework. Exploration starts us on the road not only to understanding others and their identities but also to looking within to expand our perspectives in articulating our own cultural identity. We want teachers to use their own cultural and ethnic identity as a medium for constructing empathy and promoting social justice in their classrooms. We, like Anzaldúa, feel that the transformation of self is power. She writes, "I want the freedom to carve and chisel my own face, to staunch the bleeding with ashes, to fashion my own gods out of my entrails."[13]

Now I know that I can be what I want to be, but also what I am. I can be the way I was designed to be. I can live in whatever way I choose, for I am liberated. I can shatter any space with my thoughts, my actions, my laughter, and my presence. My "wild tongues can't be tamed, they can only be cut out."[14] I am responsible for my culture, my history, my family, and for all that I honor. Anzaldúa writes, "What we say and what we do ultimately comes back to us so let us own our responsibility, place it in our hands, and carry it with dignity and strength."[15] I still have much to learn from this world, so much to still read and reflect; learning continues to nourish me. So, according to Anzaldúa, "naming is how I make my presence known, how I assert who and what I am and want to be known as. Naming myself is a survival tactic."[16]

So I will be like the huipiles that I wear, for they not only give me strength and boldness but they connect me to my essence and prepare me for action in my work, my community, my family, and my city. I, like Anzaldúa, want everyone to live in the same way with his or her own identities and supporting actions that can be strong and ever evolving. For:

> the Spanish word "nosotras" means "us." In theorizing insider/outsider I write the word with a slash between nos (us) and otras (others). Today the division between the majority of "us" and "them" is still intact. This country does not want to acknowledge its walls or limits, the places some people are stopped or stop themselves, the lines they aren't allowed to cross. [But] the future belongs to those who cultivate cultural sensitivities to differences and who use these abilities to forge a hybrid consciousness that transcends the "us" vs. "them" mentality and will carry us into a nosotras position bridging the extremes of our cultural realities.[17]

So I will continue Gloria Anzaldúa's revolutionary legacy because I am the woman who as ...*I change myself, I change the world.*

Educational activist **Genoveva Morales** (b. Uvalde, Texas, 1928) was the lead plaintiff in a watershed federal lawsuit that eroded discriminatory practices in public schools. She challenged discrimination in schools in Uvalde, Texas, in 1970 and persisted in the lawsuit for nearly forty years. In doing so, she ended institutionalized educational discrimination in Uvalde and has given thousands of Mexican American students there and elsewhere equal access to education under the law.

Genoveva Morales

ELAINE AYALA

In those prelawsuit days, a school official who
called Morales and suggested her son might be
better suited for "the Mexican school" probably
had no idea what the district was in for.

CHANGE IS A TOUGH CROP TO CULTIVATE ANYWHERE. BUT IN UVALDE, IT HAS
had an even harder time taking root. Sometimes only other people
from small-town Texas truly know what it's like to live in a place like
that. In 1928, when Genoveva Morales was born there, segregation
was blatant, and laws underscored the prejudice that existed there.
At one time, deed restrictions prohibited white people from selling
their homes to Mexicans. Before that, no Mexican wanted to be caught
walking through the frontier settlement: being Mexican while walking
was unlawful. And long before that—during the U.S.-Mexican War—
Mexicans were routinely lynched in Uvalde.

Similar conditions existed for Mexican Americans. In the county
of a thousand springs, Uvalde, where limestone rock asphalt is dug
out of the hard ground, Mexicans and Mexican Americans were one
and the same, and their civil rights were nonexistent. When they were
schooled at all, they went to the Mexican school, separate and unequal.

Morales went to the same segregated school in the 1930s that her mother had attended decades before.

By 1970, at the height of the Chicano civil rights movement characterized by student-led walkouts, Morales and other parents decided that they had had enough. They banded together to sue the Uvalde Consolidated Independent School District. The historic lawsuit that bears her name, fought in part on constitutional grounds, called for the district to desegregate and address a long list of grievances, from the dearth of Mexican American teachers and principals to the lack of equal educational opportunities for Latino children. More than forty years later, none of those parents would have imagined that the case would not reach a settlement until well into the twenty-first century, or that Uvalde schools would remain under court supervision. The judicial system, however, was never the district's biggest challenge. Morales was.

Over the years, as other parents slowly wearied of the court challenge and left the suit, the strong-willed Mexican American mother of eleven and the chief plaintiff behind *Morales v. Shannon* has remained at the center of the case. Many of the other original plaintiffs are dead. So are many of the teachers and the superintendents who worked in the district then. What they all had in common was that they disliked Morales. Over the years, they tried mightily to get out from under the court's jurisdiction. Undeterred, Morales met each of them face-to-face and vowed to outlive them. Morales did not muster such perseverance and determination at age forty, when this battle started; it was part of her DNA.

EARLY YEARS

Morales grew up in a house about a block from the home where she raised her children and where she still lives today. In addition to her Mexican American heritage, she has both Native American and German ancestry. Her father, born in Mexico, was Uvalde's blacksmith. Unlike so many other Mexican immigrants and Mexican Americans in the little town eighty miles west of San Antonio, he made a decent living. He also acquired property and ran a small farm, growing his family's vegetables and raising its livestock. "Dad didn't go to school," Morales said. "But he knew how to read and write in English and Spanish.... Considering the way we lived, we were a well-to-do family," she added. "But we had to work."

In the 1930s, children worked, but they played, too: in arroyos, running barefoot through fields. They hunted rabbits. They walked into town to buy a spool of thread when their mother needed one. In a home in which doing chores helped keep food on the table, she and her brothers and sisters milked cows, gathered eggs, and fished. Having guns was a way of life. They tended a vegetable garden and sold milk to neighbors. When a livestock animal was killed, nothing went to waste. Twice a year, a pig was slaughtered; even its blood was put into the preparation of a meal. Her mother taught her how.

Neighbors and relatives were just as important as immediate family, and they came to each other's aid in times of crisis. For leisure, they paid calls on one another. Morales's family visited the Zamoras, a family who worked for U.S. vice president John Nance Garner, who himself was born in Uvalde. "They had a little ranch," Morales recalled. "We would go to visit them." During the summer they slept outdoors on the porch. Before lying down, their father gave each of them a cigarette, hand-rolled with Prince Albert tobacco, and asked them to smoke it. Cigarette smoke kept mosquitoes away, she said.

Her mother looked after her six children—Genoveva was her fifth—and was a *curandera*, or folk healer, and a *partera*, or midwife. She also made money reading tarot cards. Sometimes she was called to San Antonio and beyond to do readings. "She was a psychic," Morales says. She had attended Uvalde schools but didn't graduate.

From this stock and into these circumstances Morales was born. She didn't start school until she was about ten years old and attended a Mexican school. "I remember the next-door neighbors were black. The woman would teach me English," she recalled. Her mother looked out for them in turn. "My mom gave them eggs or whatever we had. We were way better off. They weren't allowed in the school."

Morales gave a little sarcastic laugh when asked about the era's discrimination. "The word *discrimination* was not in the dictionary," she said.

She wasn't exactly a good student, though she enjoyed mathematics. Confidence was clearly one of her strengths. If at any time she was a little timid, that characteristic didn't surface much, even during her childhood. "Once we went to school," she said, "we didn't take nothing from no one." Even more: "I've always been an outspoken person. My English is perfect when I'm mad." And in the Mexican school where she and her siblings were sent, "we were mean. We were mean to the teachers and the students." She added later, "We were survivors."

Morales's school had no Mexican or Mexican American teachers. "They were all white," she said.

She dropped out in the ninth grade despite doing well in school. In part she blames a strong will and her attitude. Still, one asks why. She waits for the obvious question. But after all these years, she still laments the answer.

"I wasn't thinking," she said. "My parents didn't know any better. I went to a college assembly [to prepare for that possibility]. But my mother told me I was not going out of town without her."

The already combative young girl was further angered. So she quit then and there.

"Isn't that stupid?" she said. "When my children went to school, that's when I started to see things differently."

Morales married at age twenty-one, considered late for her era and culture. By then she was already seen as an old maid, but it might have played a role in her later civil rights work. She had more time to become her own person. She savored a little independence and learned to make her own money. She was a cook all her life and worked at the country club and other restaurants in town.

Her husband was the same age and also seen as old for marriage. Morales's independent, feisty spirit posed no threat to the mild-mannered man who operated large equipment in a local asphalt mine. For a time, these dusty open pits had made Uvalde the nation's asphalt mining capital. Another man might not have stood by her as she became more involved in the desegregation case and other civil rights activities. But her husband never criticized her involvement or tried to stop her. When she had to travel to San Antonio for a court hearing, or to New Orleans (to the Fifth Circuit Court of Appeals) to witness another incremental step in the judicial process, he gave his blessing and stayed home with their children. They had been married for more than sixty years.

HOW ANGER TURNED INTO ACTIVISM

When her children began attending Uvalde schools, a Mexican school still existed two blocks from her house. But Morales enrolled her children in the public school farther away "where all the Anglos would go," she said. "They'd call me because one of them would cry."

In those prelawsuit days, a school official who called and suggested her son might be better suited for "the Mexican school" probably had no idea what the district was in for. Morales wouldn't have it. "Their English is just as good as [the Anglo children's]," she said in explaining why the predominantly Anglo school was better.

Her son Eduardo Morales, a Catholic priest, recalls that his teachers gave him special instruction and attention, perhaps because he was Morales's son. "Many students were not helped. They were just passed, but they couldn't read. I was sent to speech therapy. In the whole class, I was the only one. But I wasn't the only one who couldn't pronounce *ch* and *sh* sounds. They all had the same problem. People laughed at them."

After the district institutionalized neighborhood schools, assigning children to those nearest their homes in de facto segregation, some of Morales's children ended up in migrant classes with children whose family members were seasonal farmworkers. Typically, they didn't thrive.

This angered Morales because it put her children behind in academic achievement. Such classes not only failed students but also belittled them, she thought. One of her children, who had never had a speech problem, developed a stutter. The family doctor, who was on Uvalde's school board, heard from her in marked ways, Morales said. "I told him, 'I don't want my children in separate classes.' We weren't migrants!" Even he, Morales says now, acknowledged the unfairness, if not in public, at least in private.

Later, court documents would address not only the district's "attendance zoning plan" that kept Mexican Americans separated from Anglos but also the English-language deficiencies the district failed to adequately address. Court documents also noted that the district discriminated against Mexican American applicants for faculty and administrative jobs and failed to employ Mexican Americans in adequate ways.

A MOVEMENT LED BY CHILDREN

A decade after the Supreme Court's *Brown v. Board of Education* decision (1954), which ruled school segregation unconstitutional, Chicano college students were mobilizing. It wasn't just segregation per se but the ills associated with it, such as unequal educational opportunity. Not only were Latino students dropping out of school in great numbers, those who stayed were sometimes promoted even though they were not taught to read. Latinos were discouraged from applying to college and sometimes told they weren't college material. They faced overwhelming economic obstacles to higher education, and the dropout rate was even higher than it is today.

Against this backdrop, leaders of the Mexican American Youth Organization, established in 1968 by activists who later helped create La Raza Unida, were organizing high school students. Their goal: to bring attention to wide-ranging and blatant forms of discrimination. In cities throughout South Texas, they held up placards that called attention to inadequate, deteriorating facilities and a serious lack of textbooks. They exposed not only the problem of inexperienced teachers in their schools but also unqualified and uncertified ones. In some Texas districts, students protested rodent infestations and the lack of toilet paper in school restrooms.

Morales remembers the tension that existed, how nervous and angry students and parents were about the unfolding events. "The kids were prepared for it," she said. Later they faced unimagined consequences for walking out of Uvalde schools and staying out for six weeks. What was significant about this youth activism was how the students' courage and idealism moved their parents to get involved. Parents organized in San Antonio, Uvalde, and, most notably, Crystal City, as well as other towns and cities. They didn't just protest; they planned to use the law to force change.

César Chávez, the co-founder of the United Farm Workers union, influenced students and adults alike. His inspirational movement on behalf of field-workers spread across the Southwest and grew into much more. In New Mexico, Reies Lopez Tijerina was infusing the movement with his quest to recover Spanish land grants for descendants of Mexicans who once owned them. Rodolfo "Corky" Gonzáles and his Crusade for Justice in Denver, both a spiritual quest for justice and a manifesto for self-determination, was also influential. Chicano high school students were walking out of their schools, supported by the religious community and other community members.

For her part, Morales joined the Mexican American Parents Association in Uvalde. Then she was elected its president. "I was forty," she said. "I was young, very young. I had the time. I didn't have a jealous husband. I could do as I pleased." And fighting for Mexican American children—her own and others, and those yet to be born—was what she wanted to do. She kept working as a cook and preparing her children's lunches well before they awakened.

"My mom could have given up many years ago," said Eduardo Morales, who shepherds a predominantly Anglo parish in Alamo Heights, a community north of downtown San Antonio. "But she understood from the very beginning that it wasn't about her." Before standing alongside the protesting students, "she was a homemaker. She was not politically active. My mom's interest was us kids. She didn't do it for herself. She did it for her children and those children in the future."

Several issues contributed to the incendiary moments in the student walkouts leading to the Morales lawsuit. It wasn't just Uvalde's segregation or the backroom good-old-boy politics that gave way to prejudice and pettiness in school district hiring and promotions. When a popular Mexican American teacher lost his contract and the school board reinstated a similarly dismissed Anglo teacher's contract, the movement was ignited, Morales said.

She was the spokesperson for the charge before the school board. "I'm very blunt," she said. "I'm sorry, but I am. I'm like a dog on a leash. I told [off] the superintendent in English and Spanish, and I'm not exaggerating."

Morales acknowledges that in the end it wasn't parents or lawyers who were central to the fight. At the core were Mexican American students who risked so much to walk out of their classes and into the spotlight. They did so, she said, "because they were not getting equal educational opportunities."

The Mexican American Legal Defense and Educational Fund (MAL-DEF), established in 1968 in San Antonio to fight the Latino community's civil rights cases, stepped in as students led them to evidence they could use in court. No one knew then that *Morales v. Shannon*, which MALDEF would file in 1970, was the beginning of a legal struggle that would last for decades. Some of the children, Morales's included, would suffer the worst wounds. Daniel Morales, her oldest child, didn't want to go back to school. "He cried because he lost too much time," she said. At graduation he wasn't allowed to walk across the stage.

"They were punished for the walkout," she said. "They were trying to get even with the kids. It hurt a lot to see the others graduating."

Genoveva Morales bears scars as well. For her activism and no-nonsense, take-no-prisoners style, she was labeled a Communist. She was under surveillance, she said. But the rumor that still makes her son Eduardo both laugh and wince was the one alleging that she was indoctrinated by Cuban dictator Fidel Castro. "You have to come from a small town to understand how hard it is to take on the whole town," he said.

Filed in 1970, the class-action lawsuit bearing Morales's name charged that Uvalde schools were segregated in violation of the U.S. Constitution and the Civil Rights Act of 1964. A district court "found no illegal segregation" in 1973, but two years later the U.S. Court of Appeals for the Fifth Circuit reversed the decision. The appellate court found segregation in place more than two decades after *Brown v. Board of Education,* the Supreme Court ruling that ordered U.S. schools to desegregate "with all deliberate speed."

Uvalde Consolidated ISD remained under court jurisdiction for more than thirty years. Over those decades, it asked to be released from court interference in the district's administration. The court, however, sided with Morales and MALDEF, which argued that the district showed "a lack of good-faith compliance." By the mid-1960s, the Supreme Court acknowledged widespread reluctance nationwide and stated that "the time for mere 'deliberate speed' has run out."

MALDEF's briefs contained a long series of examples of Uvalde's failure "to remove the vestiges of discrimination from the district." It also criticized the district's court appeal, saying it was making its case "without presenting any evidence of compliance and only partial, insufficient and uncorroborated evidence on the eradication of the vestiges of discrimination."

In one example, MALDEF underscored achievement gaps between Anglo and Latino students in Uvalde, along with unequal access to the gifted and talented program and advanced placement classes. It noted that 49 percent of students in advanced placement classes were Anglo, even though only 17 percent of its high school students were Anglo. Another example pointed to "the disparate treatment of disciplinary actions and disparate access to activities that 'encourage students toward higher academic levels in high school.'"

MALDEF found disparity in achievement levels between Latino and Anglo students and argued that the district did not meet state requirements for Latino students in math under the federal No Child Left Behind Act. The district, MALDEF argued in its brief, failed to make "meaningful progress toward becoming a fully integrated, non-discriminatory school with respect to all facets of its operations." In short, it argued successfully that "the district continues to struggle miserably in affording Latino students equal educational opportunities."

In June 2007 Uvalde schools again asked the appellate court to be removed from its supervision. By September 2008 the plaintiff—still Genoveva Morales—and her MALDEF attorney, David Hinojosa, reached a tentative agreement with the district. A consent order "memorialized" the settlement agreement, granting the district "dismissal in the areas of student assignments, nonfaculty staff, facilities, and transportation. The consent order also retains court supervision for a period of at least three years and provides specific remedies to further desegregate the district in the areas of bilingual education, faculty, gifted and talented, advanced placement and preadvanced placement, extracurricular and co-curricular activities, and student achievement." That three-year deadline was up in 2011.

Morales isn't convinced—not even a little bit—that the case will be shut. "On paper, the district may look good," or at least better, she said, but she knows otherwise. Segregation may be illegal, but discrimination and prejudice are alive and well in Uvalde. She points to the low number of Mexican Americans on the high school's top ten list year after year, in spite of its majority-minority status. "For the first time this past year, eight Mexican Americans made it to the top ten. Do you mean to tell me out of all those students, we're that dumb?" she asks rhetorically. "Do you think the court has been holding the case there because we have been lying all these forty-something years?"

Those who know her best say Morales went up against a whole town. A lesser person would have been intimidated, but she wasn't. Even after some Latinos agreed that she ought to stop fighting and quiet down, she didn't relent. Some criticized her and then came around when they felt a particular sting of injustice. Hopeful politicians have come around too, asking for an endorsement or a word of support on campaign material. "Still to this day, when something goes wrong, they call my mom," Father Morales said. "You have to come from a small town to understand."

Every new superintendent in the Uvalde Consolidated Independent School District gets a briefing on Morales when he or she arrives. She usually gives the new superintendent a little time to get adjusted before making her move. When she calls for an appointment, they respond in similar ways.

"They say, 'I've been expecting your call.'"

Zapatistas Indigenous peasant women from the southern Mexican state of Chiapas have helped lead the Zapatista movement for more than three decades, inspiring people worldwide with their courage. The movement stepped onto the stage on January 1, 1994, with a brief armed uprising; today it is more broadly known as a struggle for land and indigenous rights. Women have participated alongside men as insurgents, political leaders, healers, and educators. They have catalyzed dramatic changes in gender roles and continue to offer a vision of alternatives to global capitalism.

Zapatistas

HILARY KLEIN

> We are oppressed three times over, because we are
> poor, because we are indigenous, and because we
> are women.
>   Our struggle was clandestine when it first began.
> It was not easy. We couldn't organize, but then again
> we could. We had to walk from village to village to
> talk to different people and find others who felt the
> same pain as us, and the same courage to organize.[1]
> —COMANDANTA SANDRA

ON JANUARY 1, 1994, THE EJÉRCITO ZAPATISTA DE LIBERACIÓN NACIONAL
(Zapatista Army of National Liberation, or EZLN) captured the world's
imagination when it rose up to demand justice and democracy—taking
on the Mexican government and global capitalism itself. The EZLN is
named after Emiliano Zapata, a hero of the Mexican Revolution, and it
took up his rallying cry of *tierra y libertad* (land and freedom). From its
formation in 1983 until the 1994 uprising, the EZLN organized clan-
destinely, recruiting indigenous peasants throughout the mountains
and jungles of eastern Chiapas. Since its brief armed insurrection in
1994, the EZLN has been known primarily for its peaceful mobiliza-
tions, dialogue with civil society, and structures of political, economic,
and cultural autonomy.

People around the world have been inspired by Zapatista women: Major Ana María wearing a black ski mask and brown uniform, leading indigenous troops during the uprising; Comandanta Ramona standing next to Subcomandante Marcos during peace negotiations with the Mexican government, the top of her head barely reaching his shoulder; Comandanta Ester, draped in a white shawl with embroidered flowers, addressing the Mexican Congress to demand respect for indigenous rights and culture. The dignity with which these women carried themselves, set against a backdrop of centuries of racism and exploitation, embodies what the Zapatista movement has come to represent: the resistance of the marginalized and the forgotten against the powerful. Peasants turned warriors, mothers turned revolutionary leaders—dozens, hundreds, thousands of Zapatista women gather, tiny and dark-skinned, with red bandannas covering their faces and masking their individual identities, long black braids hanging down their backs, their fists in the air. They have marched, they have organized, and they have planted seeds—both real and symbolic. They have stood up to the Mexican army and to their own husbands. They have changed their own lives, and they have changed the world around them.

The indigenous communities that make up the EZLN have historically confronted extreme inequality: economic, because of the legacy of colonialism and the concentration of land and wealth in Chiapas; political, because of their exclusion from state, national, and local decision-making; and social, because of racism against indigenous people and the lack of basic services such as health care, education, electricity, and potable water. Women have also faced gender-based discrimination. In the words of Comandanta Ester, from a 2001 speech she gave in Mexico City's central plaza, "We are oppressed three times over, because we are poor, because we are indigenous, and because we are women."[2] This history of marginalization serves as a backdrop for the striking changes that have taken place in Zapatista territory.

Zapatista women have served as insurgents, political leaders, healers, educators, and key agents in autonomous economic development.

Their participation in the EZLN has helped shape the Zapatista movement, which has, in turn, opened new spaces for women and led to dramatic changes in their lives.

As the sun stretched across the sky on a warm June day in 2001, dozens of indigenous women arrived in the community of Morelia in eastern Chiapas. They came in twos and threes, each small group representing a different Zapatista village. Some had trudged for hours along dirt paths. Others stepped off a repurposed yellow school bus and shook the dust from their colorful aprons. Each woman came prepared to stay for several days, with a bundle of tostadas wrapped neatly in a clean cotton cloth.

Women sat on rough-hewn wooden benches in a large circle and shared stories of hardship as well as triumph—stories of clandestine meetings with the first women insurgents, of participating in marches and protests, and of the struggle to ban alcohol in their communities and the subsequent decrease in domestic violence. During an activity comparing their lives now and their lives before, they explained:

> Before 1994 there was no respect for women. Even our fathers told us we weren't worth anything. We didn't have the right to hold public responsibility. If we tried to speak up in the assemblies, the men made fun of us. They insulted us and said that women didn't know how to talk.
>
>   Thanks to our organization [the EZLN], we have opened our eyes and opened our hearts.[3] It was in the organization that they first began to tell us that how we were living was not right. We joined the struggle and that's when things started to change and we stopped being oppressed. Now we can participate in political work. In community and regional assemblies we participate side by side with the men. We have the right to hold any position within our organization. We also have the right to leave the house, to dance, to sing, to play sports, to go to a community party. Today there is hope and freedom in our lives. We have also found respect between men and women. Our struggle is our liberation because it gave us the courage to participate and defend our rights.[4]

Before the Zapatista uprising, women in the indigenous communities of Chiapas had limited control over their lives and many of the decisions that impacted them. They were often married against their will. With little access to birth control, it was common for women to have a dozen children or more. Domestic violence was generally considered normal and acceptable behavior, and a woman could not leave the house without her husband's permission. There was also a strict and gendered division between public and private spaces. Women's confinement to the private sphere translated into very limited participation in public life.

In the years just before and after the 1994 uprising, Zapatista women experienced social changes that often take generations to unfold. Women have established their right to decide whom to marry and when, and how many children to have. There has been a notable reduction in alcohol consumption and domestic violence. Women and girls have much greater access to health care and education, and women are exercising their right to participate in public affairs.

Isabel was one of the first women to join the EZLN. In 1984, when she was fourteen, she left home to join the rebel army. During the uprising ten years later, she led a battalion of troops as a captain. She stayed in the Zapatista army for another ten years and stepped down in 2003, having spent almost two decades as a Zapatista soldier and military leader. When I first met Isabel, she was still a military commander and quite an intimidating figure. Exuding a tremendous air of authority, she did not smile often or talk much. She was fairer skinned than most Zapatista women, and she wore her straight black hair shoulder-length and loose. When I interviewed her in 2008, she still wore pants and boots, and she still carried herself with the same air of authority, but she smiled more readily and spoke more openly.

> I was about eight or nine years old when I really began to think about my surroundings. I was already doing all [types of] a mother's work within my family. I began doing that work when I was very young because my mother is a peasant woman and she works in the fields. Since I'm the oldest daughter,

well, in our villages, a lot of responsibility falls on the shoulders of the oldest daughter. I was looking after my younger brothers and sisters, cleaning the house, and taking care of the animals.

I did very well in school with the government teacher. Everything he taught us awoke something in me, even though there were many things I didn't understand. I learned to read and write—just a little bit, not very well. But even as I began to develop more consciousness, and the sense that I wanted to better myself as a person, I had responsibilities in my family, and I had to work in the fields. I had to balance all three of these things.

I had to grow up very quickly because of the situation we lived in, the poverty, the lack of education. It was useful to study, but I felt the pressure of all the work I had to do and I couldn't be in school all day. My teacher told me that I was ahead, so I didn't have to be in class all day. "I'll put you in the higher-level class, and then you won't have to spend as many hours at school," he said. That way, I could spend more time working in the fields. Since we were the oldest, my brother and I had to plant corn or collect firewood or clear the weeds from the cornfield, far from our house. We would come home and then still go to school. I wanted to be with my teacher, to learn everything he could teach me, but there wasn't much time for that. I had to assume more responsibility at home and take care of my younger siblings.

When I was invited to join the organization, I said to myself, "I want to learn more, to move forward, but…" There's always a "but," right? You have to leave everything behind—your family, your work, community life, everything. You are taken out of that environment, away from all that. I was fourteen years old. I wanted to better myself as a person, but it was very painful. It was hard to leave all that behind. I accepted this change because I had seen the suffering of all the women around me: my mother, my sisters, my aunts, my grandmothers. I saw how unfair their lives were. So I thought to myself, "Why not now? At fourteen years old, why not commit myself to doing something for this organization called the EZLN?"

First I lived in the city for a while, in clandestine houses. I lived that way for a year. When I left my village, I went to the city. I dedicated myself to studying and learning. Why do these injustices exist? Why are there rich people and poor people? And what do we need to learn? My *compañeros* showed me, they taught me, they educated me.[5] I felt that I was beginning a new life, outside of the community, away from my family. But I found the strength because I had experienced so many injustices and the lack of opportunities within our communities and within our family life.

When I began to participate within the organization and I began a new type of education, that's when I was able to put the sadness aside, the pain of my community and my family, and I began to train and prepare myself to be responsible for all these revolutionary ideas. It was not easy to take on that responsibility. First, you have to live a clandestine life and that life closes you off in many ways.

It also depended on each one of us—how much we invested into developing our own revolutionary sensibilities. What helped me the most in living this life was to read books about other revolutionaries. The ones I liked the most were books about the Vietnam War. There are many stories of young combatants, people from villages like ours, who participated in something similar. And since I was living through a similar historical moment and at the same time in my life, those stories were very useful for me. We were the ones who had to train and prepare ourselves so that others could have a better life.

After a year of participating and studying with the *compañeros*, I had to make another decision: whether to stay in the city and continue learning about organizing and politics or go to the mountains. The EZLN had not been around for very long at that point, only about a year. It was founded in 1983, and I joined in 1984. I spent 1984 in the city and in 1985 I went to the mountains. And a new type of education—all over again! [*laughs*] But this time it was less about studying and more about learning to use weapons and the responsibility that accompanies that commitment. What came next were all the political-military lessons. That's where I landed, and I knew that's where I wanted to be and to spend my life. I began to participate, not only as a woman but also as a combatant.[6]

The intensive political education and organizing carried out by Zapatista women in the years before the uprising culminated in the Women's Revolutionary Law, a document that captured women's desire for equality and soon became a guiding framework for women's rights. Isabel, the Zapatista captain who joined the EZLN when she was fourteen, was one of the insurgent women who participated in this process.

We began to organize talks, not only with the women but with the whole community. There was a lot of work to do. First we had to explain the reason for an organization like this—in other words, educate and raise people's consciousness. But we always spoke to women about their rights and how to turn their right to participate into a reality when their husband or father still doesn't understand or doesn't see any reason to live life differently from how we're living it now. I think that was hard for men. [laughs] It was a big change, you know? To set aside what your parents, your grandparents, your great-grandparents had taught you about what it means to be a woman.

So yes, we began to have problems with the men. We told women they had rights and we analyzed with them how to make their rights into a reality. There are some men who can accept this and other men who ask themselves, "Will this change impact me? Will it change things for my wife or my daughter?" As we were doing this political, educational work, we entered a time period when women had begun to understand, to be more conscious and to make decisions, to participate more actively in the meetings, and that was how the Women's Revolutionary Law came to be.

But first we had to go through a long period when we—working as political representatives . . . we had to walk long distances with very little to eat, walk some more, talk some more, sacrifice. . . . And back then, the organization was not public, so we had to move under the cover of darkness, in the rain. It was not easy!

We gave women space to talk, to express their feelings and how they wanted to change all this: life in the family, with their husbands, with their children. That was where the ideas came from: if things are this bad, we asked ourselves, why not change it? Change men's ideas as well and find a way, as an organization, to turn these ideas into a law. And that's how the Women's Revolutionary Law was born: talking, venting, analyzing. It's not something from outside—it came from our own ideas, our experiences in our families and communities, with our parents, our husbands, our children.[7]

Isabel and the other women insurgents did not write this law. They attended meetings to help translate and coordinate, to gather ideas and demands from women throughout Zapatista territory. Each Zapatista region wrote a draft of the law, and the drafts were then compiled and sent back to each region to be reviewed—and then compiled again. In 1993 the Comité Clandestino Revolucionario Indígena (Clandestine Revolutionary Indigenous Committee, or CCRI), the EZLN's highest body of political leadership, passed the Women's Revolutionary Law. It was made public in 1994, soon after the Zapatista uprising. In a letter published in *La Jornada* in 1994, Subcomandante Marcos described the law's passage:

> In March 1993, the *compañeros* debated about what would later be the "Revolutionary Laws." Susana had been in charge of going around to dozens of communities to speak with groups of women and put together, from their thoughts, the "Women's Law." When the CCRI got together to vote on the laws, each one of the commissions got up: Justice, Agrarian Reform, War Taxes, Rights and Obligations of People in Struggle, and Women. Susana had to read the proposals that she had gathered from the ideas of thousands of indigenous women. She started to read and, as she read on, the assembly of the CCRI became more and more restless. You could hear murmurs and comments. In Chol, Tzotzil, Tojolobal, Mam, Zoque, and Spanish, the comments jumped from one side to the other. Susana, undisturbed, kept charging forward against everything and everyone: "We don't want to be forced into marriage with someone we don't want. We want to have the number of children we want and can care for. We want the right to hold positions of authority in the community. We want the right to speak up and for our opinions to be respected. We want the right to study and even be drivers."
>
> And she kept going until she was done. At the end there was a weighty silence. The Women's Laws that Susana had just read meant a true revolution for the indigenous communities. The women authorities were still receiving the translation, in their indigenous languages, of what Susana had said. The men looked at each other, nervous, restless. All of a sudden, almost at the

same time, the translators finished, and in a single movement, the women authorities began to applaud and talk among themselves. Needless to say, the Women's Laws were approved unanimously.

One of the Tzeltal men commented, "The good thing is that my wife doesn't understand Spanish, because otherwise..." A woman insurgent, Tzotzil and with the infantry rank of major, was on top of him: "You're screwed, because we're going to translate it into all the indigenous languages." The *compañero* looked down. The women authorities were singing, the men were scratching their heads. I prudently called a recess....

The EZLN's first uprising took place in March 1993 and was led by Zapatista women. There were no casualties, and they won.[8]

The text of the Women's Revolutionary Law, which created such a stir for Zapatista men and women, is as follows:

In the just fight for the liberation of our people, the EZLN incorporates women into the revolutionary struggle, regardless of their race, creed, color, or political affiliation, requiring only that they share the demands of the exploited people and that they commit to the laws and regulations of the revolution. In addition, taking into account the situation of women workers in Mexico, the revolution supports their just demands for equality and justice in the following Women's Revolutionary Law:

FIRST: Women, regardless of their race, creed, color, or political affiliation, have the right to participate in the revolutionary struggle in any way that their desire and capacity determine.

SECOND: Women have the right to work and receive a just salary.

THIRD: Women have the right to decide the number of children they will have and care for.

FOURTH: Women have the right to participate in community affairs and hold positions of authority if they are freely and democratically elected.

FIFTH: Women and their children have the right to primary care in matters of health and nutrition.

SIXTH: Women have the right to education.

SEVENTH: Women have the right to choose their partner, and to not be forced into marriage against their will.

EIGHTH: No woman shall be beaten or physically mistreated by family members or by strangers. Rape and attempted rape will be severely punished.

NINTH: Women will be able to occupy positions of leadership in the organization and hold military rank in the revolutionary armed forces.

TENTH: Women will have all the rights and obligations elaborated in the Revolutionary Laws and regulations.[9]

We saw the soldiers approaching and that's when the women started shouting, "We don't want the army here!" We didn't want the soldiers to go into our houses, to rape the women. All the women got together and we chased them out.[10]
—MARGARITA, A ZAPATISTA WOMAN FROM MORELIA

While the Mexican army has been ubiquitous in Chiapas since 1994, the low-intensity conflict escalated over the next several years. The first half of 1998 was a period of heightened state violence against Zapatista communities. From January to June, Mexican armed forces entered more than fifty Zapatista communities and "dismantled" three Zapatista autonomous municipalities. During these military offensives, carried out by federal soldiers or the *seguridad pública* (state police), hundreds of Zapatista civilians were beaten, arrested, and jailed; homes were illegally searched; municipal buildings were burned down; and property was destroyed and stolen.

In the face of this violence, women organized to confront the Mexican armed forces. Forming a barrier with their bodies, lines of women blocked soldiers from entering their communities, sometimes physically pushing them back, and sometimes armed with sticks or rocks. At countless protests and confrontations with the army, insults were hurled at the soldiers, the women's voices carrying the pent-up rage of four years of low-intensity conflict. Tiny indigenous women successfully drove heavily armed soldiers out of refugee camps, remote villages, and Zapatista strongholds. Faced with the women's fury and determination, the soldiers did not know how to respond. Many times, confused and startled, they turned on their heels and fled.

A small community high in the mountains, Galeana was likely singled out because it is a known Zapatista stronghold. To get there you have to navigate a steep, rocky walk into the mist, and it is hard to believe there is a village up there until you get to the peak, the last resting spot, and peer down into Galeana with its bright yellow adobe houses nestled in the mountains. I visited the village of Galeana for the first time not long after the confrontation with the soldiers. Visitors were rare, and children came running out of their houses to crowd around my colleague and me.

Everyone was eager to tell us how they chased the army out. They knew the soldiers were coming up the mountain path, they told us. They were angry at the carelessness with which the soldiers trampled their cornfields and ate their sugarcane. *"Nos cuesta mucho sudor"* (it was hard work), they said.[11] When the signal was given, they all rushed down the mountain to chase the soldiers away. They described in detail how big their sticks were and what they yelled: *"¡Fuera ejército! ¡No queremos dispensas!"* (Get out, army! We don't want your handouts!).

One of the women's favorite stories was about a soldier lying and saying he had been bitten by a snake when, in reality, another soldier had shot him in the foot. Several soldiers were hiding, they said, too frightened to come out. Another memorable story was about a panicked soldier who could not untangle his radio line from the bushes— he had to ask one of the Zapatista women to cut the cord so he could leave the radio behind. "We chased them all the way down to the road," the women said proudly.

It was, perhaps, a small victory in the ongoing battle between the EZLN and the Mexican government, but for the villagers in Galeana, it felt like a real success in the face of Mexican military might. News traveled quickly throughout the region, and other women referred to it as an example. Doña Manuela, a Tzeltal elder from La Garrucha, talked about the women from Galeana chasing out the soldiers, and her eyes sparkled as she spoke. Known for her sharp tongue, it is not always clear whether Doña Manuela's eyes are lit up with laughter or anger. "Those first days of January, we were ready," she said. "We even had our sticks ready. We were all prepared, all the women with our sticks, just like the women from Galeana." She stood up to demonstrate that the stick was almost as tall as her small body, with a sharp point carved on one end. She shook the stick as if at a soldier. "But they haven't come here," she concluded. "I think they were afraid."[12]

Like many Zapatista women, Celina spent her childhood on a *finca* but now lives in an all-Zapatista village and farms on reclaimed land.[13] One morning I accompanied her to her family's plot of land. We walked for more than an hour before arriving at her cornfield, climbing hills, crossing a hammock bridge, and passing through other fields on narrow dirt paths. As we walked, she recalled the hardships of her young life.

> My father worked very hard on that finca, and sometimes they paid him and sometimes they didn't. We didn't have corn, we didn't have beans. We didn't have coffee to drink because we didn't have anywhere to plant coffee. We did whatever we could to survive—we sold firewood, we sold charcoal. But I didn't think about all this until I was older. When I was younger, I thought that's just how things were.
>
> The EZLN arrived and told us that the government was oppressing us. They talked to us about land. There was never enough land for us—we only ever planted on the mountainside. No peasant or indigenous person ever farmed in the valley. So we started organizing—men and women. In the organization, they told us we should be working to organize other people.[14]

Despite having no formal education, Celina has held a number of different positions within the Zapatista movement, utilizing her natural ability to listen to others and to motivate them to act. "They had schools in some of the villages, but not on the fincas," she said. "That's why everyone who grew up on a finca—none of us know how to read or write." Recognizing her own leadership qualities, she often said ruefully that being illiterate was the only thing holding her back.

After several hours of hoeing weeds in her cornfield, we took refuge from the midday sun in the shade of a tree. Celina took a ball of ground corn out of her bag and, as she mixed it with water to make *pozol*,[15] she described one of the biggest transformations in her life—the changes that took place in her own family.

I used to think that only men have rights. I just did my work and was completely manipulated. I didn't know anything. I was always at home and I thought the only thing women were good for was working in the house. When the organization [the EZLN] arrived, we began to wake up. I began to realize that life doesn't have to be how I was living it. We heard that women can participate too. I already had children when I began thinking that the way we were living was wrong. I always thought things had to be that way, that's just how life was.

In my family, things have changed a lot. My husband is completely different. Before, he didn't want me to leave the house at all. He didn't respect me. If he didn't like something I said, he would mistreat me. But he's not like that anymore. As a woman, I learned to speak up. I learned to defend myself. Both of us have to change, that's what I realized back then. Men have to change, but so do women.

My husband worked with the organization, in the area of health care. Since they talked about women's rights there, he started to think about it, and he began to change. He allowed me to leave the house. He even encouraged me to learn too, so both of us would understand more. Sometimes I didn't want to go to meetings and he would say, "How will you learn if you don't go?" He encouraged me. It wasn't like that before.

There are men who hear this message but don't change their minds. But my *compañero* isn't like that. He changed quickly. When they chose me for the Women's Commission, he was away from home. But I accepted the responsibility and when he got back, he said, "If you already accepted, that's fine. You know what you're capable of." He always tells me, "Go as far as you can."

Zapatista women have fought tenaciously and have faced immense obstacles along the way. The young women who have grown up in the context of the Zapatista movement manifest the transformations that have taken place in Zapatista territory. Many young women are flourishing in the spaces opened for them by their grandmothers, mothers, aunts, and older sisters.

"As older women we feel happy," said Blanca Luz, a Zapatista woman in her fifties. "How could we not be happy when we see these changes, that our granddaughters have freedom in their lives?"[16] Eva, a Zapatista elder from the autonomous municipality Miguel Hidalgo, concurred, giving an example from her own family: "The children, they know. My granddaughter, when she was smaller I used to tell her, 'Come here, *mi hijita*, there's more work to do.' 'Ay, so much work, *abuelita*!' she would say. 'I'm a little girl, I should be free. Girls should be able to play.' That's what she used to tell me when she was about six. 'I have rights now, too, *abuelita*. Don't give me so much work!'"[17]

Zapatista women have a vision that extends far beyond their own communities. At the end of an interview with several Zapatista women, I asked if they wanted to add anything. Elida said, "I want to tell women around the world: 'Don't stop organizing, don't stop fighting, keep moving forward.'"[18] They all nodded, reflecting on the changes they had fought so hard to realize and expressing their desire to share this with other women. Comandanta Micaela leaned forward and said, "To all the other women who want to struggle, we want to tell you: We're with you."

EPILOGUE

NORMA ELIA CANTÚ

REVOLUTIONARY WOMEN OF TEXAS AND MEXICO IS A NECESSARY BOOK. It is necessary in our day and age because more than ever we must remember the past and celebrate the pathbreakers who forged a new way with their lives and actions. Revolutionary women are seldom recognized and acknowledged for the impact they have had on our culture and our communities. This erasure is one of the most compelling reasons for a book such as this. Many of the women profiled here are seldom recognized for their role as changemakers with a profound impact on our culture and communities. Understanding them is critical to understanding history and culture.

But the need for this book is different from the need for these stories. The individual stories carry wisdom and can be compelling, impactful guides for the younger generation. Many of the women in the book, for example, are no longer with us, but that doesn't mean we cannot learn from their stories. First we must acknowledge their legacy, but also we need their stories because they carry knowledge and transmit that knowledge to future generations. Because these women lived lives that mattered.

Each story is significant and contributes to our overall picture; each woman has power or signifies power in a different terrain and in a different panoramic view: literary, cultural, historical, political, educational, even the home front. For me, the most powerful stories, the stories I found most compelling, are those that reflect or resonate the layered history that we live in South Texas and northern Mexico. The women are not only revolutionary in their time but also in the places they inhabit. One such place is the borderlands. The U.S.–Mexico border between 1848 and 1911 is rife with women's actions and women's participation, acts that I would classify as revolutionary.

Before 1848 there was no border; the revolutionary women were Mejicanas. Sor Juana, Malintzín, Doña Josefa Ortiz de Domínguez, each in her own time and place acting in revolutionary ways, paved the way for feminists that would come later. The border divides politically; it is a geopolitical border, but the region remains one culturally, as cultural geographer Daniel Arreola claims. It is not until after World War II—a hundred years later—that the impact of that geopolitical border becomes more real. Until then, however violent it was, it remained relatively fluid with locals traveling back and forth with relative ease. At certain times, like around George Washington's birthday in Laredo, the border was open to all; *puente libre*, the open bridge, they called it. No one checked papers or collected fees.

At the Congreso Mexicanista, a gathering in September 1911, we see a surge of feminist foment led by women like Sara Estela Ramírez and Jovita Idár. It is no coincidence that the meeting happens at the border, in Laredo, Texas. The gathering lays the ground for some of the very revolutionary acts that culminate with the Movimiento Chicano.

The Texas–Mexico region, the borderlands, do not necessarily constitute a nationalist U.S. or a nationalist Mexican identity. The region, a unique cultural region with unique identity, has a language all its own. As we go through the Texas–Mexico region, there are many stories of violence—but there are also many stories of survival that are often ignored. So these essays are one way to resist that erasure and to underscore the role women have played in the survival of our culture, our stories. The women in this book have contributed to that recovery and preservation of our history.

All these women share characteristics, and not necessarily just discipline, although that is often a quality they possess. I would add tenacity and vision. They see a need to do something, and they go for it. They ask a question that hasn't been asked before and act on it. They arrive at the extraordinary through a process of reflection. It's not just knowledge acquisition; they also acquire wisdom and the gumption to go forward. All women possess the ability to go there, but not all have the wherewithal to get there. Whether it is because they are young and naive or because they're older and think, *Why not, I don't have anything to lose,* the fact is that to be revolutionary they have to act beyond the expected. They seek to find answers and to solve problems. They are also teachers who work with others, who try to get others to join the fight. In a sense, they are mentors and cultural revolutionaries.

The women profiled here have each gained revolutionary status due to their approach to life, their valor, their unique being. None of them set out to be revolutionaries—that is, they didn't have that as a life goal. But they did feel impelled to do what they must do, to take action. We can see in retrospect that often, in the midst of living their lives, they were indeed being revolutionary, but they did not see themselves as such. Others perceived them to be radical or outside the set patterns of behavior.

The women have agency. They act. Each uses her influence in a different terrain, in a different way. *Why would she even ask that?* It is one thing to ask critical questions but another to gain the courage to pursue an answer and subsequent action. That is characteristic of being revolutionary—moving curiosity or circumstance to question, and being moved to action. It requires persistence and tenacity but also following through in positive and sometimes negative ways to effect change.

These profiles present history in a broad cultural context, whereby each of these women, on some level, had superhero-like powers to see themselves in their everyday environment and manage to be extraordinary. Each found themselves in the context of their ordinary lives and arrived at an extraordinary drive to change things.

Dear reader, an epilogue is meant to give context and point forward. As you have read these chapters and gotten to know these revolutionary actors in our history, and even in our cultural reality, you may have wondered what is asked of you. Well, one possible next step is self-reflection. You may want to ask, How am I a revolutionary? In these dire times, how am I paying it forward? What in my world needs changing, and how am I adding to the narrative? How am I making a difference, adding my *granito de arena* to the incredible revolutionary moment we live in?

   ¡Adelante!

NOTES

Introduction

1. María Teresa Fernández Aceves, "La lucha por el sufragio femenino en Jalisco, 1910–1958," *Revista de estudios de género. La ventana* 2:19 (2004): 131–51.

2. There is a substantial, and growing, body of literature on women's activities and agency during the Mexican Revolution and afterward. For further reading, see Stephanie J. Smith, *Gender and the Mexican Revolution* (Chapel Hill, North Carolina, 2009); Jocelyn Olcott, Mary Kay Vaughan, and Gabriela Cano, eds., *Sex in Revolution: Gender, Politics, and Power in Modern Mexico* (Durham, North Carolina, 2006); and Gabriela Cano, "La Cruz Blanca Neutral y la Cruz Blanca Mexicana," in *Francisco I. Madero, a cien años de su muerte,* ed. Josefina MacGregor (Mexico City, 2013), 111–36.

3. Hannah Arendt, *On Revolution* (New York, 1963).

4. Karen Kampwirth, *Women and Guerrilla Movements: Nicaragua, El Salvador, Chiapas, Cuba* (University Park, Pennsylvania, 2002), 5. Kampwirth notes some recent exceptions.

5. Elizabeth Salas, *Soldaderas in the Mexican Military: Myth and History* (Austin, 1990).

6. Tabea Alexa Linhard, *Fearless Women in the Mexican Revolution and the Spanish Civil War* (Columbia, Missouri, 2005); and Eileen Mary Ford, "Women in Postrevolutionary Mexico: Politics, Culture, Identity, and the Body," *Journal of Women's History* 25, no. 3 (2013): 221–31.

7. Arendt's work on revolution addresses the French and American revolutions. She concludes that ultimately the French Revolution did not merit the term "revolution" because of its immediate failings, while the American Revolution was later a failure because the majority of citizens were still politically disenfranchised.

8. Ade Linhard, *Fearless Women*, 58. For more on this issue, see Mary Ann Tétrault, ed., *Women and Revolution in Africa, Asia, and the New World* (Columbia, South Carolina, 1994); Sahar F. Aziz, "Democracy, Like Revolution, Is Unattainable Without Women," U.S. Institute of Peace, Peace Brief 152, June 28, 2013; Adela Sloss, "Por Que en Muchos Hogares Latinos No Existe Verdadera Felicidad," *LULAC News*, March 1934, PSTC, BL.

9. Smith, *Gender and the Mexican Revolution*, 50–51.

10. Timothy Matovina, *Guadalupe and Her Faithful: Latino Catholics in San Antonio, from Colonial Origins to the Present* (Baltimore, 2005), 12–13.

11. Jeffrey M. Pilcher, *The Human Tradition in Mexico* (Lanham, Maryland, 2003), 83–84.

12. Mark Wasserman, *Everyday Life and Politics in Nineteenth-Century Mexico* (Albuquerque, 2000), 41–42.

13. Ibid., 84.

14. Luz Elena Galván Lafarga, "Teachers of Yesteryear: A Study of Women Educators During Porfiriato," in *Women and Teaching: Global Perspectives on the Feminization of a Profession*, ed. Regina Cortina and Sonsoles San Román (New York, 2006), 243–68.

15. Alan Knight, *The Mexican Revolution*, 2 vols. (Cambridge, 1986), 1:15 and 1:25.

16. Pedro Salmerón Sanginés, "Catolicismo social, mutualismo y revolución en Chihuahua," *Estudios de historia moderna y contemporánea de México* 35 (2008): 75–107. See also Stephen J. C. Andes and Julia G. Young, eds., *Local Church, Global Church: Catholic Activism in Latin America from Rerum Novarum to Vatican II* (Washington, 2016).

17. Moramay López-Alonso, *Measuring Up: A History of Living Standards in Mexico, 1850–1950* (Stanford, 2012), 46.

18. "Mexican Rebels Have Girl Leader," *Washington Herald*, August 18, 1911.

19. Robert McCaa, "Missing Millions: The Human Cost of the Mexican Revolution," University of Minnesota Population Center, 2001.

20. J. David Hacker, "Recounting the Dead," *New York Times*, September 20, 2011.

21. For further reading, see Matthew Butler, *Popular Piety and Political Identity in Mexico's Cristero Rebellion: Michoacán, 1927–1929* (Oxford, 2004).

22. María Henríques-Betancor, "Anzaldúa and 'The New Mestiza': A Chicana Dives into Collective Identity," *Language Value* 4, no. 2 (2012): 38–55.

Juana Belén Gutiérrez de Mendoza

1. The governor's office is located in the Palacio de Gobierno.

2. Chaz Bufe and Mitchell Cowen Verter, eds., *Dreams of Freedom: A Ricardo Flores Magón Reader* (Oakland, 2005).

3. Martha Eva Rocha, "The Faces of Rebellion," in *The Women's Revolution in Mexico, 1910–1953*, ed. Stephanie Mitchell and Patience A. Schell (Lanham, Maryland, 2007), 17.

4. Joel Bollinger Pouwels, *Political Journalism by Mexican Women During the Age of Revolution, 1876–1940* (Lewiston, New York, 2006), 35.

5. All historical writings on Juana refer to her as Juana Belén Gutiérrez de Mendoza, but this was not her given name. In baptismal documents I procured from the Catholic Church archives in San Juan del Río, Durango, her birth date is noted as January 27, 1875; she was baptized on February 2, 1875. Her given name reads María Juana Francisca Gutiérrez Chavez. The document's authentication can be proven through the parents' names listed (Santiago Gutiérrez and Porfiria Chavez), which are cited as her parents in all historical accounts I have read on Gutiérrez de Mendoza. She claims lineage to the Cax or Caxcan Indians through her writings from 1924 in ¡Por la tierra y por la raza!

6. The number of years that Juana attended school is not documented. At the time, many girls did not attend at all, so it would be difficult to even speculate on the level of education she received.

7. Ana Lau Jaiven, "La participación de las mujeres en la revolución mexicana: Juana Belén Gutiérrez de Mendoza (1875–1942)," *Diálogos Revista Electrónica de Historia* 5:1–2 (April 2005): 1–32.

8. Ibid.

9. Angeles Mendieta Alatorre, *Juana Belén Gutiérrez de Mendoza: Extraordinaria precursora de la revolución mexicana* (Mexico, D.F., 1983), 63.

10. Paul Garner, *Porfirio Díaz: Profile in Power* (New York, 2001), 125.

11. James D. Cockcroft, *Intellectual Precursors of the Mexican Revolution, 1900–1913* (Austin, 1968), 102.

12. Alatorre, *Juana Belén*, 16.

13. Ibid., 85. "Y el periódico se publicó con gran regocijo del impresor que en muy poco tiempo se había llevado todos mis ahorros. Cuando estos se hubieron concluido hice vender las cabras. ¡Mis cabras! Confieso que cuando llegó ese trance tuve el impulso de volverme a la montaña, un desesperado de abrazar a la 'Sancha', mi cabra favorita, de remontar a las cumbres, de ver el sol, aquel sol ardiente que reverberaba en la lomas y quemaba la frete. Sí, volver a la montaña."

14. Alicia Villaneda, *Justicia y libertad: Juana Belén Gutiérrez de Mendoza, 1875–1942* (Mexico, D.F., 1994), 129. "Antes de concluir, haremos una ligera aclaración. Nuestro periódico se ocupa de Ud. continuamente, y hemos llegado, ya ve Ud., hasta tenerle que dirigir nuestra voz directamente, esto haría suponer que venimos a combatirlo a Ud. únicamente, que es Ud. nuestro único objetivo, y esto sería perjudicial para nosotras, porque se nos confundiría con cualquier medianía raquítica de ésas que intrigan en el Palacio y la antesala por determinada personalidad; No, nuestros ideales valen algo más que un Porfirio Díaz y sí por el momento nos ocupamos de combatirlo."

15. Villaneda, *Justicia y libertad*, 17.

16. Alatorre, *Juana Belén*, 90–91.

17. The full speech can be found in Villaneda, *Justicia y libertad*, 19–22.

18. Alatorre, *Juana Belén*, 130–31.

19. "Que, ¿se figurará Porfirio Díaz que se muy humilde servidora Juana B. Gutiérrez de Mendoza quiere arrebatarle la montaña?"

20. Ibid., 137.

21. "Los cargos que hace el Sr. Bulnes a Don Profirío adulándolo, son los mismos que hacemos nosotras acusándolo."

22. Elisa assisted Juana with her newspapers and wrote several pieces. Little is known about her, however, beyond the few times she is mentioned in historical accounts.

23. Donna J. Guy, "Girls in Prison: The Role of the Buenos Aires Casa Correccional de Mujeres as an Institution for Child Rescue, 1890–1940," in *Crime and Punishment in Latin America: Law and Society Since Late Colonial Times*, ed. Ricardo D. Salvatore, Carlos A. Aguirre, and Gilbert M. Joseph (Durham, North Carolina, 2001), 369–90.

24. Ibid.

25. Villaneda, *Justicia y libertad*, 26.

26. Sara Estela Ramirez was a journalist and activist living in Laredo, Texas. For more on Ramirez, see Jessica Enoch, "*Para la Mujer*: Defining a Chicana Feminist Rhetoric at the Turn of the Century," *College English* 67 no. 1 (2004): 20–37.

27. Villaneda, *Justicia y libertad*, 27.

28. Ibid., 33.

29. Ibid., 39. "Cargos de interés colectivo, como son los que hacemos nosotras, ni se responden ni se destruyen con calumnias e insultos de carácter absolutamente personal, como pretende 'Regeneración'. Esos ultrajes y esas calumnias...no creo que le importe a nadie, ni menos creo que tales extravagancias tengan alguna relación con los intereses de la colectividad. Estos [los Flores Magón] son los patriotas, estos son los miembros de Junta Organizadora, estos son en fin los insultadores de mujeres que rugen de rabia y despecho porque hemos sido bastante dignas y amamos bastante a nuestra patria para no llevar sus desdichas al mercado, para no vender por una peseta sus infortunios."

30. Another issue that may have caused such a rift between the Flores Magón brothers and Juana was the death of compatriot, poet, and close friend Santiago de la Hoz. On March 20, 1904, he drowned in the Rio Grande in Brownsville, Texas. There were two accounts of what happened. Flores Magón told authorities that a strong current took de la Hoz, and Villaneda's account places blame on Ricardo Flores Magón for intentionally drowning de la Hoz. Juana accepted the second version and would never again see Flores Magón as an honorable man.

31. Ibid., 43.

32. Pouwels notes, in *Political Journalism* (69–70), that the newspaper *Anáhuac* had several connections with other revolutionaries. Gutiérrez de Mendoza cofounded the weekly with "José Edilberto Pinelo, who co-authored, with Jiménez y Muro, the 1911 Political and Social Plan signed by the Tacubaya conspirators. The 1907 editorial board of *Anáhuac* is listed on the front page of the January 1, 1907, issue. The officers included J. Edilberto Pinelo, Juana Gutiérrez, Elisa Acuña y Rosete, and several male representatives. The microfilm of this issue of *Anáhuac* is in the University of Texas at Austin's Benson Collection."

33. Ibid.

34. Ibid.

35. Ibid., 71.

36. Lau Jaiven, "La participación," 7.

37. Alatorre, *Juana Belén*, 147. "¿Para qué hacer elogios del hombre cuyos actos lo han dado a conocer como altamente digno de ocupar el puesto que se le designó? Para quien conozca la cobardía que tiene a la nación temblando ante el Gral. Díaz, basta con el solo hecho de que el Sr. Madero se haya puesto de pie ante ese poder que pretende someterlo todo, no porque sea un hecho extraordinario enfrentársele a un tirano que en último extremo pudiera bajar rodando por sí solo, sino porque en las actuales circunstancias, no es lo más difícil ponerse frente a Don Porfirio Díaz, como ciudadano con derechos a ejercitar, lo grave es ponerse al frente de este pueblo como ciudadano con derechos y deberes que cumplir."

38. John Lear, *Workers, Neighbors, and Citizens: The Revolution in Mexico City* (Lincoln, Nebraska, 2001), 131.

39. Ibid.

40. Ibid.

41. Enrique Krauze, *Mexico: Biography of Power: A History of Modern Mexico, 1810–1996*, trans. Hank Heifetz (New York, 1998), 225.

42. See Alan Knight, *The Mexican Revolution* (New York, 1986).

43. Eduardo Arrieta Corral, "Juana Belén Gutiérrez de Mendoza: Olvidada Heroína del periodismo político mexicano," in *Tres revolucionarios de México: Tomás Urbina, Orestes Pereyra, Juana Belén Gutiérrez* (Durango, Mexico, 1991), 15–16.

44. In Villaneda's *Justicia y libertad*, a personal letter to Madero, written on September 5, 1911, appears in her own handwriting, as well as in transcribed format (56–63). She recounted to Madero the events that led up to the capture of her son-in-law, Santiago Orozco. She asked him for his support in the matter, saying "Santiago's liberty is more important to me than my own life." He was later assassinated. Santiago Orozco would be one of several Santiagos that meant a great deal to her: her son, Santiago; her friend, Santiago de la Hoz; and her son-in-law, Santiago Orozco. They all died in her lifetime.

45. Alatorre, *Juana Belén*, 65.

46. Rocha, "The Faces of Rebellion."

47. Alatorre, *Juana Belén*, 65.

48. Villaneda, *Justicia y libertad*, 64. There is no evidence that Juana was involved in battle, but while she served as leader of the Victoria regiment, one of the members raped a woman, and upon Juana's orders the guilty member was killed as punishment. When word reached Zapata, many people thought he would not accept her actions, but he sanctioned her decision and coupled it with a decree that those who engaged in abuse against women should be severely punished.

49. The article title would in 1924 become the title for Juana's 119-page response to José Vasconcelos's *La raza cósmica*.

50. Juana Belén Gutiérrez de Mendoza, "¡Por la tierra y por la raza!," *El Desmonte*, June

15, 1919, 1, no. 1. "Antes que en un periódico ese lema fue escrito en una bandera de combate y rubricado con sangre, con la noble sangre de un soñador que en plena juventud cayó como caen los buenos, heridos por la espalda. Pero no murió con él su hermoso sueño de ver respetada la Tierra que él defendió de los que la envilecen vendiéndola y de los que la ultrajan apropiándola sin más derecho que el que les da el oro: no murió con él su generoso anhelo de ver dignificada la raza, su raza, esta raza que es una protesta contra la maldad humana. [...] El Desmonte sabrá sostener en alto la bandera recogida sobre el campo de batalla; El Desmonte sabrá llevar dignamente el lema de un soñador de esta raza."

51. Ibid. "Las revoluciones no se hacen con deseos, ni con discursos, ni con papel impreso; estos no son más que medios de insinuación, de orientación; recursos para llevar a los ánimos la decisión, el convencimiento...pero nada más. Medio de preparación muy útiles para ese objeto, pero completamente inútiles, absolutamente ineficaces cuando a eso se reduce todo."

52. Alatorre, *Juana Belén*, 149–50.

53. Diego Arenas Guzman, *El periodismo en la revolución mexicana* (Mexico, 1966), 222.

54. Pouwels, Political Journalism, 84.

55. Ibid.

Las Soldaderas

1. Palancares is the protagonist of Elena Poniatowska's 1969 novel *Hasta no verte Jesús mío*, based on the real-life story of Josefina Bórquez.

Adina De Zavala, Rena Maverick Green, and Emily Edwards

1. Luther Robert Ables, "The Work of Adina De Zavala" (master's thesis, University of Mexico City College, 1955), 1, 12, 131; Lewis F. Fisher, *Saving San Antonio: The Precarious Preservation of a Heritage* (Lubbock, 1996), 64. Her father first capitalized the "D" in De Zavala.

2. Fisher, *Saving San Antonio*, 47–52.

3. Adina De Zavala Papers, Briscoe Center for American History, University of Texas at Austin, quoted in Fisher, *Saving San Antonio*, 54–55.

4. Adina De Zavala to L. W. Kemp, undated letter in De Zavala Papers, University of Texas at Austin.

5. *San Antonio Express*, March 21, 1915, July 22, 1917.

6. Emily Edwards, oral history transcript in San Antonio Conservation Society files, 2–3.

7. Fisher, *Saving San Antonio*, 125–26, 128, 362.

8. Ibid., 148.

9. "Remarks by Mrs. Lane Taylor to San Antonio Conservation Society," December 5, 1955, in Conservation Society Library; Fisher, *Saving San Antonio*, 151.

10. Fisher, *Saving San Antonio*, 153.

11. "The Restored San José Mission Church Rededicated," April 18, 1937, program in Conservation Society Library; Fisher, *Saving San Antonio*, 166.

12. Rowena Green Fenstermaker and Mary Green in oral history transcripts, Conservation Society Library.

13. Fisher, *Saving San Antonio*, 363.

María Concepción Acevedo de la Llata

1. Conchita is listed as villain 95 in Sandra Molina, *101 vilanos de la historia de México* (Mexico City, 2014). As a heroine, her faith figures prominently in the "Corrido de Toral." Its date of composition is unknown, but it had been recorded by February 21, 1929.

2. The first version of her autobiography, which covered part of her adult life and concluded within two years of her imprisonment, was completed in 1931. It appeared as *Obregón: Memorias inéditas de la Madre Conchita*, edited and with an introduction by Armando de María y Campos (Mexico City, 1957). According to María y Campos, Conchita's memoirs were composed perhaps eight to ten pages at a time at the request of the prison warden, Francisco Múgica, who wanted to understand "the motives of that great political crime." Her initial attempts to publish them were unsuccessful. The second book is a revised and expanded version of the first, appearing as *Memorias de la madre Conchita* (Mexico City, 1962). The third book, more than six hundred pages long, is *Una mártir de México: La madre Conchita. Recuerdos históricos, escritos por ella misma* (Madrid, 1965). The fourth is *Yo, la Madre Conchita* (Mexico City, 1974). The publisher issued a slightly revised version in 1976 with the subtitle "La monja mártir de la Guerra Cristera" (Martyr Nun of the Cristero War). This essay primarily utilizes the 1957 work indicated above (hereafter, *Memorias inéditas*), and the 1976 revised edition of *Yo, la Madre Conchita: La monja mártir de la Guerra Cristera* (hereafter, *La monja mártir*). All translations are the author's.

3. Barbara Miller, "The Role of Women in the Mexican Cristero Rebellion: *Las Señoras y las Religiosas*," *Americas* 40, no. 3 (1984): 303–23, esp. 320.

4. *Memorias inéditas*, 224–28 [December 1931]. Conchita is referring to Leopoldo Ruíz y Flores, archbishop of Morelia from 1911 to 1937. Ruíz y Flores was appointed as the pope's official representative in Mexico to help broker peace between the Cristeros and the Mexican government. He served in that role from 1929 to 1937 but spent part of the Mexican Revolution and Cristero War in exile in the United States.

5. *Memorias inéditas*, 178–79 [May 1931]. In another book, she makes reference to her writing of a *diario* for her attorney and how she could not continue it once she had been moved to the prison at Mixcoac, where she remained from late August 1928 until just before the trial in early November. See *La monja mártir*, 61.

6. *La monja mártir*, 15.

7. "Ley de exclaustración de monjas y frailes," February 26, 1863. The order was directed primarily at nuns, whose secluded way of life Juárez considered to be contrary to the idea of liberty and the principles of the Republic of Mexico. Their perceived wealth and property,

too, was of interest, for the text of the law also declares that the state needs their "treasure" and that buildings such as hospitals and unoccupied properties can be utilized by poor families of those who served the *patria* against the invading French armies.

8. *Memorias inéditas*, 149.

9. *La monja mártir*, 17.

10. *Memorias inéditas*, 117. Early in her imprisonment, she recalled the difficulties of assuming control of Tlalpan, which was in a state of disarray upon her arrival. Decades later, her memory of those early days had softened.

11. Mario Ramírez Rancaño, *El asesinato de Álvaro Obregón: La conspiración y la madre Conchita* (Mexico City, 2014), 75–77.

12. By December 1927 or January 1928, Conchita's future husband had helped the community to find lodging in the town of Santa María la Ribera. *La monja mártir*, 34.

13. Ibid., 23–24.

14. "Ley que reforma el código penal para el distrito y territorios federales, sobre delitos del fuero común, y para la República sobre delitos contra la federación," in *Diario oficial* 37, no. 2 (July 2, 1926); David C. Bailey, *¡Viva Cristo Rey! The Cristero Rebellion and Church-State Conflict in Mexico* (Austin, 1974), 82.

15. Bailey, *¡Viva Cristo Rey!*, 82.

16. Robert H. Vinca, "The American Catholic Reaction to the Persecution of the Church in Mexico, 1926–1936," *Records of the American Catholic Historical Society of Philadelphia* 79 (1968): 3–38, esp. 15.

17. An overview of the coalition that became the LNDLR can be found in David Espinosa, *Jesuit Student Groups, the Universidad Iberoamericana, and Political Resistance in Mexico, 1913–1979* (Albuquerque, 2014). The U.S. Catholic hierarchy took great pains to distance itself from any direct support by the Knights of Columbus (real or perceived) on behalf of Mexican Catholics who were fighting the government, but it is likely that funds collected in the United States made their way to Cristeros in Mexico.

18. Jean Franco, *Plotting Women: Gender and Representation in Mexico* (New York, 1989), xiii, 19; *La monja mártir*, 34.

19. *La monja mártir*, 34.

20. *Memorias inéditas*, 144.

21. *La monja mártir*, 26.

22. Ibid., 39–40. Conchita uses the phrase *una tarjeta de la Mitra,* meaning "a card from the bishop."

23. Ibid., 25.

24. Ibid., 27–29. The chaplain and her spiritual adviser at that time was (Blessed) Father Félix de Jesús Rougier, a French-born Marist priest and founder of the Missionaries of the Holy Spirit. That congregation, in turn, led to the formation of three female congregations. His status as a foreign-born priest made him subject to either expulsion from Mexico or prison under federal law, and he did spend time in exile. (Félix de Jesús was inspired to found the Missionaries of the Holy Spirit by a woman named Conchita,

and some scholarship conflates the Venerable Concepción Cabrera de Armida with the Conchita of this essay.)

25. *La monja mártir*, 29.

26. In addition to Father Miguel Pro, three other men were also put to death at the same time: Miguel's brother Humberto, Luis Segura Vilchis (who had claimed responsibility and denied the involvement of the Pro brothers), and Juan Tirado Arias. Another brother, Roberto, was spared and exiled to Cuba with other members of the family.

27. *La monja mártir*, 33. Conchita and another nun from her community were permitted to assist with Father Pro's funeral mass.

28. Ibid., 33.

29. Conchita was accused of personally delivering consecrated hosts to a local jail for Catholic prisoners, which, by her own admission, she did by hiding them in a sugar bowl delivered with breakfast. A representative from the bishop decided, upon investigation, that action was to be taken against her. *La monja mártir*, 33–36.

30. Ibid., 40.

31. At one point during the trial, Toral showed jurors drawings of the many ways he had been tortured. Pablo Piccato, *A History of Infamy: Crime, Truth, and Justice in Mexico* (Berkeley, 2017), 50.

32. Jaymie Heilman, "The Demon Inside: Madre Conchita, Gender, and the Assassination of Obregón," *Mexican Studies / Estudios Mexicanos* 18 (2002): 23–60, esp. 27n7.

33. Conchita details Toral's injuries, and his obvious pain, in *La monja mártir*, 44.

34. Ibid., 45.

35. Ibid., 52. See also Heilman, "The Demon Inside," 39.

36. *La monja mártir*, 70. Conchita offers up a list of the words used to demean her by the state's prosecutors, including *crazy, possessed, heretical, delinquent, fanatical,* and many others.

37. *Memorias inéditas*, 93.

38. Piccato, *History of Infamy*, 45–50, esp. 50.

39. *La monja mártir*, 66.

40. Miller, "Role of Women," 320. Pope Pius XI had released her community from its vows in July 1928. *Memorias inéditas*, 91–93.

41. *Memorias inéditas*, 91–93.

42. *New York Times*, "Slayer of Obregón Impassive in Court," August 1, 1928, 1 and 5.

43. *La monja mártir*, 69.

44. Ibid., 107.

45. *Memorias inéditas*, 23.

46. Ibid., 40.

47. Kerstin Shands, Giulia Grillo Mikrut, Dipti R. Pattanaik, and Karen Ferreira-Meyers, "Introduction," in *Writing the Self: Essays on Autobiography and Autofiction* (Södertörn, Sweden, 2015), 7–28.

48. *La monja mártir*, 69. She quotes Pope Leo XIII, who said, "To write history one needs two things: not to lie and not to have fear of telling the truth."

Sor Juana Inés de la Cruz

1. There are two schools of thought regarding the actual year of Sor Juana's birth. Those who agree with Sor Juana's first biographer, the priest Diego de Calleja, that she was born on November 12, 1651, of whom Octavio Paz was originally a member, and those who are persuaded by the finding of a baptism certificate in a parish of Nepantla for one "Inés, hija de la Iglesia," who was baptized on December 2, 1648, by her godparents, Miguel Ramírez y Beatriz Ramírez (both names of Sor Juana's relatives). I combine the two schools by assigning November 12, 1648, as Sor Juana's birthday. Paz states that it is almost certain that the baptism certificate pertains to Sor Juana. Absent a similar certificate dated in 1651 for a "natural daughter" with Juana Inés's name and the name of her parents, the 1648 certificate seems the most definitive document of the year of her birth. See Octavio Paz, *Sor Juana Inés de la Cruz, o, las trampas de la fe* (Barcelona, 1982), 97. Hereafter cited as *Trampas*.

2. Margaret Sayers Peden, *A Woman of Genius: The Intellectual Autobiography of Sor Juana Inés de la Cruz*, translation of Sor Juana's "Respuesta a Sor Filotea de la Cruz," edited and introduced by Margaret Sayers Peden (Salisbury, Connecticut, 1982), 28. Hereafter cited as *Genius*.

3. Paz, *Trampas*, 99.

4. Criollos were the second most powerful caste in New Spain and consisted of the descendants of Spaniards born in the New World. The Spaniards themselves, those born on the peninsula of Spain (known as *peninsulares*), were the smallest demographic of New Spain, but the dominant, colonizer caste.

5. *Marisabia* was a compound word that combined two mutually exclusive identities, that of María, a generic name for a girl, and a *sabia*, or learned person. The term was mostly used pejoratively to denote a woman not behaving by the codes of her gender.

6. Peden, *Genius*, 30.

7. See Margarita López-Portillo, *Estampas de Sor Juana Inés de la Cruz* (Mexico, 1979), 57–65. Paz clarifies that Juana's grandfather had already introduced her to the texts of Homer, Ovid, and the like, as evidenced by an anthology of Latin poets in the grandfather's library, inscribed with his name and later, Juana's, as the book was passed down to her. See Paz, *Trampas*, 115–16.

8. Quoted in Paz, *Trampas*, 128.

9. Quoted in Octavio Paz, *Sor Juana, or the Traps of Faith*, trans. Margaret Sayers Peden (Cambridge, 1988), 98. Hereinafter cited as *Traps*.

10. Paz, *Trampas*, 168. "If the rules were strict, practices were lax" (translated by the author).

11. Paz, *Traps*, 99.

12. A letter detailing the transfer of property from mother to daughter for a mulatta woman named Juana de San José is also dated 1669. See Enrique A. Cervantes, *El testamento de Sor Juana y otros documentos* (Mexico, 1949). I translate portions of that letter in my novel. "Because she has immediate need of someone to attend and serve her, I make this complete and irrevocable donation for life to my daughter, Juana Ramírez de Asbaje, of this *mulata*, who is sixteen years of age [more or less]…born and raised in my house, daughter of Francesca de Jesús, also my own slave. By this letter I cede, renounce, and transfer all of my right, action, property, and ownership of said *mulata*; so that, from this day forward, my daughter may make use of her in any way she will, selling her, donating her, or transferring her without the convent or its management impeding it in any way, and even less, assuming any right over her." Alicia Gaspar de Alba, *Sor Juana's Second Dream* (Albuquerque, 1999), 73.

13. See "Petición que en forma causídica presenta al Tribunal Divino la Madre Juana Inés de la Cruz, por impetrar perdón de mis culpas," in *Fama y obras pósthumas del fénix de México, décima musa y poetisa Americana, Sor Juana Inés de la Cruz* (Madrid, 1700), 129–31.

14. Peden, *Genius*, 30.

15. Paz, *Trampas*, 190.

16. Ibid., 217.

17. Ibid.

18. In fact, in Judith Brown's hagiography *Immodest Acts: The Life of a Lesbian Nun in Renaissance Italy* (New York, 1986), we learn of one of the first documented cases of a lesbian nun, in this case a fifteenth-century Italian abbess named Benedetta Carlini. Benedetta's relationship with Bartolomea, another nun, was unwittingly discovered in a Church investigation of Benedetta's supposed mystical visions.

19. See the 2017 Netflix series *Juana Inés*, which depicted a highly erotic relationship between Sor Juana and her Divina Lysi, her endearment for la Condesa.

20. Paz, *Traps*, 111.

21. Peden, *Genius*, 42.

22. Paz, *Traps*, 217.

23. See *Fama y obras*, 126.

24. Sor Juana Inés de la Cruz, "Quéjase de la suerte: insinúa su aversión a los vicios, y justifica su divertimiento a las Musas," in *Sor Juana Inés de la Cruz: Poems, Protest, and a Dream*, trans. Margaret Sayers Peden (New York, 1997), 170. The translation of the poem's first four lines is the author's.

25. Alicia Gaspar de Alba, *[Un]Framing the "Bad Woman": Sor Juana, Malinche, Coyolxauhqui, and Other Rebels with a Cause* (Austin, 2014), 19.

26. Dorothy Schons, "First Feminist in the New World," *Equal Rights*, October 31, 1925, 11–12.

Jane McManus Storm Cazneau

1. Henry Watterson in Edward S. Wallace, *Destiny and Glory* (New York, 1957), 251; Joseph Frasier Wall, *Henry Watterson: Reconstructed Rebel* (New York, 1956), 24–25. Watterson, who received the first Pulitzer Prize for editorial writing, credited Jane with writing the Treaty of Guadalupe Hidalgo.

2. Linda S. Hudson, *Mistress of Manifest Destiny: A Biography of Jane McManus Storm* (Austin, 2001), appendix A, bibliography; most authors use "Storms" rather than "Storm." See Tom Reilly, "Jane McManus Storms: Letters from the Mexican War, 1846–1848," *Southwestern Historical Quarterly* 85 (July 1975): 230–45; Patricia Kinkade, "Jane McManus Storms Cazneau," in *Essays in History: The E. C. Barksdale Student Lectures* (Arlington, Texas, 1987–88); Anna Kasten Nelson, "Jane Storms Cazneau," 25–40; Robert E. May, "Plenipotentiary in Petticoats: Jane M. Cazneau and American Foreign Policy in the Mid-Nineteenth Century," in *Women and American Foreign Policy*, 2nd ed., ed. Edward L. Crapol (Wilmington, Delaware, 1992), 19–44; Robert E. May, "Lobbyists for Commercial Empire: Jane Cazneau, William Cazneau, and U.S. Caribbean Policy, 1846–1878," *Pacific Historical Review* 48 (1979): 383–90; William W. Freehling, *The Reintegration of American History: Slavery and the Civil War* (New York, 1994), 138–57.

3. May, "Lobbyists for Commercial Empire," 387–90, 393–412; May, "Plenipotentiary," 19, 39; Reilly, "Jane McManus Storms," 21–44; Peggy M. Cashion, "Women in the Mexican War, 1846–1848" (unpublished MA thesis, University of Texas at Arlington, 1990), 75–80; Kinkade, "Jane Cazneau," 7–34.

4. Doris R. Sheridan, *The McManus Family* (Troy, New York, 1993), 4–6, 23–24; "Lawyers of the Day," *Troy Daily Times*, November 18, 1880; "Convention of the People at Sandlake," *Troy Sentinel*, October 19, 1824; "People's Ticket," *Troy Sentinel*, October 29, 1824; "Mr. McManus," *Troy Budget and City Register*, January 10, 1826; *Biographical Directory of U.S. Congress, 1774–1989* (Washington, 1989), 1480.

5. Sheridan, *McManus Family*, 14; "Married," *Troy Sentinel*, August 23, 1825; Amos Eaton, Account Book, 1834–1844, Amos Eaton Papers, drawer 10685, box 3, Manuscript Section, New York State Library, Albany; Anthony Dey Galveston Bay and Texas Land Company Records, box 2, fol. 28, box 4, fols. 80–82, 88, 90, Western Americana Collection, Beinecke Rare Book and Manuscript Library, Yale University, New Haven, Connecticut; Burr to Judge Workman, November 16, 1832, Burr to McManus, November 17, 1832, Papers of Aaron Burr, New York Historical Society Library, New York. Tim Mabee owns the portrait and believes the artist was Ralph Earl of Albany, New York (letter to author, March 1, 2002).

6. J. McManus to Col. Burr, n.d., Eliza Jumel Papers, New York Historical Society Library, New York; Jane McManus to Justus Morton, $250, October 2, 1833, Deed Records, Matagorda County Court House, Bay City, Texas, Book A, 92–93; Matagorda County Historical Commission, *Historic Matagorda County*, 3 vols. (Houston, 1986), 1:33; Gilbert Giddings Benjamin, *Germans in Texas* (Philadelphia, 1909), 15–22. The identity of the

German indentures is unknown, but George Erath and the Biegel, Dietrich, and Ehllinger families came in 1833; J. M. Storm to M. B. Lamar, October 1845, No. 2195, Papers of Mirabeau Buonaparte Lamar, Archives and Records Division, Texas State Library, Austin; Spanish Collection, box 23, fol. 23, Archives and Records Division, Texas General Land Office, Austin; Villamae Williams, ed., *Stephen F. Austin's Register of Families* (Baltimore, 1984), Appendix, R-2. March 17, 1835, No. 2 and 3, Carancahua E. side, 1 League No. 6 deeded to Newell, 1 League No. 5, Kellers Bayou, 1 League No. 29 Prairy Creek, 1 League No. 22 Trespalacios, 1 League No. 20 Trespalacios, 1 Next west to Gulf, 1 League, No. 25 if not deeded for No. 6; Jane McManus to S. M. Williams, June 19, 1835, Samuel May Williams Papers, Galveston and Texas History Center, Rosenberg Library, Galveston.

7. Marion Tinling, *Women Remembered: A Guide to Landmarks of Women's History in the United States* (New York, 1986), 273; Gifford White, ed., *The 1840 Census of the Republic of Texas* (Austin, 1966), 103; *Galveston Semi-Weekly Journal*, February 2, 1852; R. O. W. McManus, GLO. Claims fols. 1-000231 09; 1-000297 10; 1-001397 01; B-000195 08; B-001600 01; C-005593 00; Anon. [Jane Cazneau], "Lady Hester Stanhope," *U.S. Magazine and Democratic Review* 13 (November 1843): 540–41; "Aleppo," *Our Times: A Monthly Review of Politics, Literature, Etc.,* ed. Cora Montgomery (October 1852), 114, 168; Anon. [Jane Cazneau] "Free Trade," *USDR* 9 (October 1841): 329–42; Anon. [Jane Cazneau], "Hurrah for a War with England," *USDR* 9 (November 1841): 411–15.

8. Anon. [Jane Cazneau], "The Texas Question," *USDR* 14 (April 1844): 423–27; *New York Sun*, October 17, 19, 22, 1844, March 3, 1845; C. Montgomery, "The Presidents of Texas," *USDR* 16 (Mar 1845), 282–91; Corinne Montgomery, *Texas and Her Presidents* (New York, 1845); Sam Houston to Margaret, November 10, 1845, private collection, copy furnished by descendant Madge T. Roberts, San Antonio, Texas.

9. "The Female Industrial Association," *New York Sun*, March 6, 10, 14, May 1, 1845; "Meeting of Female Industry Association," *New York Workingman's Advocate*, March 8, 22, 1845; "Women of the Nineteenth Century," *New York Sun*, July 29, 1845.

10. Julius Pratt, "The Origin of 'Manifest Destiny,'" *American Historical Review* 32 (July 1927): 795–98; "Speech of Mr. R. W. Winthrop of Mass. in H. R.," January 3, 1846, *Congressional Globe*, 29th Congress, 1st Session, appendix, 99; Wall, *Henry Watterson*, 25; Robert Dean Sampson, "'Under the Banner of the Democratic Principle': John Louis O'Sullivan, the Democracy, and the *Democratic Review*" (PhD diss, University of Illinois, 1995), 3, 159; Statistics, "Grammatik," Word Perfect, v 6.1, Novell Inc., Orem, Utah; John L. O'Sullivan, "Seeing a Friend off in a Packet," *USDR* 16 (July–Aug. 1845), 23; Anon. [Jane Cazneau], "Annexation," *USDR* 16 (July–August 1845): 8; Montgomery, "Presidents of Texas," 282; Montgomery, "Correspondence," *New York Sun*, April 3, July 11, 22, August 5, 22, 26, 1845; Storms to Lamar, n.d. October 1845, Lamar Papers, Texas State Library, Austin.

11. Anon. [Jane Cazneau], "The Mexican Question," *USDR* 16 (May 1845): 419–28; Montgomery, "Correspondence," *Sun*, March 2, 3, 17, 30, 1846; Storm to Lamar, March 27, 1846, Lamar Papers; May, "Lobbyists for Commercial Empire," 386; M. S. Beach, "A Secret Mission to Mexico," *Scribner's Monthly Century Magazine* 18 (May 1879): 136–40; Justin H.

Smith, *The War with Mexico* (New York, 1919), 11–13; Wallace, *Destiny and Glory*, 245–75; Frederick Merk, *Manifest Destiny and Mission in American History* (New York, 1963), 132–34, 167, 200n–201n; Seymour V. Connor, *Adventure in Glory* (Austin, 1965), 89; William H. Goetzmann, *When the Eagle Screamed: The Romantic Horizon in American Diplomacy, 1800–1860* (New York, 1966), 68–71; Seymour V. Connor and Odie B. Faulk, eds., *North America Divided: The Mexican War, 1846–1848* (New York, 1971), 156–57; Anna Kasten Nelson, "Mission to Mexico—Moses Y. Beach, Secret Agent," *New York Historical Society Quarterly* 59 (July 1975): 227–45; Anna Kasten Nelson, "Jane Storm Cazneau: Disciple of Manifest Destiny," *Prologue: The Journal of the National Archives* 17 (Spring 1986): 25–40; Anna Kasten Nelson, "Moses Y. Beach: Special Agent," in Robert E. Burke and Frank Freidel, eds., *Secret Agents: President Polk and the Search for Peace with Mexico* (New York, 1988), 72–96; Montgomery, "Correspondence," *New York Sun*, December 1, 1846, to May 29, 1847.

12. Reilly, "Jane McManus Storms," 21–44; Kinkade, "Jane McManus Cazneau," 7–34; Cashion, "Women in the Mexican War," 75–80; *Report of the Committee Appointed to Investigate the Affairs of the Plainfield Bank* (Trenton, New Jersey, 1847), 16.

13. May, "Plenipotentiary," 19–44.

14. Thomas Hart Benton, *Thirty Years' View; or, A History of the Working of the American Government for Thirty Years, from 1820 to 1850*, 2 vols. (New York, 1854–56; reprint, New York, 1968), 2:704.

15. Cora Montgomery, *La Verdad*, January 9, 1848, to June 17, 1848; J. M. Storm to M. S. Beach, February 20, 1849, January 8, 1850, Jane McManus Storm Cazneau Papers, New York Historical Society Library, New York. Copies, originals property of Brewster Y. Beach, Greenwich, Connecticut; Anon. [Jane Cazneau], "The King of Rivers," *U.S. Magazine and Democratic Review* 25 (December 1849): 506–15; Cora Montgomery, *The King of Rivers* (New York, 1850); Cora Montgomery, *The Queen of Islands, and the King of Rivers* (New York, 1850); J. M. Storm to James K. Polk, August 26, 1847, January 4, 1849, Polk Papers, National Archives; J. M. Storm to George Bancroft, January n.d., June 20, October 20, 1848, Bancroft Papers, Massachusetts Historical Society; J. M. Storm to James Buchanan, August 24, November n.d., December 12, 1847, February 18, July 24, 1848, January 18, 1853, November 14, 1857, June 5, 1858, Buchanan Papers, Historical Society of Pennsylvania; J. M. Cazneau to Mr. Wood, November 1, 1850, Cazneau Papers, New-York Historical Society (hereafter NYHS); J. M. Storm to William H. Seward, September 27, 1849, J. M. Cazneau to William H. Seward, December 10, 1849, William Henry Seward Papers, Rare Books, Special Collections, and Preservation, River Campus Libraries, University of Rochester, Rochester, New York (hereafter UR).

16. Cora Montgomery, "The Union of the Seas," *Merchant's Magazine* 12 (February 1850): 145–54; Joseph W. Fabens [Jane Cazneau], *The Camel Hunt* (Boston, 1851), 5–16, 28–48; Joseph W. Fabens [Jane Cazneau], *A Story of Life on the Isthmus* (New York, 1853); Wallace, *Destiny and Glory*, 267–68. In some bibliographies, Fabens is listed as author of Cazneau's books.; Anon. [Jane Cazneau], *In the Tropics: By a Settler in Santo Domingo* (New York, 1863); Cora Montgomery [Jane Cazneau], *The Prince of Kashna; A West Indies Story*

(New York, 1866); Jane Cazneau [Joseph Fabens], "The Uses of the Camel: Considered with a View to His Introduction into our Western States and Territories," paper read before American Geographical and Statistical Society, March 2, 1865 (New York, 1865); Joseph W. Fabens, *Facts about Santo Domingo* (New York, 1862); Joseph W. Fabens, *Resources of Santo Domingo* (New York, 1863, Washington, 1869, 1871); "Joseph Warren Fabens," *National Cyclopedia of American Biography*, 10 vols. (New York, 1897). Fabens was born in Salem, Massachusetts, and entered Harvard University in 1838 but dropped out. In 1843 he became U.S. consul at Cayenne, French Guiana, where he tended his father's interests. He had been a colonel in the Republic of Texas Army and met Cazneau through Henry Kinney; J. M. Cazneau to Moses Y. Beach, December 27, 1849, Cazneau Papers, NYHS; Cora Montgomery, "Peon Slavery on the Rio Grande, Eagle Pass," May 21, 1850; "American Citizens Enslaved," December 14, 1850, February 1, 1851; "A New Class of Slave States," January 18, 1851; "Enslaving American Citizens in Mexico," January 28, March 6, 1851; "Three Forms of Servitude on the Border," December 1, 1850, January 16, February 1, March 6, 8, July 15, August 2, October 17, 1851, *New York Tribune*; J. M. Cazneau to W. H. Seward, Eagle Pass, June 18, December 30, 1850; January 16, June 3, 1851, Washington, Seward Papers, UR; Cora Montgomery, *Eagle Pass, or Life on the Border* (New York, 1852).

17. Cazneau, *Eagle Pass*, 72–77, 143–47; Seventh Census of the United States, 1850, Schedule I (Free Inhabitants) Texas, Bexar County; Rosalie Schwartz, *Across the Rio to Freedom: U.S. Negroes in Mexico* (El Paso, 1975), 39; Kenneth Wiggins Porter, "The Seminole Negro-Indian Scouts," *Southwestern Historical Quarterly* 55 (January 1952): 358–60; "José María Carbajal" and "Republic of the Rio Grande," in *The New Handbook of Texas*, ed. Ronnie C. Tyler (Austin, 1996); Ernest C. Shearer, "The Carvajal Disturbances," *Southwestern Historical Quarterly* 55 (October 1951): 204–17. Seventy U.S. troops served under Captain James Todd; Colonels John Ford, Robert Wheat, and Cabasco; Majors Gonzales, McMicken, Everitt, and Andrew Walker; Captains Norton, Howell, Edmonson, Brown, and Garcia.

18. "Texan Santa Fe Expedition," in *The New Handbook of Texas*; Mexican Claims, U.S. Senate Executive Document 31, 44th Congress, 2nd Session, 24–25, 113, 131; "W. L. Cazneau," U.S. Senate Executive Document 1720, Mexican Claims, 120; U.S. Senate Executive Document 31, 44th Congress, 2nd Session, claim denied.

19. W. L. Marcy to W. L. Cazneau, November 2, 1853, Records of U.S. Department of State, Record Group 59, Special Missions, M37, National Archives, Washington, D.C.; May, "Lobbyists for Commercial Empire," 392.

20. William O. Scroggs, *Filibusters and Financiers: The Story of William Walker and His Associates* (New York, 1916), 77; J. M. Cazneau to J. M. Black, November 6, 1860, Jeremiah S. Black Papers, Library of Congress, Washington, D.C.; Ernest N. Paolina, *The Foundations of the American Empire* (Ithaca, New York, 1973), xi, 25–28; William H. Seward to W. L. Cazneau, March 11, 1861; J. M. Cazneau, account instructions, April 7, 1859, drawn on Department of State; July 1, 1861, $1,300; J. M. Cazneau, July 1, 1861, $752; office and travel, August 20, 1861, Special Missions, M37, NA.

21. J. M. Cazneau to Moses Y. Beach, January 8, 1850, Cazneau Papers, NYHS; "The Impossibility of Secession," *New York Sun*, January 2, 1861; "Letter from Dominica," *New York Sun*, February 15, 1861; "Plucking the Fat Geese," *New York Sun*, February 26, 1861; "The Struggle," *New York Sun*, February 27, 1861; "How a Southern Government Is Made," *New York Sun*, March 19, 1861; "Discontent in Alabama," *New York Sun*, March 21, 1861; "The Secession Troubles," *New York Sun*, March 26, 1861.

22. W. L. Cazneau to W. H. Seward, March 23, May 13, June 28, 1861, Special Missions, M37, National Archives; "Important from the West Indies," *New York Sun*, March 30, 1861; "The Civil War" and "The Confederate Traitors," *New York Sun*, April 15, 1861; "We Think Nothing at Present Warrants a Revolution" and "The Line Is Drawn," *New York Sun*, May 4, 1861; "More Prizes Captured," *New York Sun*, June 8, 1861; "The Object of the Conspiracy," *New York Sun*, June 11, 1861; "M. S. Beach, Editor and Sole Proprietor of the *Sun*, Shall Do Its Duty in Quelling the Unnatural Rebellion," *New York Sun*, January 1, 1862; W. L. Cazneau to W. H. Seward, August 23, 1861, Special Missions, M37, National Archives.

23. Cazneau, *Facts*; Montgomery, *Texas and Her Presidents*; J. M. Cazneau to M. S. Beach, Private, April 24, June 2, 1862, Cazneau Papers, NYHS; "Slaves Contraband of War," *New York Sun*, May 28, 1861; Philip S. Foner, *Business and Slavery: The New York Merchants and the Irrepressible Conflict* (Chapel Hill, North Carolina, 1941), 160, 200–216, 237; Louis Dow Scisco, *Political Nativism in New York State* (New York, 1901), 58, 227; Basil Leo Lee, *Discontent in New York City 1861–1865* (Washington, D.C., 1943), 103, 137–45, 163–74, 181; Charles S. Wesley, "Lincoln's Plan for Colonizing the Emancipated Negro," *Journal of Negro History* 4 (January 1919): 7–13; Floyd J. Miller, *The Search for a Black Nationality: Black Emigration and Colonization, 1787–1863* (Urbana, Illinois, 1975), 101, 114, 239, 149–51; Frederick Douglass, *Speeches, Debates, and Interviews*, vol. 4 of *Frederick Douglass Papers*, ed. John W. Blassingame and John R. McKinney (New Haven, Connecticut, 1991) 4:500.

24. J. M. Cazneau to M. S. Beach, June 6, September 24, October 7, 1862, Cazneau Papers, NYHS; Charles Callan Tansill, *The United States and Santo Domingo, 1798–1873* (Baltimore, 1938) 216–19, 225–27; Foner, *Business and Slavery*, 22, 271, 308–11; Frederick Bancroft, *The Life of Seward*, 2 vols. (New York, 1900), 2:345–47; P. J. Slaudenraus, *The African Colonization Movement, 1816–1865* (New York, 1961), 245–47; Sumner Welles, *Naboth's Vineyard: The Dominican Republic, 1844–1924*, 2 vols. (New York, 1928), 1:317; James M. McPherson, *The Struggle for Equality: Abolitionists and the Negro in the Civil War and Reconstruction* (Princeton, 1964), 154–56; Wesley, "Lincoln's Plan," 7–21; John M. Taylor, *William Henry Seward* (New York, 1991), 190–91. Kock took one hundred dollars provided for each settler and tainted others in the movement.

25. Lee, "Discontent," ix, 10, 47, 59, 82–90; McPherson, *Struggle*, 231–33; Williston Lofton, "Northern Labor and the Negro during the Civil War," *Journal of Negro History* 34 (July 1949): 251–73; Merline Pitre, "Frederick Douglass and the Annexation of Santo Domingo," *Journal of Negro History* 62 (October 1977): 390–400; Cazneau, *In the Tropics*; Cazneau, *Prince of Kashna*, preface; "Richard Kimball," *National Cyclopedia*; Tansill, *United*

States and Santo Domingo, 1:216–19; George M. Frederickson, *The Black Image in the White Mind: The Debate on Afro-American Character and Destiny, 1817–1914* (Middletown, Connecticut, 1971), 92–93, 138–39.

26. Cazneau, *In the Tropics*; Cazneau, *Prince of Kashna*; Tansill, *United States and Santo Domingo*, 1:216–19.

27. Tansill, *United States and Santo Domingo*, 1:216–19, 383; (Cora Montgomery), *Eagle Pass*; Protest of William Cazneau, October 25, 1863, with William G. W. Jaeger to William H. Seward, December 27, 1863, Dispatches from U.S. Consuls in Santo Domingo, T56, Department of State, RG59, National Archives; J. M. Cazneau to Dear Sir [Andrew Johnson], April 9, 1866, Seward Papers, UR. Mrs. Cazneau praised Lincoln's agent Jaeger.

28. Philip Sherlock, *This Is Jamaica* (London, 1968), 94; Peter Abrahams, *Jamaica: An Island Mosaic* (London, 1957), 95–96; Cazneau, *Prince of Kashna*, v, vi.

29. William Javier Nelson, *Almost a Territory: America's Attempt to Annex the Dominican Republic* (Newark, New Jersey, 1990), 49n56; Tansill, United States and *Santo Domingo*, 1:222–25; Walter R. Herrick Jr., *The American Naval Revolution* (Baton Rouge, 1966), 13; Gerald E. Poyo, "Evolution of Cuban Expansionist Thought in the Emigré Communities of the U.S., 1848–1895," *Hispanic American Historical Review* 66 (August 1986): 494–95.

30. J. M. Cazneau to M. S. Beach, August 25, 1865, Cazneau Papers, NYHS; J. M. Cazneau to James Harlan (Secretary of the Interior), September 6, 1865, Seward Papers, UR; Tansill, *United States and Santo Domingo*, 1:225.

31. Tansill, *United States and Santo Domingo*, 1:225–26; Welles, *Naboth's Vineyard*, 1:316–17; Major L. Wilson, "The Repressible Conflict: Seward's Concept of Progress and the Free Soil Movement," *Journal of Southern History* 37 (November 1971): 533, 541–42, 548; Robert W. Van Alstyne, *The Rising American Empire* (New York, 1960), 100, 146; Basil Rauch, *American Interest in Cuba, 1848–1855* (New York, 1948), 249; J. M. Cazneau to Dear Sir [Andrew Johnson], April 9, 1866, Seward Papers, UR.

32. Welles, *Naboth's Vineyard*, 1:319–20; Tansill, *United States and Santo Domingo*, 228–41; J. M. Cazneau to Dear Sir [Andrew Johnson], April 9, 1866, Seward Papers, UR; Alan Nevins, *Hamilton Fish: The Inner Workings of the Grant Administration*, 2 vols. (New York, 1936), 1:255.

33. Welles, *Naboth's Vineyard*, 1:236, 345–46, 265–66; William L. Cazneau, *To the American Press: The Dominican Negotiations* (Santo Domingo, 1870), 17–18, 20; Mrs. William L. Cazneau, *Our Winter Eden: Pen Pictures of the Tropics* (New York, 1878), 127–30; Nevins, *Hamilton Fish*, 1:255, 260–66; "William L. Halsey," "Ben Holladay," "S. L. M. Barlow," "Cyrus McCormick," "John Young," in Allan Johnson and Dumas Malone, eds., *Dictionary of American Biography* (New York, 1961); "Union Mass Meeting," *New York Times*, February 22, 1860.

34. Richard I. Lester, *Confederate Finance and Purchasing in Great Britain* (Charlottesville, Virginia, 1975), 196–99; K. Jack Bauer, *A Maritime History of the United States* (Columbia, South Carolina, 1988), 78–80, 103; C. Ernest Fayle, *A Short History of the*

World's Shipping Industry (London, 1933), 238; George Rogers Taylor, *The Transportation Revolution, 1815–1860* (Armonk, New York, 1951), 200, 204, 206. Total tonnage is deep sea, coastal, river, and lake vessels; Nevins, *Hamilton Fish*, 1:261–62; Welles, *Naboth's Vineyard*, 1:372–74; Herrick, *American Naval Revolution*, 13–18.

35. Nevins, *Hamilton Fish*, 1:270, 278, 328–35, 362; Tansill, *United States and Santo Domingo*, 1:372, 386, 393–98, 411; Bauer, *Maritime History*, 241–44; U.S. Senate, "Report of the U.S. Senate Select Committee on the Memorial of David Hatch," June 25, 1870, Senate Report No. 234, 41st Congress, 2nd Session.

36. Tansill, *United States and Santo Domingo*, 1:421, 462; Knight, *Mexican Revolution*, 16; "The Samana Bay Company," *New York Tribune*, April 7, 1874; Nevins, *Hamilton Fish*, 1:328–29; Bauer, *Maritime History*, 252–55. In 1871 it cost Alden B. Stockwell of the Pacific Mail $900,000 to get favorable legislation to build two iron and screw-propeller-driven ships. By 1875, Pacific Mail received $4 million a year from Central Pacific and Union Pacific Railroads to raise rates. Between 1875 and 1880, railroads established Occidental Shipping with British ships and brought Pacific Mail to bankruptcy. Kenneth Hagan, *The People's Navy: The Making of American Sea Power* (New York, 1991), 175–77.

37. Cazneau to Beach, December 1, 1865, Cazneau Papers, NYHS; Frank Cundall, *Historic Jamaica* (London, 1915), 146.

38. Cazneau to McManus, June 4, 24, 1875, John Herndon James Papers, Daughters of the Republic of Texas Library Collection, UTSA, San Antonio; Turpe to McManus, April 5, May 25, December 25, 1875, March 29, 1876; Turpe to Simpson and James, March 10, 1877; A. G. Carothers to R. O. W. McManus, October 29, 1876, box 3, fol. 59, 62, James Papers, UTSA; Abstract, Crawford's 1854 deed was witnessed by G. P. Devine and F. P. J. Meyer; Cazneau, *Eagle Pass*, 34; Goldfrank, Frank & Co. of San Antonio managed a cattle syndicate that filed deeds for Cazneau's unrecorded share of the Rivas Grant from Garza to Crawford and from Crawford to Devine; Ethel Mary Franklin, "Memories of Mrs. Annie P. Harris," *Southwestern Historical Quarterly* 40 (January 1937): 231–46; Obituary, "William Leslie Cazneau," *San Antonio Daily Herald*, March 22, 1876, in *Biographies of Leading Texans* (Austin), Texas State Library, Austin, 1:138–39; Cazneau to Winn, November 1877, Deed Records, Saint Catherine's Parish, Jamaica; Inventories, 1B/11/3, vol. 162, fol. 212, Spanish Town, Jamaica Archives, deed was contested, will was not recorded in Jamaica, the Cazneau school continued until 1893 (Blue Book, S19). In 1880 the school had fifty-six pupils, and in 1900 the Wesleyans closed schools (Cundall, *Historic Jamaica*, 144). Keith Hall was destroyed in an earthquake in 1907. In the 1950s ALCAN, ALCOA, Kaiser, and Reynolds began mining the solid bauxite cliffs of Bog Walk (Cazneau, *Our Winter Eden*, appendix; "Sketch," *New York Tribune*, December 31, 1878; "Lost off Cape Hatteras," *New York Sun*, December 28, 1878; "The Emily B. Souder Lost," *New York Tribune*, December 30, 1878). The ship carried a miscellaneous cargo for nineteen commission houses in New York. The manifest listed dry goods, implements, paints, seventeen cases of cartridges, eight guns, drugs, a dozen sewing machines, and fifty-three kegs of beer. The guns and cartridges were likely for Cuban rebels.

39. "Sketch," *New York Tribune*, December 31, 1878; *La Verdad*, January 8, 1848, to June 26, 1848; "Meeting of Female Industry Association," *New York Workingman's Advocate*, March 22, 1845; "The Female Industrial Association," *New York Sun*, March, 6, 10, 14, May 1, 1845; R. D. Owen to Nicholas P. Trist, July 4, 1846, Papers of Nicholas P. Trist, Library of Congress, Washington, D.C.; William L. Marcy to Prosper M. Wetmore, February 9, 1848, Marcy Papers, LOC; Col. J. W. Webb to William H. Seward, March 12, 1849, Seward Papers, UR; Storm to Bancroft, June 20, 1848, Bancroft Papers, Massachusetts Historical Society.

Nahui Olin

1. Adriana Malvido Arriaga, *Nahui Olin: La mujer del sol* (Mexico City, 1993), 17.
2. Elena Poniatowska, *Las siete cabritas* (Mexico, D.F., 2001), 82.
3. Tomás Zurian, *Nahui Olin: Una mujer en los tiempos modernos* (Mexico, D.F., 1992), 21–22.
4. Alejandra Osorio, "Nahui Olin ¿Una mujer de tiempos siempre por venir?" *Revista de Humanidades* (Monterrey) 17 (2004): 131–48; Malvido Arriaga, *Nahui Olin*; Jorge Vázquez Piñón, *Carmen Mondragón Valseca: Nahui Olin, aproximación a un misterio* (Morelia, Michoacán, 2007); Zurian, *Nahui Olin*, 143–44; Poniatowska, *Las siete cabritas*, 74.
5. Zurian, *Nahui Olin*, 150.
6. Ibid., 137.
7. Poniatowska, *Las siete cabritas*, 70. Poniatowska cites Zurian's interpretation of Nahui as an early feminist.
8. Ibid., 70.
9. Zurian, *Nahui Olin*, 116. He reports that people who met her in her later years considered her ugly and very fat.
10. Ibid., 68.
11. Nahui's original biographer, distinguished by his thoroughness and judiciousness, writes that these love poems date to the early period of their relationship. See Zurian, *Nahui Olin*, 68. Nonetheless, Atl's intention remains suspect given that he could have acknowledged in that volume her preference for the name "Nahui Olin" and that he disregarded her demand to have her letters returned by making copies for himself—which he later published without her authorization.
12. Dr. Atl, *Poemas del Dr. Atl* (Mexico, D.F., 1959), 7.
13. Atl, "Nahui Olin," in *Óptica cerebral: Poemas dinámicos*, by Nahui Olin (Mexico, D.F., n.d.).
14. Nahui Olin, "Insaciable Sed," in *Óptica cerebral*, 12.
15. The most damning testimony here comes from a painter named Nefero, a disciple of Manuel Rodríguez Lozano, who portrayed Olin as guilty of killing the child and said that Manuel was innocent and worried, and that he already detected in her back then signs of madness, probably congenital. See the reference in Zurian, *Nahui Olin*, 60. Zurian, for his part, weighs the evidence and deems it unlikely that she killed a baby. Raoul Fournier,

who was Manuel's friend, said they had a daughter or son who died under mysterious circumstances. See Poniatowska, *Las siete cabritas*, 65.

16. Nahui Olin, *Calinement: Je suis dedans* (Mexico, 1923), 53–54, as quoted in Zurian, *Nahui Olin*, 66.

17. Ibid., 36.

18. Poniatowska, *Las siete cabritas*, 72, 82.

19. In the formal program for the exhibition in Mexico dated September 29, 1921, Olin's name appears as Carmen Mondragón de Rodríguez Lozano. Yet she represented herself as XIU, interpreted by Zurian as a word derived from the Náhuatl word "Xihuitl." See Tomás Zurian, *Nahui Olin: Opera Varia* (Mexico, D.F., 2000), 12.

20. Nahui Olin, *Nahui Olin* (Mexico City, 1927), as quoted in Zurian, *Nahui Olin*, 31.

21. Olin, "Sabiduria—Lepra Humana," in *Óptica cerebral*, 21.

22. Nahui Olin, *A dix ans sur mon pupitre*, as quoted in Arriaga, *Nahui Olin*, 19.

23. Olin, "El cáncer que nos roba vida," in *Óptica cerebral*, 103–4.

24. Olin, "Bajo la mortaja de nieve duerme la Iztatzihuatl en su inercia de muerte," in *Óptica cerebral*, 57.

25. Ibid.

26. Olin, "La enorme montaña que tiene en la cima una tumba—el tiempo," in *Óptica cerebral*, 33.

27. Ibid.

28. Vázquez Piñon, *Carmen Mondragón Valseca*, 229.

29. This is according to Homero Aridjis, who met Olin in the Alameda and observed her ministrations with sympathy. As cited in Poniatowska, *Las siete cabritas*, 82.

30. Nahui Olin, "Mi alma está triste hasta morir," in *A dix ans sur mon pupitre* (Mexico, 1924).

31. Nahui Olin, *Energía cósmica* (Mexico D.F., 1937), as quoted in Vázquez Piñon, *Carmen Mondragón Valseca*, 228.

32. Ibid.

Alice Dickerson Montemayor

1. Nancy Cott, *The Grounding of Modern Feminism* (New Haven, Connecticut, 1989).

2. Cynthia E. Orozco, "The Origins of the League of United Latin American Citizens (LULAC) and the Mexican American Civil Rights Movement in Texas with an Analysis of Women's Political Participation in a Gendered Context, 1910–1929" (PhD diss., University of California at Los Angeles, 1992).

3. LULAC recognized Montemayor twice in the late 1930s with a *News* cover page and articles about her. See "Our Second Vice-President General," *LULAC News*, September 1937, and the special women's issue in May 1939, especially Esperanza E. Trevino, "Mrs. F. I. Montemayor." See also Cynthia E. Orozco, "Alice Dickerson Montemayor," in *The New Handbook of Texas*, ed. Ronnie C. Tyler (Austin, 1996).

4. For instance, see María Berta Guerra, "The Study of LULAC," in which she refers to the McAllen Ladies LULAC council as a women's council and an auxiliary (undergraduate paper, Grande Valley Collection, University of Texas–Pan American, 1979). Ladies auxiliaries were only one form of women's historical participation in LULAC; the auxiliaries existed primarily from 1932 to 1933.

5. José A. Estrada interview with Belen B. Robles, April 26–27, 1976, Institute of Oral History, University of Texas at El Paso.

6. J. Reynolds Flores, "How to Educate Our Girls," *LULAC News*, December 1931.

7. "La Mujer," *Alma Latina* 1, no. 3 (April 1932), Paul S. Taylor Collection, Bancroft Library, University of California at Berkeley (hereafter PSTC, BL).

8. Adela Sloss, "Por Que en Muchos Hogares Latinos No Existe Verdadera Felicidad," *LULAC News*, March 1934, PSTC, BL.

9. *LULAC News*, March 1937. Fidencio Guerra of McAllen held the position from 1936 to 1937. On the Guerra family, see Evan Anders, *Boss Rule in South Texas* (Austin, 1982).

10. Norma Cantú videotaped interview with Alice Dickerson Montemayor, January 26, 1986, Laredo, Texas; "Our Second Vice-President General," *LULAC News*, September 1937; Andre Guerrero interview with Alice Dickerson Montemayor, January 1983, Alice Dickerson Montemayor Collection, Benson Latin American Collection, University of Texas, Austin (hereafter ADMC, BLAC); Norma Cantú interview with Alice Dickerson Montemayor, with questions prepared by Cynthia E. Orozco, January 24, 1984. Manuela Barrera was the granddaughter of Don Desiderio de la Cruz and Doña Apolonia Reyes, who helped found Laredo ("Our Second Vice-President General"). Montemayor referred to her mother as a "clothes designer."

11. "Alicia D. Montemayor: Young at 82," *Laredo Morning Times*, July 15, 1984, ADMC, BLAC; phone conversation by author with Aurelio Montemayor, June 15, 1989, San Antonio, Texas; Guerrero interview.

12. Montemayor told Andre Guerrero that her mother prohibited her from leaving Laredo to go to college ("Our Second Vice-President General"); Veronica Salazar, "Alicia D. Montemayor," *San Antonio Express-News*, October 28, 1979; Cantú interview, January 26, 1986.

13. Cantú interview, January 26, 1986; Salazar, "Alicia D. Montemayor." Montemayor set up three apple crates under a tree to conduct her work. The San Antonio newspaper noted that two other Mexican Americans had been sent to Cotulla "but were not accepted because they were Mexican-Americans."

14. Phone conversation with Aurelio Montemayor, June 15, 1989.

15. Cantú interview, January 26, 1986.

16. "Outstanding Councils of the League, Laredo Ladies Council No. 15," *LULAC News*, June 1937; "Around the LULAC Shield, Laredo Ladies Council No. 15," *LULAC News*, July 1937; "Our Second Vice-President General." The first names of some of these women were not readily available.

17. "Around the LULAC Shield, Laredo Ladies Council No. 15," *LULAC News*, December 1936.

18. "Around the LULAC Shield, Laredo, Ladies Council No. 15," *LULAC News*, February 1937. Elena Leal replaced Montemayor as secretary for 1937–38; see "Around the LULAC Shield, Laredo Ladies Council No. 15," *LULAC News*, July 1937 and August 1938.

19. "Around the LULAC Shield, Laredo Ladies Council No. 15," *LULAC News*, March 1937.

20. "Outstanding Councils of the League, Laredo Ladies Council No. 15," *LULAC News*, June 1937; "Minutes of the Tenth Annual Convention of the League of Latin American Citizens," *LULAC News*, July 1938; "Convention Proceedings, Minutes of the Ninth Annual General Convention of the LULAC held in Houston, Texas, June 5th & 6th 1937," *LULAC News*, July 1937; Cantú interview, January 26, 1986. A nominating committee, not a general election, selected officers. See "Convention Proceedings," *LULAC News*, July 1937, and "Our Second Vice-President General."

21. "We Need More Ladies Councils," *LULAC News*, July 1937. The article is unsigned but written by Montemayor. See also Mrs. F. I. Montemayor, "A Message from Our Second Vice-President General," *LULAC News*, September 1937, and Mrs. F. I. Montemayor, "Echoes of the Installation of Officers of Council No. 1, Corpus Christi, Texas," *LULAC News*, December 1937.

22. "Son Muy Hombres (?)" (editorial), *LULAC News*, March 1938.

23. Ibid.

24. Garza, "LULAC," 24; "Special Convention Minutes, Minutes of the Special Convention Held in Laredo, Texas, February 20, 1938," *LULAC News*, December 1937; "Around the LULAC Shield, Laredo Junior Council No. 1," *LULAC News*, February 1938; Francisco I. Montemayor Jr., "Laredo Junior Council," *LULAC News*, December 1938. Mrs. Charles Ramirez was the 1937–38 ladies organizer general for Junior LULAC. Montemayor served from 1939 to 1940. M. C. Gonzales, a man, replaced her in 1940–41. The first two official field organizers of youth councils were Sergio Gonzalez Jr., a lawyer from Del Rio, and Fidencio M. Guerra of McAllen, but the men did not offer assistance until December 1938 when a Junior LULAC member noted that now the groups would have "not only MAMAS but PAPAS as well."

25. Mrs. F. I. Montemayor, "Let's Organize Junior Councils," *LULAC News*, August 1938; "Around the LULAC Shield, the Laredo Junior Council," *LULAC News*, December 1938.

26. Cantú interview, January 26, 1986; Cantú interview, January 24, 1984.

27. Leonor Montes, "Who Is Who in the Laredo Junior Council," *LULAC News*, August 1938; Francisco Montemayor Jr., "Laredo Junior Council," *LULAC News*, December 1938.

28. See Mrs. F. I. Montemayor, "A Message from Our Second Vice-President General"; "Take Stock of Yourself," *LULAC News*, September 1937; Mrs. F. I. Montemayor, "Women's Opportunity in LULAC," *LULAC News*, October 1937; "Son Muy Hombres (?)"; Mrs. F. I. Montemayor, "Echoes of the Installation of Officers of Council No. 1," *LULAC News*,

February 1938; Montemayor, "Let's Organize Junior Councils"; Mrs. F. I. Montemayor, "President General and Three Laredo Councils"; Mrs. F. I. Montemayor, "When…and Then Only," *LULAC News*, March 1939; Mrs. F. I. Montemayor, "Our Ladies Organizer General," *LULAC News*, May 1939; Mrs. F. I. Montemayor, "Why and How More Junior Councils," *LULAC News*, April 1940. See also "Our Second Vice-President General."

29. Montemayor, "Let's Organize Junior Councils."

30. "We Need More Ladies Councils," *LULAC News*, July 1937.

31. Mrs. F. I. Montemayor, "A Message."

32. Mrs. F. I. Montemayor, "Women's Opportunity in LULAC."

33. "Son Muy Hombres (?)."

34. Ibid.

35. Montemayor, "When…and Then Only"; Montemayor, "Let's Organize Junior Councils."

36. "Around the LULAC Shield, Laredo, Ladies Council No. 15," *LULAC News*, February 1937.

37. Cantú interview, January 24, 1984, and Cantú interview, January 26, 1986. Carmen Cortes of Houston Ladies LULAC 14, a member in the 1930s, also mentioned Laredo men's opposition to Montemayor in an interview. Thomas Kreneck and Cynthia E. Orozco interview with Carmen Cortes, December 16, 1983, Houston, Texas.

38. Cantú interview, January 24, 1984.

39. Mrs. F. I. Montemayor, "Echoes of the Installation of Officers," "Dedicatoria del Nuevo Parque Ben Garza," *El Paladín*, March 3, 1939; Cantú interview, January 26, 1986 (here Montemayor named a Dr. Canales among her male supporters, but I assume she was referring to Dr. Carlos Castaneda *and* J. T. Canales); Cantú interview, January 24, 1984.

40. *LULAC News*, July 1945.

41. "Outstanding Councils of the League."

42. Ezequiel Salinas, "My Junior LULAC Activities," *LULAC News*, June 1937.

43. Phone conversation with Aurelio Montemayor, June 15, 1989; Guerrero interview.

44. "We Need More Ladies Councils"; "Women's Opportunity in LULAC."

Frida Kahlo

1. Amalia Mesa-Bains, "Frida Kahlo: Chicano Inspiration, Galería de la Raza," *Studio 24 Newsletter* 1, no. 2 (April–May 1987).

Gloria Anzaldúa

1. Gloria Anzaldúa, *Borderlands / La frontera: The New Mestiza* (San Francisco, 1987), 205.

2. Cherrie Moraga and Gloria Anzaldúa, eds., *This Bridge Called My Back: Writings by Radical Women of Color* (Albany, New York, 2015), 108.

3. Ibid., 109.

4. Anzaldúa, *Borderlands*.

5. Founded by Octavio Romano, Quinto Sol Publications supported the careers of Chicano writers and published journals of Mexican American culture and philosophy, such as *El Grito* and *El Espejo*.

6. Anzaldúa, *Borderlands*, 101.

7. Ibid., 242.

8. Anzaldúa, *Borderlands*, 305.

9. Ibid., 25–26.

10. Gloria Anzaldúa and AnaLouise Keating, *This Bridge We Call Home: Radical Visions for Transformation* (New York, 2013), 109.

11. AnaLouise Keating, "From Borderlands and New *Mestizas* to *Nepantlas* and *Nepantleras*: Anzaldúan Theories for Social Change," *Human Architecture: Journal of the Sociology of Self-Knowledge* 4, no. 3 (2006): 4, 5.

12. Anzaldúa, *Borderlands*, 306.

13. Ibid., 21–22.

14. Ibid., 44.

15. Anzaldúa and Keating, *This Bridge We Call Home*, 87.

16. Ibid., 164.

17. Anzaldúa, *Borderlands*, 76.

Zapatistas

1. Testimony from the Third Gathering between the Zapatista People and the Peoples of the World, "Comandanta Ramona and the Zapatistas," La Garrucha, Chiapas, Mexico, December 29, 2007.

2. Comandanta Ester's complete speech from March 11, 2001, can be found at http://palabra.ezln.org.mx/comunicados/2001/2001_03_11_a.htm.

3. Zapatistas often refer to the EZLN simply as "the organization."

4. Regional women's gathering, handwritten transcription, Morelia, Chiapas, Mexico, June 9–10, 2001.

5. A *compañero* is a comrade or companion. In a political context, *compañero* generally refers to someone who belongs to a particular organization or movement. For the EZLN, *compañero*, or *compa*, is synonymous with "Zapatista."

6. Isabel, interview by author, digital recording, San Cristóbal de las Casas, Chiapas, Mexico, June 27, 2008.

7. Ibid.

8. Subcomandante Insurgente Marcos, "Carta de Marcos sobre la vida cotidiana en el EZLN" (communiqué, January 26, 1994). The communiqué can be found at http://palabra.ezln.org.mx/comunicados/1994/1994_01_26.htm.

9. The Women's Revolutionary Law was first published in *El Despertador Mexicano*,

Órgano Informativo del EZLN, Mexico, no. 1, December 1993. The text of the law can be found at http://palabra.ezln.org.mx/comunicados/1994/1993_12_g.htm.

10. Ernestina, Elida, and Margarita, interview by author, tape recording, Morelia, Chiapas, Mexico, January 20, 1998.

11. Collective interview with Zapatista women, interview by author, handwritten transcription, Galeana, Chiapas, Mexico, January 1998.

12. Manuela, interview by Mariana Mora, handwritten transcription, La Garrucha, Chiapas, Mexico, November 1999.

13. A *finca* is an extensive and largely self-sufficient agricultural estate that often controlled indigenous laborers through debt peonage, many times from generation to generation; also known as an *hacienda* in other parts of Latin America.

14. Celina, interview by author, handwritten transcription, Diez de Abril, Chiapas, Mexico, August 2001.

15. A drink made of corn dough mixed with water.

16. Blanca Luz, interview by author, digital recording, Tulanca, Chiapas, Mexico, December 7, 2006.

17. Paula, Amelia, Eva, Nora, and Guadalupe, interview by author, digital recording, San Caralampio, Chiapas, Mexico, December 5, 2006.

18. Ernestina, Elida, Micaela, and Margarita, interview by author, tape recording, Morelia, Chiapas, Mexico, February 18, 2001.

ACKNOWLEDGMENTS AND CREDITS

My gratitude to *mis amigas*, Sandra Cisneros and Ellen Riojas Clark, without whose encouragement at the outset and participation all along, this project would never have become reality. To Jennifer Speed, whose dedication and exquisite scholarship made the project bloom so beautifully. To Arturo Suarez, who suggested the book would not be complete without La Malinche. To my grandmother, Ethel Corley Chapman, who, after the death of her young husband, raised and sent five children to college in the middle of the Great Depression. To my mother, who deemed conventionality overrated. To all the revolutionary women and girls in my family and in my life. And especially to Lionel, for supporting every dream I have ever had and for sharing the stories of his grandmothers, who had the courage to flee the chaos and violence of the Mexican Revolution with their small children and make the long journey to begin anew in San Antonio, and who helped change the face of Texas forever.
—*Kathy Sosa*

To all the women upon whose shoulders we stand, I, Ellen Riojas Clark, salute and evoke their souls. Those spirits, that power, and the indomitable energy that has permeated my being, I thank my mother, a most revolutionary woman who gave me life, who gave me the will to overcome, to survive, to excel, I honor. Of my two daughters, Judy

and Jennifer, revolutionary women in their engineering fields, I am most proud. And I am heartened by the legacy of my granddaughters: Erica, Emily, and Melony, the new revolutionaries in fusion and aeronautical engineering, and Madeline, who with her degrees in museum studies and a bicultural and bilingual lens can create change. For the men in our lives, my dad and Hector, who encouraged us to do what we are meant to do, *mi cariño y gracias.*
    —*Ellen Riojas Clark*

A special thanks to Kathy Sosa for her vision, her revolutionary spirit, and her friendship, and to my colleagues at the University of Dayton—especially those in the Department of Religious Studies and the Office of the Dean of the College of Arts and Sciences—for nourishing and sustaining my scholarship. And, finally, a special debt of gratitude is owed to Helena and Dan for supporting this project from the very beginning.
    —*Jennifer Speed*

CREDITS

"Las Soldaderas," by Elena Poniatowska, was translated by Tony Beckwith.
Excerpt from *Malinche*, by Laura Esquivel. Copyright © 2006 by Laura Esquivel. Reprinted with permission of Atria Books, a division of Simon & Schuster, Inc. All rights reserved.
"The Girl Who Became a Saint: Teresa Urrea" and "Chavela Vargas" reprinted from *A House of My Own: Stories from My Life*. Copyright © 2015 by Sandra Cisneros. Reprinted by permission of Susan Bergholz Literary Services, New York, New York, and Lamy, New Mexico. All rights reserved.
"A Plaza, a Revolution, and a Young Girl: Emma Tenayuca and La Plaza del Zacate," by Carmen Tafolla. Printed with permission of the author. All rights reserved.
"Indigenous Women of Chiapas and Their Role in the Zapatista Movement" excerpted from *Compañeros: Zapatista Women's Stories*. Copyright © 2015 by Hilary Klein. Reprinted by permission of Seven Stories Press.

CONTRIBUTOR NOTES

Elaine Ayala has worked in the newspaper business for more than thirty years as a reporter, editor, columnist, and blogger, including at the *San Antonio Express-News*, the *Cleveland Plain Dealer*, the *Austin American-Statesman*, and the *El Paso Times*. Her Metro column appears in both the *Express-News* and the bilingual weekly *Conexión*.

Norma Elia Cantú is the Murchison Professor in the Humanities at Trinity University. Her research and creative writing focus on the cultural and literary production along the U.S.–Mexico borderland. She is the author, co-author, or co-editor of more than a dozen books, including the award-winning *Canícula: Snapshots of a Girlhood en la Frontera*.

Sandra Cisneros celebrates more than fifty years as an activist poet, fiction writer, essayist, educator, and artist. Her novel *The House on Mango Street* has been translated into multiple languages and utilized in school curricula around the world. She has received a MacArthur Fellowship, the Texas Medal of the Arts, the National Medal of Arts, and many other awards.

Virgilio P. Elizondo spent his life serving the pastoral and spiritual needs of Hispanic Catholics in San Antonio and around the world. He was rector of San Fernando Cathedral from 1983 to 1995 and a professor of pastoral and Hispanic theology at the University of Notre Dame from 1999 until his death in 2016. He authored or co-authored twelve books on Catholic culture and theology, two of which explore the significance of the Virgin of Guadalupe.

Laura Esquivel's breakout novel, *Como Agua Para Chocolate*, is set during the Mexican Revolution and has sold more than six million copies worldwide. The movie *Like Water for Chocolate* became the highest-grossing foreign film in U.S. history. Esquivel is the author of numerous screenplays and novels. She was elected a federal representative for Coyoacán in 2012 and serves in Mexico's Cámara de Diputados.

Lewis F. Fisher is the author of numerous books, including *Chili Queens, Hay Wagons, and Fandangos: The Spanish Plazas in Frontier San Antonio*, winner of the 2015 San Antonio Conservation Society Publication Award, and *Saving San Antonio: The Preservation of a Heritage*. He has received numerous local, state, and national writing awards and was named a Texas Preservation Hero by the Conservation Society in 2014.

Alicia Gaspar de Alba is a professor of Chicana/o studies, English, and gender studies at the University of California at Los Angeles, where she is also chair of the LGBTQ Studies Program. She is the author or co-author of eleven books. Her debut work of historical fiction, *Sor Juana's Second Dream*, won the 2001 historical fiction prize from the Latino Literary Hall of Fame.

Linda Hudson is a former history professor at East Texas Baptist University and a past president of the East Texas Historical Association. She is the author of *Mistress of Manifest Destiny: A Biography of Jane McManus Storm Cazneau, 1807–1878*, which won the T. R. Fehrenbach Award, and numerous essays on women in early Texas and the South.

Dolores Huerta is a civil rights activist and U.S. labor leader. She co-founded the National Farmworkers Association, now known as United Farm Workers, with César E. Chávez, and in 2002 founded the Dolores Huerta Foundation, which creates leadership opportunities for community organizing, civic engagement, and policy advocacy. She has received the Presidential Eleanor Roosevelt Award for Human Rights, the Presidential Medal of Freedom, and the Radcliffe Medal.

Hilary Klein spent six years in Chiapas, Mexico, working with women's projects in Zapatista communities. She is the author of *Compañeras: Zapatista Women's Stories* and the national coordinator of Make the Road, a family of membership organizations that builds the power of immigrant and working-class communities.

Amalia Mesa-Bains is a professor emerita and former director of the Visual and Public Arts Department at California State University, Monterey Bay. Her artwork has been exhibited and collected in museums around the world. In 1992 she received a MacArthur Fellowship, and in 2005 she took part in an international exhibit on Frida Kahlo at the Tate Modern in London.

Cynthia Orozco is a professor of history and humanities at Eastern New Mexico State University in Ruidoso. She is the author of *No Mexicans, Women, or Dogs Allowed: The Rise of the Mexican American Civil Rights Movement* and the co-editor of *Mexican Americans in Texas History*. She serves on the advisory board of the forthcoming *Handbook of Texas Women's History*.

Elena Poniatowska began her writing career with the newspaper *Excélsior* in the early 1950s. Her 1969 book, *Hasta no verte Jesús mío*, is based on the oral history of a washer woman who fought in the Mexican Revolution. Beginning in the 1970s she published a series of books exploring human rights, inequality, and structural problems in Mexico. Among other honors, she was the first woman to receive the Mexican National Award for Journalism (1979) and remains the only woman to be awarded a title by the French Legion of Honor (2003). She also received the Courage in Journalism Lifetime Achievement Award from the International Women's Media Foundation (2006) and the Cervantes Prize in 2013.

Cristina Devereaux Ramírez is an assistant professor at the University of Arizona and spent more than a decade as an educator in the El Paso public school system. Her research focuses on women journalists in late nineteenth- and early twentieth-century Mexico. She is the author of *Occupying Our Space: The Mestiza Rhetorics of Mexican Women Journalists, 1875–1942*.

Lionel Sosa is an independent marketing consultant and a nationally known portrait artist. He has served on the teams of eight national presidential campaigns and is a member of the Political Consultants Hall of Fame. He is the author or co-author of five books, including *El Vaquero Real: The Original American Cowboy*, and the producer of the award-winning documentary *Children of the Revolución*.

Carmen Tafolla is a professor of bicultural-bilingual studies at the University of Texas at San Antonio and the author of numerous television screenplays, works of poetry and nonfiction, and illustrated children's books, including *That's Not Fair! / ¡No Es Justo!: Emma Tenayuca's Struggle for Justice / La lucha de Emma Tenayuca*. She was poet laureate of San Antonio from 2012 to 2014 and poet laureate of Texas from 2015 to 2016.

Teresa Van Hoy is a professor of history at Saint Mary's University, where she specializes in the history of Texas, Mexico, and the borderlands. She is the author of *A Social History of Mexico's Railroads: Peons, Prisoners, and Priests* and a forthcoming book, tentatively titled *Cinco de Mayo and Civil War in the Borderlands*.

EDITORS

Kathy Sosa has been a teacher, marketer, political consultant, designer, curator, entrepreneur, activist, and artist. Her art has been featured in national media, and she has participated in more than three dozen exhibitions, including with the Smithsonian Latino Center and at Smithsonian-affiliated museums. In 2010 Sosa began investigating the Mexican Revolution's impact on the demographics, culture, and future of Texas and the United States. She conceived and helped develop a series of multimedia projects to promote a clearer understanding of this cataclysmic event. *Revolutionary Women of Texas and Mexico* is one of those projects.

Ellen Riojas Clark is professor emerita at the University of Texas at San Antonio. Her research examines ethnic and cultural identity and cultural studies topics. She received three National Endowment for the Humanities grants and was cultural director for *Maya and Miguel*, a PBS program. She is executive producer for the *Latino Artist Speaks: Exploring Who I Am* series, and her many publications include *Multicultural Literature for Latino Children: Their Words, Their Worlds; Don Moisés Espino del Castillo y sus Calaveras;* and a forthcoming book, *Pan Dulce: A Compendium of Mexican Pastries.*

Jennifer Speed is a research development strategist in the office of the Dean for Research at Princeton University. She was formerly research professor of religious studies at the University of Dayton, where she specialized in Spanish historical writing and narratives, biography, theology, and law. She has taught Western, world, medieval, and Latin American history for more than twenty years. She served as historian for the award-winning PBS documentary *Children of the Revolución* and is a co-project director of a major NEH-funded, multiyear project on the African American poet Paul Laurence Dunbar.

CPSIA information can be obtained
at www.ICGtesting.com
Printed in the USA
JSHW042227290721
17291JS00003B/4